CASENOTE® Legal Briefs®

WILLS, TRUSTS, AND ESTATES

Keyed to Courses Using
Sitkoff and Dukeminier's
Wills, Trusts, and Estates
Twelfth Edition

Authored by: Publisher's Editorial Staff

ASPEN PUBLISHING

To contact Customer Service, e-mail customer.service@aspenpublishing.com, call 1-800-950-5259, or mail correspondence to:

Aspen Publishing
Attn: Order Department
1 Wall Street
Burlington, MA 01803

1 2 3 4 5 6 7 8 9 0

ISBN 979-8-8996-4110-7

ABOUT ASPEN PUBLISHING

Aspen Publishing is a leading provider of legal education content and digital learning solutions in the United States and globally. Our innovative products and platforms—designed based on best practices in learning science—engage students and enhance outcomes. From textbooks and audiobooks authored by renowned experts to digital platforms and products like LEAF, Connected eBooks, Connected Quizzing, PracticePerfect, and JD-Next, we empower the next generation of legal professionals with innovative, trusted, and accessible resources.

The Aspen Casebook Series, affectionately known as the "red and black" casebooks among law faculty and students, includes hundreds of highly regarded textbooks across more than 80 disciplines. These range from foundational courses like Torts and Contracts to emerging electives such as Sustainability and the Law of Policing. Our study aids, including the popular *Examples & Explanations* series, help law students master complex topics with clarity and confidence.

Aspen's expertise extends to undergraduate education with our Paralegal, Criminal Justice, and Business Law series, offering the same hallmark quality to a broader audience. JD-Next, our groundbreaking online law school prep course and admissions test, provides a realistic preview of law school, equips students with essential skills for academic success, and evaluates their readiness for legal studies.

Aspen Publishing Is Proud to Be a UWorld Company

Since 2003, UWorld has been a global leader in developing high-quality learning tools for students preparing for high-stakes exams. With a commitment to excellence, UWorld has helped millions of students in undergraduate, graduate, and professional programs in fields such as medicine, nursing, finance, and law achieve their academic and career goals.

Founded by Chandra S. Pemmasani, M.D., during his medical residency, UWorld began focusing on medical education and has since expanded into various academic fields, including law. In 2020, UWorld launched its Legal vertical, starting with its comprehensive Multistate Bar Exam (MBE®) Question Bank, followed by the acquisition of Themis Bar Review, which integrated resources to provide a complete bar exam preparation experience. In 2024, UWorld expanded its offerings by acquiring Aspen Publishing, enhancing its suite of legal education products.

Today, UWorld offers an unparalleled range of study materials that blend active learning methods with expert content, ensuring students and educators can access the most effective resources. From bar preparation to law school success, UWorld is committed to supporting the next generation of legal professionals. Learn more at uworld.com.

Format for the Casenote® Legal Brief

Nature of Case: This section identifies the form of action (e.g., breach of contract, negligence, battery), the type of proceeding (e.g., demurrer, appeal from trial court's jury instructions) or the relief sought (e.g., damages, injunction, criminal sanctions).

Fact Summary: This is included to refresh your memory and can be used as a quick reminder of the facts.

Rule of Law: Summarizes the general principle of law that the case illustrates. It may be used for instant recall of the court's holding and for classroom discussion or home review.

Facts: This section contains all relevant facts of the case, including the contentions of the parties and the lower court holdings. It is written in a logical order to give you a clear understanding of the case. The plaintiff and defendant are identified by their proper names throughout and are always labeled with a (P) or (D).

Issue: The issue is a concise question that brings out the essence of the opinion as it relates to the section of the casebook in which the case appears. Both substantive and procedural issues are included if relevant to the decision.

Palsgraf v. Long Island R.R. Co.

Injured bystander (P) v. Railroad company (D)

N.Y. Ct. App., 248 N.Y. 339, 162 N.E. 99 (1928).

NATURE OF CASE: Appeal from judgment affirming verdict for plaintiff seeking damages for personal injury.

FACT SUMMARY: Helen Palsgraf (P) was injured on R.R.'s (D) train platform when R.R.'s (D) guard helped a passenger aboard a moving train, causing his package to fall on the tracks. The package contained fireworks which exploded, creating a shock that tipped a scale onto Palsgraf (P).

RULE OF LAW

The risk reasonably to be perceived defines the duty to be obeyed.

FACTS: Helen Palsgraf (P) purchased a ticket to Rockaway Beach from R.R. (D) and was waiting on the train platform. As she waited, two men ran to catch a train that was pulling out from the platform. The first man jumped aboard, but the second man, who appeared as if he might fall, was helped aboard by the guard on the train who had kept the door open so they could jump aboard. A guard on the platform also helped by pushing him onto the train. The man was carrying a package wrapped in newspaper. In the process, the man dropped his package, which fell on the tracks. The package contained fireworks and exploded. The shock of the explosion was apparently of great enough strength to tip over some scales at the other end of the platform, which fell on Palsgraf (P) and injured her. A jury awarded her damages, and R.R. (D) appealed.

ISSUE: Does the risk reasonably to be perceived define the duty to be obeyed?

HOLDING AND DECISION: (Cardozo, C.J.) Yes. The risk reasonably to be perceived defines the duty to be obeyed. If there is no foreseeable hazard to the injured party as the result of a seemingly innocent act, the act does not become a tort because it happened to be a wrong as to another. If the wrong was not willful, the plaintiff must show that the act as to her had such great and apparent possibilities of danger as to entitle her to protection. Negligence in the abstract is not enough upon which to base liability. Negligence is a relative concept, evolving out of the common law doctrine of trespass on the case. To establish liability, the defendant must owe a legal duty of reasonable care to the injured party. A cause of action in tort will lie where harm, though unintended, could have been averted or avoided by observance of such a duty. The scope of the duty is limited by the range of danger that a reasonable person could foresee. In this case, there was nothing to suggest from the appearance of the parcel or otherwise that the parcel contained fireworks. The guard could not reasonably have had any warning of a threat to Palsgraf (P), and R.R. (D) therefore cannot be held liable. Judgment is reversed in favor of R.R. (D).

DISSENT: (Andrews, J.) The concept that there is no negligence unless R.R. (D) owes a legal duty to take care as to Palsgraf (P) herself is too narrow. Everyone owes to the world at large the duty of refraining from those acts that may unreasonably threaten the safety of others. If the guard's action was negligent as to those nearby, it was also negligent as to those outside what might be termed the "danger zone." For Palsgraf (P) to recover, R.R.'s (D) negligence must have been the proximate cause of her injury, a question of fact for the jury.

ANALYSIS

The majority defined the limit of the defendant's liability in terms of the danger that a reasonable person in defendant's situation would have perceived. The dissent argued that the limitation should not be placed on liability, but rather on damages. Judge Andrews suggested that only injuries that would not have happened but for R.R.'s (D) negligence should be compensable. Both the majority and dissent recognized the policy-driven need to limit liability for negligent acts, seeking, in the words of Judge Andrews, to define a framework "that will be practical and in keeping with the general understanding of mankind." The Restatement (Second) of Torts has accepted Judge Cardozo's view.

Quicknotes

FORESEEABILITY A reasonable expectation that change is the probable result of certain acts or omissions.

NEGLIGENCE Conduct falling below the standard of care that a reasonable person would demonstrate under similar conditions.

PROXIMATE CAUSE The natural sequence of events without which an injury would not have been sustained.

Party ID: Quick identification of the relationship between the parties.

Concurrence/Dissent: All concurrences and dissents are briefed whenever they are included by the casebook author.

Analysis: This last paragraph gives you a broad understanding of where the case "fits in" with other cases in the section of the book and with the entire course. It is a hornbook-style discussion indicating whether the case is a majority or minority opinion and comparing the principal case with other cases in the casebook. It may also provide analysis from restatements, uniform codes, and law review articles.

Holding and Decision: This section offers a clear and in-depth discussion of the rule of the case and the court's rationale. It is written in easy-to-understand language and answers the issue presented by applying the law to the facts of the case. When relevant, it includes a thorough discussion of the exceptions to the case as listed by the court, any major cites to the other cases on point, and the names of the judges who wrote the decisions.

Quicknotes: Conveniently defines legal terms found in the case.

Note to Students

Aspen Publishing is proud to offer *Casenote® Legal Briefs*—continuing thirty years of publishing America's best-selling legal briefs.

Casenote® Legal Briefs are designed to help you save time when briefing assigned cases. Organized under convenient headings, they show you how to abstract the basic facts and holdings from the text of the actual opinions handed down by the courts. Used as part of a rigorous study regimen, they can help you spend more time analyzing and critiquing points of law than on copying bits and pieces of judicial opinions into your notebook or outline.

Casenote® Legal Briefs should never be used as a substitute for assigned casebook readings. They work best when read as a follow-up to reviewing the underlying opinions themselves. Students who try to avoid reading and digesting the judicial opinions in their casebooks or online sources will end up shortchanging themselves in the long run. The ability to absorb, critique, and restate the dynamic and complex elements of case law decisions is crucial to your success in law school and beyond. It cannot be developed vicariously.

In addition to *Casenote® Legal Briefs*, Aspen Publishing offers the following study aids:

- *Casenote® Legal Briefs*
- *Emanuel Law Outlines®*
- Emanuel *Law in a Flash Flash Cards®*
- Emanuel *CrunchTime® Series*

Each of these series is designed to provide you with easy-to-understand explanations of complex points of law. Each volume offers guidance on the principles of legal analysis and, consulted regularly, will hone your ability to spot relevant issues. We have titles that will help you prepare for class, prepare for your exams, and enhance your general comprehension of the law along the way.

To find out more about our law school tools for success, visit us at *www.AspenPublishing.com* or e-mail us at *customer.service@aspenpublishing.com*. We'll be happy to assist you.

How to Brief a Case

A. Decide on a Format and Stick to It

Structure is essential to a good brief. It enables you to arrange systematically the related parts that are scattered throughout most cases, thus making manageable and understandable what might otherwise seem to be an endless and unfathomable sea of information. There are, of course, an unlimited number of formats that can be utilized. However, it is best to find one that suits your needs and stick to it. Consistency breeds both efficiency and the security that when called upon you will know where to look in your brief for the information you are asked to give.

Any format, as long as it presents the essential elements of a case in an organized fashion, can be used. Experience, however, has led *Casenote® Legal Briefs* to develop and utilize the following format because of its logical flow and universal applicability.

NATURE OF CASE: This is a brief statement of the legal character and procedural status of the case (e.g., "Appeal of a burglary conviction").

There are many different alternatives open to a litigant dissatisfied with a court ruling. The key to determining which one has been used is to discover *who is asking this court for what.*

This first entry in the brief should be kept as *short as possible.* Use the court's terminology if you understand it. But since jurisdictions vary as to the titles of pleadings, the best entry is the one that addresses who wants what in this proceeding, not the one that sounds most like the court's language.

RULE OF LAW: A statement of the general principle of law that the case illustrates (e.g., "An acceptance that varies any term of the offer is considered a rejection and counteroffer").

Determining the rule of law of a case is a procedure similar to determining the issue of the case. Avoid being fooled by red herrings; there may be a few rules of law mentioned in the case excerpt, but usually only one is *the* rule with which the casebook editor is concerned. The techniques used to locate the issue, described below, may also be utilized to find the rule of law. Generally, your best guide is simply the chapter heading. It is a clue to the point the casebook editor seeks to make and should be kept in mind when reading every case in the respective section.

FACTS: A synopsis of only the essential facts of the case, i.e., those bearing upon or leading up to the issue.

The facts entry should be a short statement of the events and transactions that led one party to initiate legal proceedings against another in the first place. While some cases conveniently state the salient facts at the beginning of the decision, in other instances they will have to be culled from hiding places throughout the text, even from concurring and dissenting opinions. Some of the "facts" will often be in dispute and should be so noted. Conflicting evidence may be briefly pointed up. "Hard" facts must be included. Both must be *relevant* in order to be listed in the facts entry. It is impossible to tell what is relevant until the entire case is read, as the ultimate determination of the rights and liabilities of the parties may turn on something buried deep in the opinion.

Generally, the facts entry should not be longer than three to five *short* sentences.

It is often helpful to identify the role played by a party in a given context. For example, in a construction contract case the identification of a party as the "contractor" or "builder" alleviates the need to tell that that party was the one who was supposed to have built the house.

It is always helpful, and a good general practice, to identify the "plaintiff" and the "defendant." This may seem elementary and uncomplicated, but, especially in view of the creative editing practiced by some casebook editors, it is sometimes a difficult or even impossible task. Bear in mind that the *party presently* seeking something from this court may not be the plaintiff, and that sometimes only the cross-claim of a defendant is treated in the excerpt. Confusing or misaligning the parties can ruin your analysis and understanding of the case.

ISSUE: A statement of the general legal question answered by or illustrated in the case. For clarity, the issue is best put in the form of a question capable of a "yes" or "no" answer. In reality, the issue is simply the Rule of Law put in the form of a question (e.g., "May an offer be accepted by performance?").

The major problem presented in discerning what is *the* issue in the case is that an opinion usually purports to raise and answer several questions. However, except for rare cases, only one such question is really the issue in the case. Collateral issues not necessary to the resolution of the matter in controversy are handled by the court by language known as *"obiter dictum"* or merely *"dictum."* While dicta may be included later in the brief, they have no place under the issue heading.

To find the issue, ask *who wants what* and then go on to ask *why did that party succeed or fail in getting it.* Once this is determined, the "why" should be turned into a question.

The complexity of the issues in the cases will vary, but in all cases a single-sentence question should sum up the issue. *In a few cases,* there will be two, or even more rarely, three issues of equal importance to the resolution of the case. Each should be expressed in a single-sentence question.

Since many issues are resolved by a court in coming to a final disposition of a case, the casebook editor will reproduce the portion of the opinion containing the issue or issues most relevant to the area of law under scrutiny. A noted law professor gave this advice: "Close the book; look at the title on the cover." Chances are, if it is Property, you need not concern yourself with whether, for example, the federal government's treatment of the plaintiff's land really raises a federal question sufficient to support jurisdiction on this ground in federal court.

The same rule applies to chapter headings designating sub-areas within the subjects. They tip you off as to what the text is designed to teach. The cases are arranged in a casebook to show a progression or development of the law, so that the preceding cases may also help.

It is also most important to remember to *read the notes and questions* at the end of a case to determine what the editors wanted you to have gleaned from it.

HOLDING AND DECISION: This section should succinctly explain the rationale of the court in arriving at its decision. In capsulizing the "reasoning" of the court, it should always include an application of the general rule or rules of law to the specific facts of the case. Hidden justifications come to light in this entry: the reasons for the state of the law, the public policies, the biases and prejudices, those considerations that influence the justices' thinking and, ultimately, the outcome of the case. At the end, there should be a short indication of the disposition or procedural resolution of the case (e.g., "Decision of the trial court for Mr. Smith (P) reversed").

The foregoing format is designed to help you "digest" the reams of case material with which you will be faced in your law school career. Once mastered by practice, it will place at your fingertips the information the authors of your casebooks have sought to impart to you in case-by-case illustration and analysis.

B. Be as Economical as Possible in Briefing Cases

Once armed with a format that encourages succinctness, it is as important to be economical with regard to the time spent on the actual reading of the case as it is to be economical in the writing of the brief itself. This does not mean "skimming" a case. Rather, it means reading the case with an "eye" trained to recognize into which "section" of your brief a particular passage or line fits and having a system for quickly and precisely marking the case so that the passages fitting any one particular part of the brief can be easily identified and brought together in a concise and accurate manner when the brief is actually written.

It is of no use to simply repeat everything in the opinion of the court; record only enough information to trigger your recollection of what the court said. Nevertheless, an accurate statement of the "law of the case," i.e., the legal principle applied to the facts, is absolutely essential to class preparation and to learning the law under the case method.

To that end, it is important to develop a "shorthand" that you can use to make marginal notations. These notations will tell you at a glance in which section of the brief you will be placing that particular passage or portion of the opinion.

Some students prefer to underline all the salient portions of the opinion (with a pencil or colored underliner marker), making marginal notations as they go along. Others prefer the color-coded method of underlining, utilizing different colors of markers to underline the salient portions of the case, each separate color being used to represent a different section of the brief. For example, blue underlining could be used for passages relating to the rule of law, yellow for those relating to the issue, and green for those relating to the holding and decision, etc. While it has its advocates, the color-coded method can be confusing and time-consuming (all that time spent on changing colored markers). Furthermore, it can interfere with the continuity and concentration many students deem essential to the reading of a case for maximum comprehension. In the end, however, it is a matter of personal preference and style. Just remember, whatever method you use, underlining must be used sparingly or its value is lost.

If you take the marginal notation route, an efficient and easy method is to go along underlining the key portions of the case and placing in the margin alongside them the following "markers" to indicate where a particular passage or line "belongs" in the brief you will write:

N	(NATURE OF CASE)
RL	(RULE OF LAW)
I	(ISSUE)
HL	(HOLDING AND DECISION, relates to the RULE OF LAW behind the decision)
HR	(HOLDING AND DECISION, gives the RATIONALE or reasoning behind the decision)
HA	(HOLDING AND DECISION, applies the general principle(s) of law to the facts of the case to arrive at the decision)

Remember that a particular passage may well contain information necessary to more than one part of your brief, in which case you simply note that in the margin. If you are using the color-coded underlining method instead of marginal notation, simply make asterisks or checks in the margin next to the passage in question in the colors that indicate the additional sections of the brief where it might be utilized.

The economy of utilizing "shorthand" in marking cases for briefing can be maintained in the actual brief writing process itself by utilizing "law student shorthand" within the brief. There are many commonly used words and phrases for which abbreviations can be substituted in your briefs (and in your class notes also). You can develop abbreviations that are personal to you and which will save you a lot of time. A reference list of briefing abbreviations can be found on page x of this book.

C. Use Both the Briefing Process and the Brief as a Learning Tool

Now that you have a format and the tools for briefing cases efficiently, the most important thing is to make the time spent in briefing profitable to you and to make the most advantageous use of the briefs you create. Of course, the briefs are invaluable for classroom reference when you are called upon to explain or analyze a particular case. However, they are also useful in reviewing for exams. A quick glance at the fact summary should bring the case to mind, and a rereading of the rule of law should enable you to go over the underlying legal concept in your mind, how it was applied in that particular case, and how it might apply in other factual settings.

As to the value to be derived from engaging in the briefing process itself, there is an immediate benefit that arises from being forced to sift through the essential facts and reasoning from the court's opinion and to succinctly express them in your own words in your brief. The process ensures that you understand the case and the point that it illustrates, and that means you will be ready to absorb further analysis and information brought forth in class. It also ensures you will have something to say when called upon in class. The briefing process helps develop a mental agility for getting to the *gist* of a case and for identifying, expounding on, and applying the legal concepts and issues found there. The briefing process is the mental process on which you must rely in taking law school examinations; it is also the mental process upon which lawyers rely in serving their clients and in making a living.

Abbreviations for Briefs

acceptance	acp
affirmed	aff
answer	ans
assumption of risk	a/r
attorney	atty
beyond a reasonable doubt	b/r/d
bona fide purchaser	BFP
breach of contract	br/k
cause of action	c/a
common law	c/l
Constitution	Con
constitutional	con
contract	K
contributory negligence	c/n
cross	x
cross-complaint	x/c
cross-examination	x/ex
cruel and unusual punishment	c/u/p
defendant	D
dismissed	dis
double jeopardy	d/j
due process	d/p
equal protection	e/p
equity	eq
evidence	ev
exclude	exc
exclusionary rule	exc/r
felony	f/n
freedom of speech	f/s
good faith	g/f
habeas corpus	h/c
hearsay	hr
husband	H
injunction	inj
in loco parentis	ILP
inter vivos	I/v
joint tenancy	j/t
judgment	judgt
jurisdiction	jur
last clear chance	LCC
long-arm statute	LAS
majority view	maj
meeting of minds	MOM
minority view	min
Miranda rule	Mir/r
Miranda warnings	Mir/w
negligence	neg
notice	ntc
nuisance	nus
obligation	ob
obscene	obs
offer	O
offeree	OE
offeror	OR
ordinance	ord
pain and suffering	p/s
parol evidence	p/e
plaintiff	P
prima facie	p/f
probable cause	p/c
proximate cause	px/c
real property	r/p
reasonable doubt	r/d
reasonable man	r/m
rebuttable presumption	rb/p
remanded	rem
res ipsa loquitur	RIL
respondeat superior	r/s
Restatement	RS
reversed	rev
Rule Against Perpetuities	RAP
search and seizure	s/s
search warrant	s/w
self-defense	s/d
specific performance	s/p
statute	S
statute of frauds	S/F
statute of limitations	S/L
summary judgment	s/j
tenancy at will	t/w
tenancy in common	t/c
tenant	t
third party	TP
third party beneficiary	TPB
transferred intent	TI
unconscionable	uncon
unconstitutional	unconst
undue influence	u/e
Uniform Commercial Code	UCC
unilateral	uni
vendee	VE
vendor	VR
versus	v
void for vagueness	VFV
weight of authority	w/a
weight of the evidence	w/e
wife	W
with	w/
within	w/i
without	w/o
without prejudice	w/o/p
wrongful death	wr/d

Table of Cases

A A. v. B. *5*
Allard v. Pacific National Bank *109*
Anton, In re Estate of *65*
Arnheiter v. Arnheiter *56*

B Beck, Matter of Estate of *23*
Bitetzakis v. Bitetzakis *17*
Breeden v. Stone *41*
Brown, In re Estate of *116*
Brown v. Miller *134*

C Cessac v. Stevens *131*
Clark v. Campbell *72*
Clark v. Greenhalge *32*
Clobberie's Case *137*
Clymer v. Mayo *83*
Cole, In re Estate of *55*
Cook v. Equitable Life Assurance Society *84*

D Davis v. U.S. Bank National Association *121*
Dawson v. Yucus *64*
Dewire v. Haveles *138*
Duke, In re Estate of *58*

E Egelhoff v. Egelhoff *86*

F Fournier, In re Estate of *74*
Fulp v. Gilliland *78*

G Gibbs' Estate, In re *57*
Gibney v. Hossack *62*
Gleeson's Will, In re *101*
Gonzalez, In re Estate of *25*
Gray v. Gray *96*

H Hall, In re Estate of *19*
Hall v. Vallandingham *8*
Harrison v. Bird *28*
Hartman v. Hartle *100*
Hebrew University Assn. v. Nye (1961) *69*
Hebrew University Assn. v. Nye (1966) *70*
Hodges v. Johnson *119*
Horton, In re Estate of *21*
Huber v. Huber *113*

I Irwin Union Bank & Trust Co. v. Long *130*
In re Estate of. *See name of party*

J Jackson, In re Estate of *98*
Janes, In re Estate of *104*
Jimenez v. Lee *68*

K Keith v. Lulofs *33*
Kimmel's Estate, In re *24*
Kuralt, In re Estate of *26*
Kurrelmeyer, In re Estate of *88*

L LaCroix v. Senecal *30*
Lambeff v. Farmers Co-operative Executors & Trustees Ltd. *93*
Latham v. Father Divine *49*
Lipper v. Weslow *47*

M Macool, In re Probate of Will and Codicil of *20*
Mahoney, In re Estate of *13*
Mahoney v. Grainger *54*
Marsman v. Nasca *103*
Minary v. Citizens Fidelity Bank & Trust Co. *9*
Moses, In re Will of *44*
Myers, In re Estate of *91*

N National Academy of Sciences v. Cambridge Trust Co. *110*
Neher's Will, In re *125*
Nunnenman v. Estate of Grubbs *85*

O Old Colony Trust Co. v. United States *142*
Olliffe v. Wells *75*
Omega Trust, In re *80*
O'Neal v. Wilkes *10*

P Prestie, In re Estate of *94*

R Reece v. Elliott *92*
Riddell, In re *117*
Rigsby, In re Estate of *31*
Rothko, In re *102*
Russell, In re Estate of *61*

S Scheffel v. Krueger *112*
Schilling v. Herrera *51*
Searight's Estate, In re *73*
Shapira v. Union National Bank *2*
Sharis, In re Estate of *42*
Shaw Family Archives Ltd. v. CMG Worldwide, Inc. *3*
Shenandoah Valley National Bank v. Taylor *124*
Simpson v. Calivas *4*
Smithers v. St. Luke's-Roosevelt Hospital Center *126*
State Street Bank and Trust Co. v. Reiser *82*
Stoker, In re Estate of *29*
Strittmater's Estate, In re *40*
Sullivan v. Burkin *90*

T Tait v. Community First Trust Co. *136*
Thompson v. Royall *27*
Timmons v. Ingrahm *133*

U Unthank v. Rippstein *71*

V Varela v. Bernachea. *87*
Vissering, Estate of, v. Commissioner *143*

W Will of Kline, Matter of *105*
Wilson v. Lane *38*
Wilson v. Wilson. *107*
Woodward v. Commissioner of Social Security *11*
Woodworth, Estate of. *140*
Wright's Estate, In re. *36*

CHAPTER 1

Introduction: Freedom of Disposition

Quick Reference Rules of Law

PAGE

1. *Shapira v. Union National Bank.* A testator may validly impose a restraint on the religion of the spouse of a beneficiary as a condition precedent to inheriting under the will. *2*
2. *Shaw Family Archives Ltd. v. CMG Worldwide, Inc.* A postmortem right of publicity does not pass through the residuary clause in a decedent's will when the decedent did not have a statutory right of publicity at the time of the decedent's death. *3*
3. *Simpson v. Calivas.* Attorneys drafting wills owe a duty of reasonable care to the intended beneficiaries. *4*
4. *A. v. B.* Rule of Professional Conduct 1.6(c) permits a lawyer to disclose a confidential communication to the extent the lawyer believes necessary "to rectify the consequences of the client's criminal, illegal or fraudulent act in furtherance of which the lawyer's services had been used." *5*

Shapira v. Union National Bank

Beneficiary (P) v. Bank (D)

Ohio Com. Pl. Ct., 315 N.E.2d 825 (1974)

NATURE OF CASE: Declaratory judgment action.

FACT SUMMARY: Daniel's (P) interest under his father's will was conditioned on the requirement that he marry a Jew whose parents were both Jewish within seven years of his father's death.

RULE OF LAW

A testator may validly impose a restraint on the religion of the spouse of a beneficiary as a condition precedent to inheriting under the will.

FACTS: Under Shapira's will, his son Daniel (P) could inherit only if, at the time of Shapira's death or within seven years thereafter, he was married to a Jewish woman whose parents were both Jewish. Daniel (P) sought a declaration that the will was unconstitutional since it restricted his right to marry or that such a clause violated public policy.

ISSUE: May a testator validly impose a restraint on the religion of the spouse of a beneficiary as a condition precedent to inheriting under the will?

HOLDING AND DECISION: (Henderson, J.) Yes. A testator may validly impose a restraint on the religion of the spouse of a beneficiary as a condition precedent to inheriting under the will. The right to receive property by will is a matter of statutory law. A testator may either disinherit his children or condition their taking in any manner without offending the Constitution. While the right to marry is a constitutionally protected right, there is no state action present herein that would trigger the Due Process or Equal Protection Clause. The courts are not being asked to enforce covenants. The only official action involves the probate of the will, and this is, in itself, insufficient to be deemed state action. Therefore, a testator may restrict a beneficiary's right to marriage without offending the Constitution. Public policy does not prohibit a limited restriction on the right to marriage restricted to members of one religion. A partial restraint of marriage that imposes only reasonable restrictions is not void as violative of public policy. Gifts conditioned on marrying within a certain religious grouping are deemed reasonable restrictions in a majority of jurisdictions. We find that it is not violative of public policy to condition a bequest on the marriage to one of a particular religion. The clause is valid, and Daniel (P) is bound by its terms.

ANALYSIS

A condition requiring the beneficiary not to marry a member of a specific religion is also deemed valid. *In re Clayton's Estate*, 13 Pa. D. & C. 413 (Pa. Orphan's Ct. 1930). Where the restriction based on religion unreasonably limits the beneficiary's right to marriage, it will be deemed void, e.g., *Maddox v. Maddox*, 52 Va. (11 Grattan's) 804 (1854), where there were only four or five unmarried members of the particular sect.

Quicknotes

BENEFICIARY A third party who is the recipient of the benefit of a transaction undertaken by another.

DUE PROCESS The constitutional mandate requiring the courts to protect and enforce individuals' rights and liberties, consistent with prevailing principals of fairness and justice and prohibiting the federal and state governments from such activities that deprive its citizens of a life, liberty, or property interest.

EQUAL PROTECTION A constitutional guarantee that no person shall be denied the same protection of the laws enjoyed by other persons in life circumstances.

TESTATOR One who executes a will.

Shaw Family Archives Ltd. v. CMG Worldwide, Inc.

Intellectual property owner (D) v. Decedent's successor-in-interest (P)

486 F. Supp. 2d 309 (S.D.N.Y. 2007)

NATURE OF CASE: Cross-motions for summary judgment in suit alleging violation of right of publicity.

FACT SUMMARY: Shaw Family Archives, LLC (SFA) (D), a limited liability company that owned photographs taken by professional photographer Sam Shaw, sold T-shirts bearing Marilyn Monroe's image and also allowed customers to purchase licenses for the use of pictures and images of Monroe that Shaw created. CMG Worldwide, Inc. (P), one of the successors in interest to Monroe's estate, filed suit against SFA (D), alleging that SFA's (D) use of Monroe's likeness violated Indiana's Right of Publicity Act.

RULE OF LAW

A postmortem right of publicity does not pass through the residuary clause in a decedent's will when the decedent did not have a statutory right of publicity at the time of the decedent's death.

FACTS: Marilyn Monroe died in 1962, leaving the remainder of her estate to Lee Strasberg and naming her attorney Aaron Frosch as her executor. Strasberg died in 1982 and left his estate to his wife, Anna. When Frosch died in 1989, Anna was appointed Administratrix of the Monroe Estate, which remained open until 2001. When the estate was closed, the residuary assets were transferred to Marilyn Monroe, LLC (MMLLC) (P). In 2006, MMLLC (P) and CMG Worldwide, Inc. (P) discovered that Shaw Family Archives, LLC (SFA) (D)—the company that owned the photographs taken by the famous photographer Sam Shaw—was selling T-shirts bearing Monroe's likeness, and was also issuing licenses for others to reproduce Monroe's image from photographs that Shaw had taken. MMLLC (P) sued SFA (D) under Indiana's Right of Publicity Act, alleging that as the successor-in-interest to Monroe's estate, it could prevent SFA (D) from selling Monroe's image because Monroe's right of publicity passed to MMLLC (P) through the residuary clause of Monroe's will. Both parties filed motions for summary judgment.

ISSUE: Does a postmortem right of publicity pass through the residuary clause in a decedent's will when the decedent did not have a statutory right of publicity at the time of the decedent's death?

HOLDING AND DECISION: (McMahon, J.) No. A postmortem right of publicity does not pass through the residuary clause in a decedent's will when the decedent did not have a statutory right of publicity at the time of the decedent's death. Here, regardless of any rights purportedly conferred after her death, Monroe could not devise by will a property right she did not own at the time of her death in 1962. Descendible postmortem publicity rights were not recognized in New York, California (the two states of which she could have been a domiciliary), or Indiana at the time of Monroe's death in 1962. As a result, any publicity rights she enjoyed during her lifetime were extinguished at her death by operation of law. MMLLC (P) makes much of Ms. Monroe's purported intent to include in her residuary estate all property "to which [she] shall be in any way entitled." In the absence of any other evidence concerning her intent, this boiler-plate language is much too slender a reed on which to hang a devise of postmortem publicity rights that did not come into being until 22 years after her death. Summary judgment granted to SFA (D) and denied to CMG Worldwide, Inc. (P).

ANALYSIS

In 2007, in a direct refutation of *Shaw Family Archives*, California amended its right of publicity statute to create generally devisable publicity rights, even for wills created before the enactment of the statute. The amendment was of no use to MMLLC (P) in this case because two separate courts determined that Monroe was a New York domiciliary and therefore not subject to California law.

Quicknotes

RESIDUARY ESTATE That portion of the estate that remains after all the estate has been distributed through the satisfaction of all claims.

RIGHT OF PUBLICITY The right of a person to control the commercial exploitation of their name or likeness.

SUCCESSOR IN INTEREST One who comes after another in ownership or control of property.

Simpson v. Calivas

Beneficiary (P) v. Attorney (D)

N.H. Sup. Ct., 650 A.2d 318 (1994)

NATURE OF CASE: Appeal from summary judgment and dismissal of negligence and breach of contract actions.

FACT SUMMARY: Calivas (D) drafted a will for Robert Simpson, Sr. that was intended to leave property to his son, but was ambiguous, causing Robert Simpson, Jr. (P) to bring suit.

RULE OF LAW

Attorneys drafting wills owe a duty of reasonable care to the intended beneficiaries.

FACTS: In March 1984, Robert Simpson, Sr. executed a will that had been drafted by Calivas (D). The will was ambiguously written, causing the probate court to award a life estate in Simpson's property to the stepmother of Robert Simpson, Jr. (Robert Jr.) (P), although notes from meetings with Calivas (D) showed that the intent was for Simpson Jr. (P) to receive most of the property outright. Since Robert Jr. (P) had to pay his stepmother $400,000 for the life estate, he sued Calivas (D) for malpractice in improperly drafting his father's will. The trial court dismissed the action and Robert Jr. (P) appealed.

ISSUE: Do attorneys drafting wills owe a duty of reasonable care to the intended beneficiaries?

HOLDING AND DECISION: (Horton, J.) Yes. Attorneys drafting wills owe a duty of reasonable care to the intended beneficiaries. In order to recover for negligence a plaintiff must show that the defendant owed a duty of care. Generally, duty arises out of relation between the parties and the scope of such a duty is limited to those in privity of contract. However, there are exceptions to this privity rule. One such exception has been accepted by the overwhelming majority of jurisdictions: attorneys owe a duty to the intended beneficiary of a will. This exception to privity is accepted because of the obvious foreseeability of injury upon malpractice. Accordingly, in the present case, the trial court should not have dismissed Simpson Jr.'s (P) negligence action. Reversed and remanded.

ANALYSIS

The court also rejected Calivas's (D) argument that collateral estoppel barred the suit. The court found that the probate court had not expressly ruled on the question of Simpson Sr.'s (P) actual intent. Another situation in which privity is not required is where investigators for insurance companies look into claims of the insureds.

Quicknotes

COLLATERAL ESTOPPEL A doctrine whereby issues litigated and determined in a prior proceeding are binding upon all subsequent litigation between the parties regarding that issue.

DUTY OF REASONABLE CARE Duty to exercise the degree of care as would a reasonably prudent person under like circumstances.

A. v. B.

[Parties not identified.]

N.J. Sup. Ct., 726 A.2d 924 (1999)

NATURE OF CASE: Paternity action.

FACT SUMMARY: Father sought to restrain his former law firm from revealing to his present wife the existence of his illegitimate child.

RULE OF LAW

Rule of Professional Conduct 1.6(c) permits a lawyer to disclose a confidential communication to the extent the lawyer believes necessary "to rectify the consequences of the client's criminal, illegal or fraudulent act in furtherance of which the lawyer's services had been used."

FACTS: In this paternity action, the mother's former law firm, which simultaneously represented the father and his wife in planning their estates, sought to disclose to the wife the existence of the father's illegitimate child. The devises in the father and wife's wills created the possibility that the other spouse's issue, whether legitimate or illegitimate, ultimately would acquire the decedent's property. Because of a clerical error, the firm's computer check did not reveal the conflict of interest in its representation of the mother and the husband. On learning of the conflict, the firm withdrew from representation of the mother in the paternity action. The husband, represented by new counsel, requested restraints against the firm from disclosing to his wife the existence of the child. The restraints were denied and the appellate division reversed and remanded.

ISSUE: Does Rule of Professional Conduct 1.6(c) permit a lawyer to disclose a confidential communication to the extent the lawyer believes necessary "to rectify the consequences of the client's criminal, illegal or fraudulent act in furtherance of which the lawyer's services had been used?"

HOLDING AND DECISION: (Pollock, J.) Yes. Rule of Professional Conduct 1.6(c) permits a lawyer to disclose a confidential communication to the extent the lawyer believes necessary "to rectify the consequences of the client's criminal, illegal or fraudulent act in furtherance of which the lawyer's services had been used." This appeal involves the conflict between two fundamental obligations of lawyers: the duty of confidentiality and the duty to inform clients as to material facts. The conflict arises from the representation of two clients whose interests were, but are no longer, compatible. Rule of Professional Conduct 1.6(a) imposes a duty on the lawyer not to reveal confidential information learned in the course of representation unless the client consents after consultation. A lawyer's obligation to communicate to one client all information needed to make an informed decision qualifies the firm's duty to maintain the confidentiality of a co-client's information. The firm argues that Rule of Professional Conduct 1.6 mandates, or at least permits, the firm to disclose the existence of the husband's illegitimate child. Rule of Professional Conduct 1.6(b) requires that a lawyer disclose information relating to a client to the proper authorities if the lawyer reasonably believes that such disclosure is necessary to prevent a client from committing an unlawful act likely to result in death or substantial bodily harm or substantial injury to the financial interest or property of another. Despite the firm's argument that this section applies here, the facts of this case do not justify mandatory disclosure. The possible inheritance of the wife's estate by the husband's illegitimate child is too remote to constitute such substantial injury within the meaning of Rule of Professional Conduct 1.6(b). However, in limited circumstances Rule of Professional Conduct 1.6(c) permits a lawyer to disclose a confidential communication to the extent the lawyer believes necessary "to rectify the consequences of the client's criminal, illegal or fraudulent act in furtherance of which the lawyer's services had been used." In construing the "crime or fraud" exception to the attorney-client privilege the term fraud has been given an expansive meaning. So construed, the husband's deliberate omission of the existence of his illegitimate child constitutes a fraud on the wife. In executing reciprocal wills, the husband and wife could reasonably expect that each would disclose information material to the distribution of their estates, including the existence of children who are contingent residuary beneficiaries. The husband breached that duty. The existence of the illegitimate child could affect the distribution of the wife's estate if she predeceased him or deplete that part of his estate that would otherwise pass to the wife. The firm may inform the wife of the existence of the illegitimate child. Reversed and remanded.

ANALYSIS

The court states that an attorney who is jointly representing co-clients, should first expressly agree with the clients on the sharing of confidential information. That prior agreement would clarify the expectations of the parties and preclude the need for future litigation.

Continued on next page.

Quicknotes

CONFIDENTIAL COMMUNICATION A communication made between specified classes of persons that is privileged.

DEVISE The conferring of a gift of real or personal property by means of a testamentary instrument.

RECIPROCAL WILLS Testamentary instruments, pursuant to which two or more individuals make reciprocal provisions in favor of the other.

CHAPTER 2

Intestacy: An Estate Plan by Default

Quick Reference Rules of Law

	PAGE
1. *Hall v. Vallandingham.* An adopted child is no longer considered a child of either natural parent and loses on adoption all rights of inheritance from the child's natural parents.	*8*
2. *Minary v. Citizens Fidelity Bank & Trust Co.* One who adopts a spouse or other adult cannot thereby make the adoptee an heir to an estate created by an existing testamentary instrument executed by an ancestor of the adopter.	*9*
3. *O'Neal v. Wilkes.* A contract to adopt may not be specifically enforced unless the contract was entered into by a person with the legal authority to consent to the adoption.	*10*
4. *Woodward v. Commissioner of Social Security.* A child resulting from posthumous reproduction may enjoy the inheritance rights of "issue" under the intestacy statute where there is a genetic relationship between the child and the decedent and the decedent consented to posthumous conception and to the support of any resulting child.	*11*
5. *In re Estate of Mahoney.* A conviction of voluntary manslaughter disables the party convicted of killing the decedent from taking under the decedent's will or from the decedent's estate through intestate succession.	*13*

Hall v. Vallandingham

[Parties not identified.]

Md. Ct. Spec. App., 540 A.2d 1162 (1988)

NATURE OF CASE: Appeal from judgment disinheriting relatives.

FACT SUMMARY: After Earl Vallandingham died, his children were adopted by Killgore, his wife's new husband.

RULE OF LAW

An adopted child is no longer considered a child of either natural parent and loses on adoption all rights of inheritance from the child's natural parents.

FACTS: Earl Vallandingham died, survived by his wife Elizabeth and their four children. Elizabeth then married Jim Killgore. Killgore adopted Vallandingham's children. Earl's brother William died childless, unmarried, and intestate. His sole heirs were his surviving brothers and the children of brothers (like Earl) and sisters who predeceased him. Earl's children alleged that they were entitled to their distributive share. The court held that they were not entitled to inherit from William because they had been adopted by Killgore. They appealed.

ISSUE: Is an adopted child no longer considered a child of either natural parent, and does the child lose on adoption all rights of inheritance from the child's natural parents?

HOLDING AND DECISION: (Gilbert, C.J.) Yes. An adopted child is no longer considered a child of either natural parent and loses on adoption all rights of inheritance from the child's natural parents. The Maryland Estates and Trust Code provide that on adoption, "a child no longer shall be considered a child of either natural parent." To construe this statute so as to allow dual inheritance would bestow upon an adopted child a superior status. Because an adopted child has no right to inherit from the estate of a natural parent who dies intestate, it follows that the same child may not inherit through the natural parent by way of representation. Affirmed.

ANALYSIS

The states disagree whether or not a child continues to have inheritance rights from both natural parents when the child is adopted by a step-parent. Only a few states draw a distinction between adoption of a minor and adoption of an adult. Adult adoption has been used more frequently to prevent will contests.

Quicknotes

MARYLAND ESTATES AND TRUSTS CODE ANN. §1-207(a) (1) An adopted child shall be treated as a natural child of the child's adopting parent or parents; (2) Except as provided in paragraph (3) of this subsection, on adoption a child may not be considered a child of either natural parent; (3) On adoption by the spouse of a natural parent, the child shall still be considered the child of that natural parent.

Minary v. Citizens Fidelity Bank & Trust Co.

Daughter-in-law of deceased (P) v. Trustee (D)

Ky. Ct. App., 419 S.W.2d 340 (1967)

NATURE OF CASE: Action seeking to have a will provision construed.

FACT SUMMARY: Amelia Minary placed property in trust for eventual distribution "to [her] then-surviving heirs." One of Amelia's sons adopted his own wife (P), but the Bank (D) refused to distribute the trust property to the wife (P) as Amelia's heir.

RULE OF LAW

One who adopts a spouse or other adult cannot thereby make the adoptee an heir to an estate created by an existing testamentary instrument executed by an ancestor of the adopter.

FACTS: Amelia Minary's will created a trust, the income of which was to be paid to her husband and her three sons. Upon the death of the last surviving beneficiary, the property which Amelia had placed in the trust was to be distributed "to [her] then-surviving heirs, according to the laws of descent and distribution then in force in Kentucky, and, if no such heirs, then to the First Christian Church, Louisville, Kentucky." Amelia died in 1932. Her husband passed away three years later. Two of her three sons had predeceased their father and had left no issue. Amelia's husband was survived by the couple's daughter and by Alfred, the last of the three sons who had been named beneficiaries of Amelia's trust. In 1934, Alfred married and, prior to his death, he adopted his wife (P). When Alfred died in 1959, Myra (P), the wife, demanded that the Citizens Fidelity Bank & Trust Co. (D), the trustee, distribute the corpus of Amelia's trust to her. A suit was eventually filed in which Myra (P) claimed to be, by virtue of having been adopted as Alfred's child, an heir of Amelia Minary. The trial court ruled that Myra (P) was an heir of Amelia, but the trustee (D) appealed.

ISSUE: Can one who adopts a spouse or other adult thereby make the adoptee an heir to an estate created by an existing testamentary instrument executed by an ancestor of the adopter?

HOLDING AND DECISION: (Osborne, J.) No. One who adopts a spouse or other adult cannot thereby make the adoptee an heir to an estate created by an existing testamentary instrument executed by an ancestor of the adopter. It is clear that any adopted person, including an adult adoptee, may inherit from their adoptive parent. Moreover, the adoptee may ordinarily inherit, through an adoptive parent, the estate of an adoptive ancestor. In this case, it is probable that Amelia Minary intended her heirs to include any adopted children of her sons. Nonetheless, despite precedent to the contrary, a descendant should not be able to frustrate the declared intentions of an ancestor by adopting an adult for the sole purpose of making them an heir of the ancestor. Such a tactic, although permitted by the adoption laws, would thwart the ancestor's testamentary scheme. Therefore, the finding that Myra (P) is an heir of Amelia Minary must be reversed.

ANALYSIS

Adoption is entirely a creature of statute and was not recognized in earliest common law times. Traditionally, an adopted child was entitled to inherit from, but not through, their adoptive parents. The modern statutory trend, however, is to permit the adoptee to inherit from the ancestors of their adoptive parents. Of course, once a legal adoption has been consummated, the adopted child loses all right to inherit from or through their natural parents.

Quicknotes

RESIDUARY ESTATE The portion of the estate remaining following distribution of the assets and the payment of costs.

TESTAMENTARY INSTRUMENT An instrument that takes effect upon the death of the maker.

O'Neal v. Wilkes

Virtual adoptee (P) v. Estate executor (D)

Ga. Sup. Ct., 439 S.E.2d 490 (1994)

NATURE OF CASE: Appeal from judgment n.o.v. denying equitable adoption claim.

FACT SUMMARY: O'Neal (P), who had been raised by testator but never formally adopted, petitioned the court for a declaration of virtual (equitable) adoption.

RULE OF LAW

A contract to adopt may not be specifically enforced unless the contract was entered into by a person with the legal authority to consent to the adoption.

FACTS: Hattie O'Neal's (P) mother died in 1957, when O'Neal (P) was eight years old. O'Neal's (P) father never recognized her as his daughter. After O'Neal (P) had lived with a maternal aunt for four years, she was taken to live with her paternal aunt, Page. Page ultimately sent O'Neal (P) to live with the testator. She lived with the testator for more than ten years, until she was married. The testator referred to O'Neal (P) as his daughter and her children as his grandchildren. After he died intestate, O'Neal (P) claimed she was entitled to inherit, under the theory of equitable adoption, the property she would have been entitled to had she been the testator's statutorily adopted daughter. Wilkes (D), the executor of the estate, contested O'Neal's (P) claim. The court granted a judgment n.o.v. (notwithstanding the verdict) in favor of Wilkes (D) on the grounds that Page, the paternal aunt who sent O'Neal (D) to live with the testator, had no legal authority to enter into an adoption contract with the testator. O'Neal (P) appealed.

ISSUE: May a contract to adopt be specifically enforced if it is entered into by a person without authority to consent to the adoption?

HOLDING AND DECISION: (Fletcher, J.) No. A contract to adopt cannot be specifically enforced if it is entered into by a person without authority to consent to the adoption. Consent to an adoption may only be given by a child's parent or legal guardian. O'Neal's (P) Aunt Page was not O'Neal's (P) legal guardian; she was merely taking over a familial obligation in caring for the child. Because Page had no legal relationship with O'Neal (P), she could not consent to her adoption by the testator. The adoption contract was, therefore, invalid, and thus, O'Neal's (P) claim for an equitable adoption is defeated. Affirmed.

DISSENT: (Sears, J.) Equity treats as done that which ought to be done. By insisting that a person be appointed as a legal guardian before agreeing to a contract to adopt, the majority is harming the very person the requirement is designed to protect— the child.

ANALYSIS

The majority does not grant the adoption in this case because the aunt was not the proper party to consent. The opinion, however, recognizes that O'Neal's (P) biological father also had no right to consent since he had abandoned her. The question the court fails to address is whether the child should be punished when there is no proper party to consent through no fault of her own. The result is anything but equitable toward the child.

Quicknotes

EQUITABLE ADOPTION An oral contract to adopt a child not executed in accordance with statutory requirements, giving rise to rights of inheritance in the child, upon the death of the promisor.

INTESTATE To die without leaving a valid testamentary instrument.

JUDGMENT NOTWITHSTANDING THE VERDICT (J.N.O.V) A judgment entered by the trial judge reversing a jury verdict if the jury's determination has no basis in law or fact.

LEGAL CUSTODIAN Person having responsibility for a person or the person's property pursuant to law.

TESTATOR One who executes a will.

Woodward v. Commissioner of Social Security

Applicant for survivor benefits (P) v. Federal agency (D)

Mass. Sup. Jud. Ct., 760 N.E.2d 257 (2002)

NATURE OF CASE: Certified question regarding the inheritance rights of a child created through posthumous reproduction in an action for survivor benefits.

FACT SUMMARY: Woodward (P) sought survivor benefits for herself and her children, who were conceived using her deceased husband's previously preserved semen.

RULE OF LAW

A child resulting from posthumous reproduction may enjoy the inheritance rights of "issue" under the intestacy statute where there is a genetic relationship between the child and the decedent, and the decedent consented to posthumous conception and to the support of any resulting child.

FACTS: Three years after the Woodward's wedding, the husband was diagnosed with leukemia. The Woodwards subsequently arranged for a quantity of the husband's semen to be medically withdrawn and preserved in case he was left sterile after treatment. Shortly thereafter the husband died. Two years later, the wife (P) gave birth to twin girls conceived through artificial insemination using the husband's preserved semen. The Social Security Administration (SSA) (D) rejected the wife's (P) application for mother and child survivor benefits on the ground that she had not established that the twins were the husband's children within the meaning of the applicable law. While a series of appeals of the SSA (D) decision were pending, the Probate and Family Court entered a judgment of paternity and an order to amend both birth certificates declaring the deceased husband to be the children's father. A United States administrative law judge concluded that the children did not qualify for benefits because they were not entitled to inherit from the husband under the Massachusetts intestacy and paternity laws. The appeals counsel of the SSA (D) affirmed. The wife (P) appealed to the United States District Court for the District of Massachusetts seeking a declaratory judgment to reverse the commissioner's ruling and the United States District Court judge certified the question to this court.

ISSUE: May a child resulting from posthumous reproduction enjoy the inheritance rights of "issue" under the intestacy statute where there is a genetic relationship between the child and the decedent, and the decedent consented to posthumous conception and to the support of any resulting child?

HOLDING AND DECISION: (Marshall, C.J.) Yes. A child resulting from posthumous reproduction may enjoy the inheritance rights of "issue" under the intestacy statute where there is a genetic relationship between the child and the decedent, and the decedent consented to posthumous conception and to the support of any resulting child. Although the intestacy statute does not limit the class of posthumous children to those in utero at the time of the decedent's death, posthumous reproduction may at times conflict with the purpose of the intestacy law and implicate other interests. This holding reconciles that conflict. The term "issue" means all genetic descendants and both marital and nonmarital descendants. Provisions of the intestacy statute regarding nonmarital children and posthumous children of an intestate are an expression of the legislature's intent to ensure that wealth passes from and to the actual family. The former requires that such a child must obtain a judicial determination that he or she is the father's child. Under our intestacy law, there is no reason that children conceived after the decedent's death, who are the decedent's direct genetic descendants, may not enjoy the same succession rights as children conceived before the decedent's death who are the decedent's direct genetic descendants. Massachusetts's interests in the best interests of the children, the orderly administration of estates, and the reproductive rights of the genetic parents are balanced and harmonized by this holding to effect the legislature's overall purposes. It can be assumed based on precedent and public policy, the legislature intended that posthumously conceived children be entitled to the same rights and protections of law, such as financial support from their parents, as children conceived before death. The protection of minor children has been a forefront issue in legislative action and jurisprudence. Despite the long existence of assistive reproductive technologies, the legislature has not acted to narrow the broad statutory class of posthumous children to restrict posthumously conceived children from taking in intestacy. According succession rights under our intestacy laws to posthumously conceived children will also not deteriorate the legislative purpose of providing certainty to heirs and creditors. The orderly, prompt, and accurate administration of intestate estates will not be affected. Since death ends a marriage, a posthumously conceived child is a nonmarital child. As such, our intestacy law mandates that a nonmarital child must obtain a judicial determination of paternity as a prerequisite to succeeding to a portion of the father's intestate estate. Posthumous maternity is uncertain until judicially established as is posthumous paternity, and neither more nor less difficult

Continued on next page.

to prove. The final state interest implicated by this certified question is the reproductive rights of the genetic parent. Individuals have a protected right to control the use of their gametes. A decedent's silence or equivocal indications of a desire to parent posthumously, ought not to be construed as consent, but rather the prospective donor parent must clearly and unequivocally consent not only to posthumous reproduction but also to the support of any resulting child. That a man has medically preserved his gametes for use by his spouse may indicate only that he wished to reproduce after some contingency while he was alive, and not that he consented to the different circumstances of creating a child after his death. A rule that just required a genetic tie or the election to preserve gametes would thus be insufficient. In the present case, it is up to the wife (P) to prove that her husband consented to posthumously conceived children and that he consented to support such children.

ANALYSIS

This case demonstrates what effect modern technology is having on the definition of the family in the context of intestate succession. New Jersey has come out similarly to Massachusetts on this issue, whereas Virginia and North Dakota have enacted the Uniform Status of Children of Assisted Conception Act (1988), which provides that a donor of an egg or sperm is not the parent of a child conceived through assisted conception. This case also brings up the yet-to-be-determined issue of the conflict between the state's interest in the orderly administration of estates effectuated by establishing a limitations period for the commencement of paternity claims against the intestate estate and the burdens such limitations period imposes on the surviving parent and child.

Quicknotes

DECEDENT A person who is deceased.

INTESTATE To die without leaving a valid testamentary instrument.

INTESTATE SUCCESSION The scheme pursuant to which property is distributed in the absence of a valid will or of a disposition of particular property.

In re Estate of Mahoney

Widow (P) v. Decedent's parents (D)

Vt. Sup. Ct., 220 A.2d 475 (1966)

NATURE OF CASE: Appeal from an estate distribution order.

FACT SUMMARY: Mrs. Mahoney (P) was convicted of manslaughter for killing her husband.

RULE OF LAW

A conviction of voluntary manslaughter disables the party convicted of killing the decedent from taking under the decedent's will or from the decedent's estate through intestate succession.

FACTS: Mrs. Mahoney (P) was convicted of voluntary manslaughter for shooting her husband. Mr. Mahoney died intestate. His estate was ordered distributed to his mother (D) and father (D) since the probate court found that a conviction of voluntary manslaughter disabled Mrs. Mahoney (P) from taking any part of her husband's estate.

ISSUE: Does a conviction of voluntary manslaughter disable the party convicted of killing the decedent from taking under the decedent's will or from the decedent's estate through intestate succession?

HOLDING AND DECISION: (Smith, J.) Yes. A conviction of voluntary manslaughter disables the party convicted of killing the decedent from taking under the decedent's will or from the decedent's estate through intestate succession. Any inheritance in the killer's favor is held as a constructive trust in favor of the other heirs or next of kin. While decisions in other jurisdictions vary with respect to voluntary manslaughter, the rule imposing a constructive trust appears to be the best solution. Although in this case there was no special finding concerning the voluntariness of Mrs. Mahoney's (P) actions, the court obviously concluded that she had been convicted of the felonious killing of her husband. While a constructive trust could be imposed on the bequest, the probate court could only apply the laws of distribution and descent and incorrectly awarded the property directly to Mr. Mahoney's parents (D). We must reverse and remand to allow a constructive trust action to be brought in a proper court of chancery.

ANALYSIS

In a majority of states, a killer is barred by statute, sometimes referred to as a slayer statute, from inheriting any interest in the estate of his victim. In jurisdictions where no such statute has been enacted, courts have shown a reluctance to impose any restraints on the killer's right to inherit. Sometimes, however, a court of equity will adopt the constructive trust approach favored by the Mahoney court, although the trust device seems to unduly complicate the nature of the relief granted. Note that at earliest common law, the commission of any felony, not only murder, deprived the wrongdoer of the right to inherit property.

Quicknotes

CONSTRUCTIVE TRUST A trust that arises by operation of law whereby the court imposes a trust upon property lawfully held by one party for the benefit of another, as a result of some wrongdoing by the party in possession so as to avoid unjust enrichment.

RESIDUE That property which remains following the distribution of the assets of the testator's estate.

SLAYER STATUTE Statute providing that a person who feloniously and intentionally kills another individual is prohibited from receiving any property from the victim decedent's estate either by will or inheritance or from receiving the proceeds of any life insurance policies.

CHAPTER 3

Wills: Formalities and Forms

Quick Reference Rules of Law

PAGE

1. *Bitetzakis v. Bitetzaklis.* Where a testator who ordinarily signs their full name on a document only signs part of their name on a document purporting to be their last will and testament, the testator has not signed the document in strict compliance with statutory will execution requirements. *17*

2. *In re Estate of Hall.* It is irrelevant that a document offered for probate as a will has not been properly witnessed where clear and convincing evidence establishes the testator's intent that the document be the testator's will. *19*

3. *In re Probate of Will and Codicil of Macool.* For a writing to be admitted into probate as a will, the proponent of the document must prove by clear and convincing evidence that the decedent actually reviewed the document and gave their assent to it. *20*

4. *In re Estate of Horton.* In a jurisdiction that permits the probate of a will that does not meet will execution formalities, where the proponent of a document or writing establishes by clear and convincing evidence that the decedent intended the document or writing to constitute the decedent's will, an undated and unwitnessed electronic note on a decedent's cellphone can be probated as the decedent's will where the note's contents, and extrinsic evidence of all relevant circumstances, indicate that the decedent intended the note to constitute the decedent's will. *21*

5. *Matter of Estate of Beck.* A video recording, even if it manifests testamentary intent, cannot qualify as an intended will where a will must be a "document." *23*

6. *In re Kimmel's Estate.* An informal document evidencing intent of a conditional gift and an intent to execute may serve as a testamentary document. *24*

7. *In re Estate of Gonzalez.* Printed portions of a will form can be incorporated into a holographic will where the trial court finds a testamentary intent, considering all of the evidence in the case. *25*

8. *In re Estate of Kuralt.* A letter written by the deceased while in extremis, expressing an intent that another "inherit" a specific bequest of the deceased's property and not the entirety of the deceased's estate, is a valid holographic codicil to the deceased's formal will. *26*

9. *Thompson v. Royall.* Revocation of a will by cancellation is accomplished only if the written words of the document are mutilated or otherwise impaired. *27*

10. *Harrison v. Bird.* A rebuttable presumption of revocation exists where a will cannot be found among a deceased's personal effects. *28*

11. *In re Estate of Stoker.* A will is valid if the proponent of the will proves by clear and convincing evidence that at the time the testator executed the will, the testator intended the document to constitute their last will. *29*

12. *LaCroix v. Senecal.* The doctrine of dependent relative revocation sustains a gift by will when such a gift has been revoked in a codicil that substantially reaffirms the gift but is void by reason of the interest of a subscribing witness. *30*

13. *In re Estate of Rigsby.* In regard to handwritten or holographic wills that consist of more than one page, it must be clearly apparent that the testator intended that all pages constitute the testator's last will and testament. *31*

14. *Clark v. Greenhalge.* A properly executed will may incorporate by reference into its provisions any document or paper not so executed and witnessed if it was in existence at the time of the execution of the will and is identified by clear and satisfactory proof as the paper referred to therein. *32*

15. *Keith v. Lulofs.* When reciprocal testamentary provisions are made in mutual or reciprocal wills for the benefit of a third party, sufficient consideration is present to entitle the beneficiary to enforce the wills as a contract, provided there is clear and convincing evidence the parties intended to create a contract. *33*

Bitetzakis v. Bitetzakis

Decedent's child (P) v. Decedent's spouse (D)

Fla. Ct. App., 264 So. 3d 297 (2019)

NATURE OF CASE: Appeal from order admitting will to probate.

FACT SUMMARY: Alice Bitetzakis (P) contended that her father, George Bitetzakis (George), had not complied with the statutory requirements for signing a will where George, who ordinarily signed his full name on documents, signed only his first name to his will, notwithstanding that George did so because his wife, Ana (D), had interrupted the signing and directed George to stop signing because she mistakenly believed he needed to sign before a notary, and notwithstanding that George went to a notary the next day to sign the will, but accidentally took a self-proving affidavit.

RULE OF LAW

Where a testator who ordinarily signs their full name on a document only signs part of their name on a document purporting to be their last will and testament, the testator has not signed the document in strict compliance with statutory will execution requirements.

FACTS: George Bitetzakis had his wife, Ana (D), and two close friends come to a breakfast at his house for the purpose of executing his will. The two witnesses signed first, at George's request, and then George started to sign. He had completed his first name, when Ana (D) interrupted the signing because she mistakenly believed he needed to sign in front of a notary. George normally signed his full name when signing documents. The next day, Ana (D) took George to a notary. Unfortunately, George accidentally brought a self-proving affidavit to the notary, not the will. George signed the self-proving affidavit, and it contained the notary's stamp, but it incongruously averred that George served as a witness to the execution of his own will. After George died, his grandson (D) was appointed the personal representative and petitioned for the administration of the document George had signed only with his first name. George's daughter, Alice Bitetzakis (P), responded to the petition by asserting that George's will failed to conform to statutory requirements because George did not sign at the end of the will, and because his later signing of the self-proving affidavit was insufficient to rectify his incomplete signature. The probate court determined that George had intended the document to be his last will and testament, reasoning that his stopping to sign before he completed his full name did not do away with his intent, and that his efforts to have the document signed the next day before a notary further demonstrated his intent, notwithstanding that he brought the wrong document to the notary. The state's intermediate appellate court granted review.

ISSUE: Where a testator who ordinarily signs their full name on a document only signs part of their name on a document purporting to be their last will and testament, has the testator signed the document in strict compliance with statutory will execution requirements?

HOLDING AND DECISION: (Northcutt, J.) No. Where a testator who ordinarily signs their full name on a document only signs part of their name on a document purporting to be their last will and testament, the testator has not signed the document in strict compliance with statutory will execution requirements. Although any mark a testator makes that the testator intends to be their signature qualifies as a valid signature, where a testator regularly signs their full name to documents, and there is no evidence that the testator intends a partially signed name to be their signature, regardless of the circumstances, under strict compliance the partial signature does not qualify as a valid signature because that is not what the testator intended as the testator's signature. Therefore, the probate court erred because the evidence did not establish that George signed at the end of the will or directed another to subscribe his name in his stead, as required by statute. To the contrary, George's intentionally ceasing signing the will and later signing the self-proving affidavit in an apparent attempt to ratify it dispels any notion that he believed or intended that his first name serve as his signature and assent to the will. Accordingly, the will was unsigned and should not have been admitted to probate. Reversed and remanded.

ANALYSIS

This case illustrates the principle that, as a matter of strict compliance, although the primary consideration in construing a will is the intent of the testator, when testamentary intent is contained in a will, it can only be effectuated if the will has been validly executed. Here, because the appellate court determined that the will had not been validly executed, it did not give weight to the circumstances surrounding George's attempt to sign his will to show his intent, as the probate court had done.

Continued on next page.

Quicknotes

PROBATE The administration of a decedent's estate.

SELF-PROVING AFFIDAVIT An affidavit accompanying a will and signed by the testator and witnesses; it certifies that the will has been executed according to statutory requirements.

TESTATOR One who executes a will.

In re Estate of Hall

[Parties not identified.]

Mont. Sup. Ct., 51 P.3d 1134 (2002)

NATURE OF CASE: Appeal from admittance of joint will to probate.

FACT SUMMARY: Hall's daughter argued that a draft of a joint will executed by Hall and his wife and notarized by their attorney in the absence of any other witnesses was invalid because it was not properly witnessed.

RULE OF LAW

It is irrelevant that a document offered for probate as a will has not been properly witnessed where clear and convincing evidence establishes the testator's intent that the document be the testator's will.

FACTS: Hall had executed a will in 1984. Then, in 1997, at the suggestion of Cannon, Hall's attorney, Hall and his wife agreed to execute a joint will. They met at Cannon's office and ironed out the will's terms. Although the document they had worked on was a draft, Hall asked Cannon if the draft could stand as a will until Cannon sent them a final version. Cannon said that it would be valid if Hall and Hall's wife executed the draft and he notarized it, and accordingly, the couple executed the draft, and Cannon notarized it with no other witnesses present. When they returned home from the meeting, Hall apparently told his wife to tear up his 1984 will, which his wife did. After Hall's death, his wife applied to informally probate the joint will. Hall's daughter objected, arguing that the draft had been improperly witnessed (the state's law requires at least two witnesses). The lower court ordered the joint will admitted to probate, and the daughter appealed. The state's highest court granted review.

ISSUE: Is it irrelevant that a document offered for probate as a will has not been properly witnessed where clear and convincing evidence establishes the testator's intent that the document be the testator's will?

HOLDING AND DECISION: (Regnier, J.) Yes. It is irrelevant that a document offered for probate as a will has not been properly witnessed where clear and convincing evidence establishes the testator's intent that the document be the testator's will. Typically, the probate statute requires that for a will to be valid, two people must witness the testator signing the will and then sign the will themselves. However, the statute also provides that if two individuals do not properly witness the document, it may still be treated as if it had been executed under certain circumstances. One such circumstance is if the proponent of the document establishes by clear and convincing evidence that the decedent intended the document to be the decedent's will. Thus, here the issue is whether the lower court erred in concluding that Hall intended the joint will to be his will. The evidence indicates that the lower court did not err. First, the joint will specifically revoked all previous wills and codicils made by either Hall or his wife. Second, Hall directed that his prior will be destroyed. The evidence demonstrated that Hall and his wife believed that the joint will would stand as a will until Cannon provided one in cleaner, more final form. Affirmed.

ANALYSIS

The doctrine under which a court may probate a document that was not properly executed if the court is satisfied that there can be no reasonable doubt that the deceased intended the document to constitute the deceased's will is known as the dispensing power doctrine. The dispensing power doctrine, applied in this case, is found at Uniform Probate Code § 2-503.

Quicknotes

PROBATE The administration of a decedent's estate.

TESTATOR One who executes a will.

In re Probate of Will and Codicil of Macool

Niece of decedent (P) v. Decedent's step-children (D)

N.J. Super. Ct. App. Div., 3 A.3d 1258 (2010)

NATURE OF CASE: Plaintiff's appeal from lower court decision finding that the decedent's will was not valid, because she did not review or sign it prior to her death.

FACT SUMMARY: Louise Macool sought to amend her existing will and codicil after her husband passed away. She gave her attorney a handwritten note that allegedly added her niece to her will. Her attorney then created a rough draft of her will, but Macool passed away before reviewing or signing the new will.

RULE OF LAW

For a writing to be admitted into probate as a will, the proponent of the document must prove by clear and convincing evidence that the decedent actually reviewed the document and gave their assent to it.

FACTS: Louise and Elmer Macool were married for forty years. Both were previously married. Louise was the step-mother to Elmer's seven children, including Muriel Macool (D) and Michael Macool (D), and raised them as her own. Louise was also very close to her niece, Mary Rescigno (P). Louise created her own will in 1995 and added a codicil in 2007 that named Elmer as her sole beneficiary. After Elmer died, Louise sought to amend her will. She provided her attorney with a handwritten note that, among other things, stated Mary Rescigno (P) should be included as a beneficiary. After Louise met and discussed the new changes to the will with her attorney, her attorney's office then created a draft will that had the word "rough" handwritten at the top of it. Louise passed away an hour after her meeting with the attorney. The trial court found that Louise never reviewed the draft will or assented to it. Accordingly, the trial court rejected Mary Resigno's (P) argument that the draft will constituted a valid will under state law. Resigno (P) appealed.

ISSUE: For a writing to be admitted into probate as a will, must the proponent of the document prove by clear and convincing evidence that the decedent actually reviewed the document and gave their assent to it?

HOLDING AND DECISION: (Fuentes, J.) Yes. For a writing to be admitted into probate as a will, the proponent of the document must prove by clear and convincing evidence that the decedent actually reviewed the document and gave their assent to it. The trial court properly distinguished between evidence that Louise desired to amend her will, which was undisputed, and evidence that she reviewed and assented to the draft will created by her attorney. Louise's death prevented her from ever reading or reviewing the document. The rough draft was clearly a work in progress that was not meant to be a final draft. Because Louise never read the document or approved it, it cannot constitute a valid will. The court also finds that a testamentary or traditional will, created by a third party for the decedent's benefit, need not actually be signed by the decedent. It is enough that the decedent reviews and assents to it, with both of those elements proved by clear and convincing evidence. Conversely, holographic wills are handwritten documents created by a decedent. These types of wills must be executed by the decedent to be valid. Affirmed.

ANALYSIS

This decision codifies the "harmless error doctrine." The doctrine is a relaxation of the formal requirement that a will must be signed for it to be valid. It allows a will to be probated where there is clear and convincing evidence that the decedent reviewed the will and assented to it. For example, in another recent state case, a decedent's actions of reviewing a will, failing to sign it but then sending it to the executor to review and sign was enough evidence to hold that the will was final and valid.

Quicknotes

CLEAR AND CONVINCING EVIDENCE An evidentiary standard requiring a demonstration that the fact sought to be proven is reasonably certain.

In re Estate of Horton

[Decedent's sole heir (Petitioner) v. Decedent's conservator (Petitioner)]

Mich. Ct. App., 925 N.W.2d 207 (2018)

NATURE OF CASE: Appeal from order recognizing an electronic document as a valid will.

FACT SUMMARY: Duane Francis Horton II (decedent) committed suicide, leaving a handwritten journal entry that directed whoever found it to an electronic, final "farewell" note that was a typed document that existed only in electronic form. The electronic note included a paragraph disposing of his property after his death. Decedent's court-appointed conservator, Guardianship and Alternatives, Inc. (GAI), petitioned for probate of the electronic note, contending it was decedent's last will and testament. Decedent's mother, Lanora Jones (Jones), decedent's sole heir, filed a separate petition to be named as the personal representative, contending that decedent had died intestate on the grounds that the note was not a validly executed will.

RULE OF LAW

In a jurisdiction that permits the probate of a will that does not meet will execution formalities, where the proponent of a document or writing establishes by clear and convincing evidence that the decedent intended the document or writing to constitute the decedent's will, an undated and unwitnessed electronic note on a decedent's cellphone can be probated as the decedent's will where the note's contents, and extrinsic evidence of all relevant circumstances, indicate that the decedent intended the note to constitute the decedent's will.

FACTS: Duane Francis Horton II (decedent) committed suicide when he was 21, leaving a handwritten journal entry that directed whoever found it to an undated and unwitnessed electronic, final "farewell" note that was a typed document which existed only in electronic form. The journal entry provided an e-mail address and password for the note, which was on an app on decedent's cellphone. Decedent had left the journal and the cellphone in his room. The note contained apologies and explanations for his suicide, comments relating to decedent's views on God and the afterlife, final farewells and advice to loved ones and friends, and it contained requests regarding his funeral. The note then clearly dictated the distribution of his property after his death. Decedent's note provided nothing for his mother and sole heir, Lanora Jones (Jones), but provided for other relatives and for a couple he had been living with. The note also expressly affirmed that decedent wanted none of his property to go to his mother after his death. The note had decedent's name at its end. During his lifetime, decedent was subject to a conservatorship. Guardianship and Alternatives, Inc. (GAI) served as the court-appointed conservator. GAI filed a petition for probate and appointment of a personal representative, nominating itself to serve as the personal representative of decedent's estate. GAI maintained that decedent's electronic note qualified as decedent's will. Jones filed a competing petition for probate and appointment of a personal representative in which she nominated herself to serve as the personal representative of decedent's estate. In that petition, Jones alleged that decedent died intestate on the grounds that the note was not a validly executed will. She also averred that she was decedent's sole heir. The state's will execution statutes were modeled on the Uniform Probate Code (UPC), and, although providing for will execution formalities, also provided that no particular formalities were necessary to create a valid will, provided it could be shown that the decedent intended the writing or document offered for probate to be the decedent's will. After an evidentiary hearing involving testimony from several witnesses, the probate court concluded that GAI presented clear and convincing evidence that decedent's electronic note was intended by decedent to constitute his will. At that hearing, it was brought out that decedent had a strained relationship with his mother. The probate court recognized the document as a valid will, Jones appealed, and the state's intermediate appellate court granted review.

ISSUE: In a jurisdiction that permits the probate of a will that does not meet will execution formalities, where the proponent of a document or writing establishes by clear and convincing evidence that the decedent intended the document or writing to constitute the decedent's will, can an undated and unwitnessed electronic note on a decedent's cellphone be probated as the decedent's will where the note's contents, and extrinsic evidence of all relevant circumstances, indicate that the decedent intended the note to constitute the decedent's will?

HOLDING AND DECISION: (Per curiam) Yes. In a jurisdiction that permits the probate of a will that does not meet will execution formalities, where the proponent of a document or writing establishes by clear and convincing evidence that the decedent intended the document or writing to constitute the decedent's will, an undated and unwitnessed electronic note on a decedent's cellphone can be probated as decedent's will where the note's contents, and extrinsic evidence of all relevant circumstances, indicate that the decedent intended the note to constitute

Continued on next page.

the decedent's will. The state's statutory will execution scheme permits the probate of a will that does not meet will execution formalities. Pursuant to that scheme, any document or writing can constitute a valid will provided that the proponent of the document or writing establishes by clear and convincing evidence that the decedent intended the document or writing to constitute the decedent's will. In considering the decedent's intent, the statutory scheme permits the admission of extrinsic evidence to determine whether the decedent intended a document to constitute the decedent's will. Application of these principles here shows that the probate court did not err in its conclusion that decedent's electronic note constituted his will. It is beyond dispute that the note did not meet the formal requirements for a will or the requirements of a holographic will. Therefore, the issue is whether clear and convincing evidence shows that decedent intended the electronic note to be his will. The ultimate question is whether decedent intended the note to govern the posthumous distribution of his property. In light of the circumstances surrounding the creation of the note, the contents of the note, the unequivocal expression of the decedent's wishes concerning the disposition of his property following his death, the circumstances surrounding the creation of the note, the circumstances surrounding his death, and the circumstances surrounding the writings he left to ensure the electronic note could be found, there was clear and convincing evidence the decedent intended the electronic document to constitute his will. Therefore, the note constitutes a valid will. Affirmed.

ANALYSIS

Will execution formalities, or a lack thereof, are not irrelevant in a will contest involving statutory provisions like the ones in this case that permit the probating of a writing or document that is shown to have been intended by a decedent to constitute the decedent's will by clear and convincing evidence. Formalities are considered indicative of intent. Restatement (Third) of Property: Will and Other Donative Transfers, § 3.3, comment a. Consequently, an adherence to some formalities, or conversely the extent of the departure from formalities, can be considered when determining whether a document was intended to be a will. As the comment to UPC § 2-503—on which the statute in this case, permitting of a writing or document that does not meet will execution formalities, was modeled—indicates, "The larger the departure from . . . formality, the harder it will be to satisfy the court that the instrument reflects the testator's intent." The more formal requirements for a will (under UPC § 2-502) remain a viable—and perhaps more straightforward—means for expressing intent to create a will. See Restatement (Third), § 3.3, comment a. MCL 700.2503 (based on UPC § 2-503) simply makes plain that other evidence clearly and convincingly demonstrating intent to adopt a will should not be ignored simply because the decedent failed to comply with formalities.

Quicknotes

CONSERVATOR A court-appointed custodian of property belonging to a person found to be unable to manage their property.

EXTRINSIC EVIDENCE Evidence that is not contained within the text of a document or contract, but that is derived from the parties' statements or the circumstances under which the agreement was made.

GUARDIANSHIP A legal relationship whereby one party is responsible for the care and control over another, called the "ward," and the ward's property, resulting from the ward's legal incapacity.

HOLOGRAPHIC WILL A will that is handwritten by the testator.

Matter of Estate of Beck

Brother of decedent (P) v. Daughter of decedent (D)

Mont. Sup. Ct., 557 P.3d 1255 (2024)

NATURE OF CASE: Appeal from denial of petition to probate a video recording as an intended will.

FACT SUMMARY: Jason Beck (P) sought to have a video his brother, Jesse Beck (Jesse), sent to Jason (P) four days before Jesse died, accepted as an intended will.

RULE OF LAW

A video recording, even if it manifests testamentary intent, cannot qualify as an intended will where a will must be a "document."

FACTS: Jesse Beck died in a motorcycle accident. He was survived by one child, Alexia (D). Four days prior to his death, Jesse sent his brother, Jason (P), a phone video of himself in which he stated that all of his possessions should go to his brother upon his death and not a named woman. The woman he named was a nonrelative who would not have been entitled to anything from Jesse's estate if he died intestate. Alexia (D) filed a petition to be appointed as personal representative to administer Jesse's estate and filed a wrongful death action in connection with Jesse's death. Jason (P) filed a subsequent complaint seeking intervention in the wrongful death action and a petition to probate Jesse's video as an enforceable will and appoint him as personal representative instead of Alexia (D). Alexia (D) objected, arguing the video was not a valid will under Montana's probate code. The District Court found in Alexia's (D) favor on the grounds that a video will did not meet the definition of a "document or writing added upon a document" as required by Montana's probate code. Jason (P) appealed, and the state's highest court granted review.

ISSUE: Can a video recording, even if it manifests testamentary intent, qualify as an intended will where a will must be a "document"?

HOLDING AND DECISION: (Rice, J.) No. A video recording, even if it manifests testamentary intent, cannot qualify as an intended will where a will must be a "document." Montana's probate code, which is based on the Uniform Probate Code (UPC), states that a "document or writing added upon a document" that was not executed in compliance with the Code's requirements for a will can still be valid if it meets certain criteria. Jason (P) argued that the Montana legislature intended "in writing" to encompass video recordings and that allowing a video recording to serve as a will would further the legislature's goals of honoring testamentary intent and promoting justice. In response, Alexia (D) argued that the statute does not authorize nonwritten wills.

No state legislative authority or court applying the UPC has recognized nonwritten, video wills. The plain language of the statute clearly implies that a "document" is a physical paper or possibly digital file with words that could be signed and witnessed; it does not include audio or video recordings. The purpose of the section Jason (P) references regarding a writing added upon a document is intended to excuse harmless errors in the creation of a written will, not to authorize audio or video wills. Affirmed.

ANALYSIS

Though video wills were rejected as a valid will substitute, in *In re Estate of Horton*, 925 N.W.2d 207 (Mich. App. 2018), a Michigan appellate court found that a written note on a decedent's phone that was referenced in a handwritten note as his "farewell" was considered part of a valid will. As audio, video, and other digital technology continues to develop, legislatures may need to revisit the traditional constraints of a written will.

Quicknotes

TESTAMENTARY INTENT A determination that a document was intended to be a will and, as such, reflects the writer's true wishes.

TESTATOR One who executes a will.

WILL An instrument setting forth the distribution to be made of an individual's estate upon their death; since a will is not effective until the death of its maker, it is revocable during their life.

WILL SUBSTITUTE A legal method that enables an individual to transfer property to a beneficiary without going through the probate process, typically taking effect upon the individual's death, but also possibly during the individual's lifetime, including, for example, joint bank accounts, joint tenancy, life insurance, payable on death accounts, and revocable trusts.

In re Kimmel's Estate

[Parties not identified.]

Pa. Sup. Ct., 123 A. 405 (1924)

NATURE OF CASE: Appeal from entry of a letter into probate.

FACT SUMMARY: Kimmel, the decedent, wrote a letter to his sons mentioning, among other things, what was to happen to his possessions if anything were to happen to him. His sons attempted to probate the letter.

RULE OF LAW

An informal document evidencing intent of a conditional gift and an intent to execute may serve as a testamentary document.

FACTS: Kimmel wrote a letter to his sons, which was mailed by him on the day of his death. The letter was very poorly written but contained a discussion of the weather, butchering, and a possible trip to town. It also stated, "if enny thing hapens all the scock money in the 3 Bank liberty lones Post office stamps and my home on Horner St goes to George Darl and Irvin Kepp [my two sons] this letter lock it up it may help you out." The letter was dated and signed "Father." The heirs at law protested the entry of the letter into probate.

ISSUE: Can an informal document evidencing intent of a conditional gift and an intent to execute serve as a testamentary document?

HOLDING AND DECISION: (Simpson, J.) Yes. An informal document evidencing intent of a conditional gift and an intent to execute can serve as a testamentary document. In this case, Kimmel's language, however poor, telling his sons what should happen if he were not to survive clearly shows a gift that is conditional upon the occurrence of something, namely Kimmel's death. Most holographic wills are informal in character, and the fact that the weather is discussed in the document does not change its testamentary effect. Also, the fact that Kimmel signed all his letters "Father" shows that he considered this letter a final and executed document. The intent to execute is more important than Kimmel's knowledge of the formal requirements for execution. Affirmed.

ANALYSIS

Most courts interpret conditional wills as stating the testator's inducement to execute the will rather than an actual condition that must be fulfilled before the will can be probated. For example, in *Eaton v. Brown*, 193 U.S. 411 (1904), the testator's holographic will stated, "I am going on a journey and may not return. If I do not, I leave everything to my adopted son." The testator did in fact return, only to die several months later. The court held the will entitled to probate on the grounds that her statement about not returning was merely an expression of her thoughts at the time she wrote the will, not an event that must occur in order to make the will effective.

Quicknotes

HOLOGRAPHIC WILL A will that is handwritten by the testator.

TESTAMENTARY INTENT A determination that the document was intended to be a will and, as such, reflects the writer's true wishes.

In re Estate of Gonzalez

[Parties not identified.]

Maine Sup. Jud. Ct., 855 A.2d 1146 (2004)

NATURE OF CASE: Appeal from decree allowing holographic will for probate.

FACT SUMMARY: Gonzalez filled out a preprinted will naming three of his five children as beneficiaries, but he did not have the will properly witnessed. The three named beneficiaries submitted the will for probate as a holographic will and the two omitted children objected.

RULE OF LAW

Printed portions of a will form can be incorporated into a holographic will where the trial court finds a testamentary intent, considering all of the evidence in the case.

FACTS: Before going on a trip to Florida, Fermin Gonzalez filled in a preprinted will leaving his estate in equal shares to three of his five children. Gonzalez showed his brother Joseph, and his brother's wife Elizabeth, the completed form, and Elizabeth saw Gonzalez sign it. However, no one signed the form as a witness. Gonzalez told Joseph and Elizabeth that he was going to copy the document onto a new form so that it would be more legible, and Joseph, Elizabeth, and Gonzalez's mother all signed the blank form as witnesses. However, Gonzalez died before he filled out the second form. Because the first form was not properly witnessed, it did not qualify as a will under Maine law. Therefore, Gonzalez's three children named in the form petitioned the court to admit the form for probate as a holographic will, which is admissible as a testamentary instrument when "the signature and the material provisions are in the handwriting of the testator." Gonzalez's other two children, who were omitted on the form, objected. They claimed the material provisions of the will were preprinted and not in Gonzalez's handwriting. The Probate Court found that the form was a valid holographic will, and the omitted children appealed.

ISSUE: Can printed portions of a will form be incorporated into a holographic will where the trial court finds a testamentary intent, considering all of the evidence in the case?

HOLDING AND DECISION: (Alexander, J.) Yes. Printed portions of a will form can be incorporated into a holographic will where the trial court finds a testamentary intent, considering all of the evidence in the case. Most jurisdictions have dealt with this issue in one of two ways. Some courts have looked to the preprinted language in order to determine the context of the handwritten notes. Other courts have ignored all of the preprinted words, and determined whether the handwritten words, taken alone, fulfill the requirements of a holographic will. We agree with the first method. The Uniform Probate Code comment states that "a holograph may be valid even though immaterial parts such as date or introductory wording be printed or stamped." The preprinted words in Gonzalez's will are introductory and may be preprinted. When filled in by Gonzalez's handwriting, they become a valid statement of testamentary intent in a holographic will. Affirmed.

ANALYSIS

Not all states have statutes permitting holographic wills, and the requirements in the states that do permit them vary widely. Some states require that the entire will is written, signed, and dated in the testator's handwriting. Others, like the one at issue in this case, require that the material provisions of the document be written by hand. More modern statutes call for handwritten material portions and allow the introduction of extrinsic evidence to show testamentary intent.

Quicknotes

HOLOGRAPHIC WILL A will that is handwritten by the testator.

In re Estate of Kuralt

[Parties not identified.]

Mont. Sup. Ct., 15 P.3d 931 (2000)

NATURE OF CASE: Appeal from determination that a letter was a valid holographic codicil to the deceased's formal will.

FACT SUMMARY: Kuralt (famous for his "On the Road" television show) wrote a letter to his mistress, Shannon, a couple of weeks before he died, while very sick, expressing an intent that Shannon "inherit" property they had shared. Kuralt's estate argued that the letter was not a valid holographic codicil to his formal will.

RULE OF LAW

A letter written by the deceased while in extremis, expressing an intent that another "inherit" a specific bequest of the deceased's property and not the entirety of the deceased's estate, is a valid holographic codicil to the deceased's formal will.

FACTS: Charles Kuralt (Kuralt), who was a "homespun American icon" known for his television show "On the Road," had a 30-year intimate personal relationship with Shannon. Both Kuralt and Shannon desired to keep their relationship secret and were successful in doing so. In 1989, Kuralt executed a holographic will that bequeathed all of Kuralt's interest in particular real property to Shannon. Then, in 1994, Kuralt executed a formal will that did not specifically mention any of the real property owned by Kuralt. Apparently, Kuralt had intended to transfer a 90-acre parcel to Shannon in 1997, but he suddenly became very ill that year. The day he checked into a hospital, he wrote a letter to Shannon expressing his intent that she "inherit" the parcel. He sent about $17,000 with the letter. He died two weeks later, and Shannon sought to probate the letter as a valid holographic codicil to Kuralt's formal 1994 will. The estate objected, but the trial court eventually entered judgment in favor of Shannon. The state's highest court granted review.

ISSUE: Is a letter written by the deceased while in extremis, expressing intent that another "inherit" a specific bequest of deceased's property and not the entirety of the deceased's estate, a valid holographic codicil to deceased's formal will?

HOLDING AND DECISION: (Trieweiler, J.) Yes. A letter written by the deceased while in extremis, expressing an intent that another "inherit" a specific bequest of the deceased's property and not the entirety of the deceased's estate is a valid holographic codicil to deceased's formal will. The intent of the testator must be followed. Here, the record supports the lower court's decision. The relevant facts are that Kuralt and Shannon continued to have a family-like relationship until the day he died; that along with the letter at issue he sent Shannon significant sums of money; there was extrinsic evidence that he intended to convey the parcel to Shannon; he was in extremis (practically on his death bed); he used the word "inherit"; and the letter made a specific bequest, and did not purport to bequeath the entirety of the estate. For these reasons, the letter was a valid holographic codicil to Kuralt's formal 1994 will. Affirmed.

ANALYSIS

The estate, and in a case that preceded this one, the dissent, argued that the letter, which said, "I'll have the lawyer visit the hospital to be sure you inherit the rest of the place . . . " was not a codicil, but was instead an expression of a future intent to make a will. That argument focused on the precatory, versus imperative, language of the letter; the majority clearly went beyond just the letter's language in rendering its decision.

Quicknotes

CODICIL A supplement to a will.

HOLOGRAPHIC WILL A will that is handwritten by the testator.

Thompson v. Royall

[Parties not identified.]

Va. Sup. Ct., 175 S.E. 748 (1934)

NATURE OF CASE: Action to probate a will.

FACT SUMMARY: Kroll attempted to revoke her will and codicil by signing notations on the back of each that purported to render them void.

RULE OF LAW

Revocation of a will by cancellation is accomplished only if the written words of the document are mutilated or otherwise impaired.

FACTS: Kroll executed an attested will that she gave to Brittain, her executor, for safekeeping. She then executed a codicil, which she signed in the presence of two attesting witnesses, and gave to Coulling, the attorney who prepared both documents. She later instructed Coulling to destroy both documents but was persuaded by Coulling to retain the documents for her use in case she decided to execute a new will. She signed a statement written on the back of the will by Coulling, which read, "This will null and void and to be only held by H.P. Brittain instead of being destroyed as a memorandum for another will if I desire to make same." An identical statement, but substituting Coulling's name for Brittain's, was written by Coulling on the back of the codicil and was signed by Kroll. Upon her death, Kroll left an estate valued at approximately $200,000. The will and codicil were offered for probate and contested by various nieces and nephews who were not mentioned in the instruments. The jury found the documents to be the last will and testament of Kroll, and from an order sustaining that verdict and probating the will, contestants brought this writ of error.

ISSUE: Is revocation of a will by cancellation accomplished only if the written words of the document are mutilated or otherwise impaired?

HOLDING AND DECISION: (Hudgins, J.) Yes. Revocation of a will by cancellation is accomplished only if the written words of the document are mutilated or otherwise impaired. A memorandum written in another's handwriting on the reverse side of a testamentary instrument and signed by the testator, purporting to void the document, may not effect a revocation by cancellation of the instrument. In order to effect revocation by cancellation, the testator must actually mutilate, erase, deface, or otherwise mark the written portions of the testamentary instrument. It is true that in *Warner v. Warner's Estate*, 37 Vt. 356 (1864), one court permitted cancellation by a writing that did not actually touch written portions of the will, but that decision has not been followed and has been justly criticized by commentators. Thus, although the testatrix obviously intended to revoke her will, she did not revoke it by cancellation. Furthermore, the contestants agree that the memorandum did not constitute a "writing indicating an intention to revoke" under the appropriate statute since it was not in testatrix's own handwriting or attested to by witnesses. Therefore, the will and codicil were not revoked, and the order admitting them to probate must be affirmed.

ANALYSIS

Thompson v. Royall accords with authorities generally. If words purporting to effect the cancellation of a will are written in the margin or on the reverse side of the instrument, they are ineffective to accomplish their purpose. However, the writing of words such as "void" or "canceled" will affect a revocation of a will if written across material portions of the will. The ruling of *Warner v. Warner's Estate*, disapproved by the court, is in general disrepute.

Quicknotes

CODICIL A supplement to a will.

DEVISAVIT VEL NON A matter transferred from a court of chancery to a court of law to determine whether a certain document was intended to be a will.

REVOCATION The cancellation or withdrawal of some authority conferred or an instrument drafted, such as the withdrawal of a revocable contract offer prior to the offeree's acceptance.

SUBSCRIBING WITNESS A person who witnesses the execution of a document and signs their name thereto.

TESTATRIX *(Archaic)* A female who executes a will.

Harrison v. Bird

Beneficiary (P) v. Decedent's cousin (D)

Ala. Sup. Ct., 621 So. 2d 972 (1993)

NATURE OF CASE: Appeal from a judgment of intestacy.

FACT SUMMARY: After Speer died, Harrison (P), the sole beneficiary of Speer's will, filed for probate a document purporting to be Speer's last will and testament, despite the fact that Speer's attorney had torn Speer's will into four pieces after Speer informed him that she wanted to revoke her will.

RULE OF LAW

A rebuttable presumption of revocation exists where a will cannot be found among a deceased's personal effects.

FACTS: A year and a half after Speer executed a will naming Harrison (P) as the main beneficiary of her estate, she advised her attorney that she wanted to revoke her will. Her attorney tore the will into four pieces, informing Speer by letter that he had "revoked" her will as instructed and was sending the pieces of the will to her. State law required that, to be lawfully revoked, a will must be destroyed in the testator's presence. When Speer died, the letter was found but not the four pieces of the will. The probate court granted letters of administration to Bird (D), Speer's cousin. Harrison (P) filed for probate a duplicate of the original will. The court ruled that, although Speer's will was not lawfully revoked, there arose a presumption that Speer had revoked the will herself since the destroyed will was not found. The court held that Harrison (P) had not rebutted the presumption of revocation and that the estate should be administered as an intestate estate and confirmed the letters of administration issued to Bird (D). Harrison (P) appealed.

ISSUE: Does a rebuttable presumption of revocation exist where a will cannot be found among a deceased's personal effects?

HOLDING AND DECISION: (Houston, J.) Yes. A rebuttable presumption of revocation exists where a will cannot be found among a deceased's personal effects. Under Alabama state law, Speer's will was not lawfully revoked because her attorney destroyed it at her direction and consent but not in her presence. However, where a testator destroys the copy of the will in her possession, a presumption arises that she has revoked her will and all duplicates, even though a duplicate exists that is not in her possession. The burden of rebutting the presumption is on the proponent of the will. Under the facts of this case, there existed a presumption that Speer destroyed her will, thus revoking it. Harrison (P) did not present sufficient evidence to rebut the presumption, i.e., to convince the trier of fact that the absence of the will was not due to Speer's destroying and thus revoking the will. Affirmed.

ANALYSIS

A will may be revoked either by executing a subsequent will that revokes the previous one (expressly or by inconsistency) or by physical destruction of the will, known as "performing a revocatory act on the will." Revocatory acts include tearing, burning, or obliterating the will, either completely or partially. If neither of the two steps above is taken, the will, if duly executed, will be admitted to probate.

Quicknotes

EXECUTRIX ***(Archaic)*** A female designated by a deceased individual to effectuate the disposition of the deceased's property pursuant to a testamentary instrument.

INTESTATE ESTATE The property of an individual who dies without executing a valid will.

In re Estate of Stoker

Decedent's former girlfriend (P) v. Decedent's children (D)

Cal. Ct. App., 122 Cal. Rptr. 3d 529 (2011)

NATURE OF CASE: Plaintiffs' appeal from lower court decision finding that the decedent created a will in 2005 that revoked an earlier 1997 will naming them as beneficiaries.

FACT SUMMARY: Decedent Steven Stoker created a will in 1997 that named his former girlfriend and two others as his beneficiaries. In 2005, Stoker created a handwritten document expressly revoking the 1997 will and naming his children as his sole beneficiaries. He signed the new will in the presence of one other person.

RULE OF LAW

A will is valid if the proponent of the will proves by clear and convincing evidence that at the time the testator executed the will, the testator intended the document to their last will.

FACTS: Steven Stoker created a will in 1997 that named his former girlfriend, Destiny Gularte (P), and two others as beneficiaries. In 2005, Stoker drafted a handwritten will that revoked the 1997 will and named his two children, Danine Pradia (D) and Darrin Stoker (D), as sole beneficiaries. Both wills were submitted to the probate court. At trial, a witness, Anne Meier, testified that Stoker dictated the will to her in 2005 and that she wrote it down word for word. She then gave the handwritten document to Stoker who signed it. The 2005 will specifically states that Gularte (P) and the other beneficiaries in the 1997 will should receive nothing. The trial court found the 2005 will, coupled with the eyewitness testimony of the creation of the will, evidenced the intent of Stoker and that the 1997 will was validly revoked. Gularte (P) appealed.

ISSUE: Is a will valid if the proponent of the will proves by clear and convincing evidence that at the time the testator executed the will, the testator intended the document to constitute their last will?

HOLDING AND DECISION: (Gilbert, J.) Yes. A will is valid if the proponent of the will proves by clear and convincing evidence that at the time the testator executed the will, the testator intended the document to constitute their last will. Dularte's (P) argument at the trial court level and here on appeal is that Stoker's handwritten will, while executed, did not include the signature of two witnesses as required by statute. The Probate Code does allow defective written wills to be submitted to probate if the will is consistent with the decedent's intent. Dularte (P) argues the legislature did not intend this provision to apply to handwritten wills. However, there is nothing in the statute that excludes handwritten wills. Dularte (P) also argues the 2005 will did not contain any proper testamentary language. However, no specific words are necessary as long as the language provides evidence that the document constitutes the testator's last will. Here, the 2005 will clearly states that his children will be his sole beneficiaries. The document also expressly revokes the 1997 will and states that the prior beneficiaries shall receive nothing. Meier was also present at the creation of the will. There was also separate testimony that in 2001 Stoker burned and urinated on the original 1997 will. The trial court's ruling below was correct. Affirmed.

ANALYSIS

When necessary, a court will allow extrinsic or outside evidence to determine the intent of the testator as stated in the document. In this case, Meier's testimony was particularly supportive of the validity of the will. She was not only present but actually drafted the will as dictated to her by Stoker.

Quicknotes

CLEAR AND CONVINCING EVIDENCE An evidentiary standard requiring a demonstration that the fact sought to be proven is reasonably certain.

EXTRINSIC EVIDENCE Evidence that is not contained within the text of a document or contract, but that is derived from the parties' statements or the circumstances under which the agreement was made.

TESTATOR One who executes a will.

LaCroix v. Senecal

Deceased's niece (P) v. Deceased's friend (D)

Conn. Sup. Ct., 99 A.2d 115 (1953)

NATURE OF CASE: Appeal from judgment holding that a residuary devise and bequest under a codicil, that was virtually identical to a similar residuary devise and bequest in deceased's will, was void, but that there was no resulting intestacy as to that portion of the residue because it was valid under the will.

FACT SUMMARY: Dupre's niece, LaCroix (P), argued that a residuary clause in Dupre's codicil, which replaced a virtually identical clause in Dupre's will, was void because it was witnessed by the spouse of a beneficiary.

RULE OF LAW

The doctrine of dependent relative revocation sustains a gift by will when such a gift has been revoked in a codicil that substantially reaffirms the gift but is void by reason of the interest of a subscribing witness.

FACTS: Dupre executed a will leaving the residue of her estate in equal shares to her nephew and her friend, Senecal (D). She then executed a codicil revoking the residuary clause of the will and replaced it with an almost identical clause. The only change was that in the will she had used her nephew's nickname and in the codicil she used both his formal name and nickname. However, Senecal's (D) husband witnessed the codicil. Under the applicable purging statute, the codicil would be valid, but the gift to Senecal (D) would be invalid. The lower court nonetheless held that the gift to Senecal (D) was valid, on the theory that the gift under the will remained valid. Dupre's niece, LaCroix (P), argued that the gift was void, and the state's supreme court granted review.

ISSUE: Does the doctrine of dependent relative revocation sustain a gift by will, when such a gift has been revoked in a codicil that substantially reaffirms the gift but is void by reason of the interest of a subscribing witness?

HOLDING AND DECISION: (Brown, J.) Yes. The doctrine of dependent relative revocation sustains a gift by will when such a gift has been revoked in a codicil that substantially reaffirms the gift but is void by reason of the interest of a subscribing witness. That doctrine provides that if a testator cancels or destroys a will with a present intention of making a new one immediately and as a substitute and the new will is not made or, if made, fails of effect for any reason, it will be presumed that the testator preferred the old will to intestacy, and the old one will be admitted to probate in the absence of evidence overcoming the presumption. It is a rule of presumed intention. As to the case at hand, it would be difficult to conceive of a more deserving case for the application of the doctrine of dependent relative revocation. There is no room for doubt that the sole purpose of the testatrix in executing the codicil was, by making the very minor change in referring to her nephew, to eliminate any uncertainty as to his identity. Obviously, it was furthest from her intention to make any change in the disposition of her residuary estate. When the will and codicil are considered together, as they must be, to determine the intent of the testatrix, it is clear that her intention to revoke the will was conditioned upon the execution of a codicil that would be effective to continue the same disposition of her residuary estate. Affirmed.

ANALYSIS

Most courts place limitations on the doctrine of dependent relative revocation. They require that the doctrine applies only (1) if there is an alternative plan of disposition that fails or (2) where the mistake is recited in the terms of the revoking instrument, or is established by clear and convincing evidence.

Quicknotes

CODICIL A supplement to a will.

DEPENDENT RELATIVE REVOCATION Doctrine that states that if the same person executes a will that revokes an earlier will, the earlier will is revoked only if the latter will is effective; otherwise the earlier will remains in full effect and force.

TESTATRIX ***(Archaic)*** A female who executes a will.

In re Estate of Rigsby

Decedent's sister (P) v. Decedent's husband (D)

Okla. Ct. App., 843 P.2d 856 (1992)

NATURE OF CASE: Plaintiff's appeal from lower court decision finding that a second page of an alleged handwritten will should not be considered part of the will.

FACT SUMMARY: Decedent Jessaline Rigsby drafted a one-page handwritten will with instructions to disperse various personal property and money. Found with that one page was a second handwritten page listing various personal items with names of individuals next to each item. The two pages were not connected to each other and the first page did not reference the second page.

RULE OF LAW

In regard to handwritten or holographic wills that consist of more than one page, it must be clearly apparent that the testator intended that all pages constitute the testator's last will and testament.

FACTS: Decedent Jessaline Rigsby drafted a one page handwritten will. The document clearly stated, "Inasmuch as I do not have a will, I would like to make the following arrangements in the event of my death." After her death, her husband, Don Rigsby (D), found the will. Next to the will, but not attached to it, was a second handwritten page. The second page included a list of personal items with names next to each item. The first page of the will made no mention of the second page. At trial, the decedent's sister, Betty Dorsey (P), argued the court should consider the second page as part of the will. The trial court found that the second page was not part of the will because the first page did not incorporate or reference the second page. There were also some inconsistencies between instructions on the first page and the second page. For example, the first page stated any money she had in the bank should go to a group that sponsored horse breeding. The second page stated the money should go to her husband. Dorsey (P) appealed.

ISSUE: In regard to handwritten or holographic wills that consist of more than one page, must it be clearly apparent that the testator intended that all pages constitute the testator's last will and testament?

HOLDING AND DECISION: (Jones, J.) Yes. In regard to handwritten or holographic wills that consist of more than one page, it must be clearly apparent that the testator intended that all pages constitute the testator's last will and testament. The trial court correctly concluded that it is not clearly apparent that the second page was intended to be part of the will. The decedent signed and dated the first page only. The first page did not reference or incorporate the second page at all. The second page also conflicts with various instructions clearly stated on the first page. The second page could be interpreted as a worksheet listing various items, but without clear language in the first page incorporating that list, the second page cannot be considered part of the will. Affirmed.

ANALYSIS

This decision deals with the doctrine of integration. Traditional testamentary wills are usually in typewritten form and stapled together. There typically is little dispute regarding the pages that constitute the will. With handwritten or holographic wills, there are often disputes over which handwritten documents constitute the testator's last will and testament. If one document clearly references another, the second document will be integrated into the will. That was not the case here.

Quicknotes

HOLOGRAPHIC WILL A will that is handwritten by the testator.

Clark v. Greenhalge

Beneficiary (P) v. Executor (D)

Mass. Sup. Jud. Ct., 582 N.E.2d 949 (1991)

NATURE OF CASE: Appeal from a judgment incorporating a notebook by reference into the terms of a will.

FACT SUMMARY: Although Nesmith reserved the right in her will to make a further disposition of personal property by a memorandum, Greenhalge (D), the executor, refused to comply with one of Nesmith's bequests written in a notebook.

RULE OF LAW

A properly executed will may incorporate by reference into its provisions any document or paper not so executed and witnessed if it was in existence at the time of the execution of the will and is identified by clear and satisfactory proof as the paper referred to therein.

FACTS: Nesmith executed a will, naming Greenhalge (D) as executor of her estate and also the principal beneficiary, but reserved the right to make further disposition of tangible personal property as designated by a memorandum. In addition to a memorandum list of items to be distributed, Nesmith periodically made entries into a notebook, designating bequests of personal property. One of those bequests gave Clark (P) an oil painting of a farm scene. After Nesmith's death, Greenhalge (D) complied with all her bequests, except the one for the painting. Clark (P) commenced this action to compel Greenhalge (D) to deliver the painting to her. The probate judge awarded the painting to Clark (P), and Greenhalge (D) appealed.

ISSUE: May a properly executed will incorporate by reference into its provisions any document or paper not so executed and witnessed if it was in existence at the time of the execution of the will and is identified by clear and satisfactory proof as the paper referred to therein?

HOLDING AND DECISION: (Nolan, J.) Yes. A properly executed will may incorporate by reference into its provisions any document or paper not so executed and witnessed if it was in existence at the time of the execution of the will and is identified by clear and satisfactory proof as the paper referred to therein. Here, the parties agree that the memorandum document was incorporated into the will, but Greenhalge (D) contends that the notebook was not incorporated. However, the statements in the notebook unquestionably reflect Nesmith's exercise of her right to restructure the distribution of her tangible personal property upon her death. That the notebook is not entitled "memorandum" is of no consequence. The evidence supports the conclusion that Nesmith intended that the bequests in her notebook be accorded the same power and effect as those contained in the memorandum referenced in her will. Affirmed.

ANALYSIS

The cardinal rule in the interpretation of wills is that the intention of the testator shall prevail, provided it is consistent with the rules of law. To narrowly construe the will to exclude the notebook contents as "a memorandum" would undermine that long-standing policy. The most recent (1991) version of the Uniform Probate Code requires that a will may refer to a separate memo or list disposing of personal property, but such a list must be signed by the testator in order to be given effect.

Quicknotes

CODICIL A supplement to a will.

SPECIFIC BEQUEST A transfer of property that is accomplished by means of a testamentary instrument.

TESTATRIX *(Archaic)* A female who executes a will.

Keith v. Lulofs

Step-brother (P) v. Step-sister (D)

Va. Sup. Ct., 724 S.E.2d 695 (2012)

NATURE OF CASE: Plaintiff's appeal from lower court decision finding that the 1987 "mirror image" wills executed by his parents were revocable and not an enforceable contract.

FACT SUMMARY: Arvid Keith and Lucy Keith executed mirror image wills in 1987, leaving their entire estate to the other in the event one of them died. The couple each had a child from a prior marriage and both were named equal beneficiaries in the 1987 wills. Arvid died in 1996 and his estate passed to Lucy. Lucy then modified her will in 2006, removing her stepson Walter Keith (P) from her will and giving her entire estate to her daughter, Venocia Lulofs (D).

RULE OF LAW

When reciprocal testamentary provisions are made in mutual or reciprocal wills for the benefit of a third party, sufficient consideration is present to entitle the beneficiary to enforce the wills as a contract, provided there is clear and convincing evidence the parties intended to create a contract.

FACTS: In 1987, Arvid Keith and his wife, Lucy Keith, executed reciprocal or mirror image wills. The wills provided that if either one of them died, their estate would pass first to the surviving spouse and then equally to the couple's two children. Walter Keith (P) was Arvid's son from a prior marriage and Lulofs (D) was Lucy's daughter from a prior marriage. Arvid died in 1996 leaving his estate to Lucy. In late 1996, Lucy modified her will to exclude Walter (P) and leave her entire estate to Lulofs (D). Also, in 1994, Arvid and Lucy took out a life insurance policy naming Walter (P) and Lulofs (D) equal beneficiaries. After Arvid died, Lucy modified the policy to give Lulofs (D) 78 percent of the proceeds and Walter 22 percent. Walter (P) also testified at trial that he had several conversations with Arvid and Lucy wherein they informed him that Walter (P) and Lulofs (D) would receive equal shares of their estate and the insurance policy. At trial, Walter (P) argued that the 1987 wills were irrevocable and constituted a contract for the benefit of Walter (P) and Lulofs (D). The trial court denied his arguments and found in favor of Lulofs (D). Walter (P) appealed.

ISSUE: When reciprocal testamentary provisions are made in mutual or reciprocal wills for the benefit of a third party, is sufficient consideration present to entitle the beneficiary to enforce the wills as a contract, provided there is clear and convincing evidence the parties intended to create a contract?

HOLDING AND DECISION: (Powell, J.) Yes. When reciprocal testamentary provisions are made in mutual or reciprocal wills for the benefit of a third party, sufficient consideration is present to entitle the beneficiary to enforce the wills as a contract, provided there is clear and convincing evidence the parties intended to create a contract. The proof may be express language in the documents, or it can be provided by competent witnesses who can testify to admissions of the testators, or can be provided by implication based upon the relationship of the parties. Here, there is no evidence the parties intended their mutual wills to constitute a contract and be irrevocable. The wills do not contain such language themselves. Agreeing with Walter's argument would mean that any surviving spouse who had executed a reciprocal will could not modify it to provide for a future spouse. That position is untenable. Also, the attorney who assisted Arvid and Lucy to draft the wills could not recall whether or not the parties intended the wills to constitute a binding contract between them. Lastly, Walter (P) cannot provide as evidence his recollection of statements made to him by Arvid and Lucy, as they have both passed away. In these circumstances, Walter (P) is required to provide independent evidence to corroborate his testimony regarding Arvid's and Lucy's statements relating to the contractual nature of the wills. The existence of the insurance policy does not assist his argument as it was created seven years after the wills were created. Accordingly, Walter (P) has not proven by clear and convincing evidence the 1987 wills constituted an enforceable, irrevocable contract. Affirmed.

ANALYSIS

In regard to joint or reciprocal wills, courts will be hesitant to find that a contract exists to benefit a third party unless the documents include express language to that effect. Also, Walter's (P) inability to testify as to his parents' statements was in accordance with the Dead Man's statute. Most states have such statutes that prevent a beneficiary from testifying as to the testator's statements unless those statements can be corroborated by independent evidence.

Continued on next page.

Quicknotes

DEAD MAN'S STATUTE Evidence of a deceased's promises or statements may not be introduced by a claimant against the deceased's estate.

JOINT WILLS A jointly signed single instrument that is made the will of two or more persons.

RECIPROCAL WILL Testamentary instruments pursuant to which two or more individuals make reciprocal provisions in favor of the other.

CHAPTER 4

Wills: Capacity and Contests

Quick Reference Rules of Law

PAGE

1. *In re Wright's Estate.* Testamentary capacity to create a will cannot be destroyed by testimony regarding a testator's few isolated acts, idiosyncrasies or mental irregularities unless they bear directly upon the testamentary act of creating the will itself. *36*

2. *Wilson v. Lane.* Evidence that a testator was eccentric, elderly, and feeble at the time the testator signed the will by itself is not indicative of a lack of testamentary capacity. *38*

3. *In re Strittmater's Estate.* A will that is the product of an insane delusion will not be probated. *40*

4. *Breeden v. Stone.* An objector to a will may challenge a testator's capacity based on both or either of the *Cunningham* and insane delusion tests. *41*

5. *In re Estate of Sharis.* Circumstantial evidence may support a finding that a will is the product of undue influence, and therefore invalid, where such evidence supports a finding that a named beneficiary was in a fiduciary relationship to the testator, the testator did not have independent legal counsel, the testator was susceptible to the fiduciary's influence, and the fiduciary's actions were made in secret and without an accounting. *42*

6. *In re Will of Moses.* (1) Where an attorney and client have an intimate relationship, a presumption of undue influence arises where the client leaves most of her estate to the attorney, even if the attorney had no knowledge of the will until after the client's death. (2) The presumption of undue influence that arises when a client leaves most of her estate to her attorney, with whom she has an intimate relationship, may be rebutted by evidence that, in making will, she acted upon independent advice and counsel of a third-party, disinterested attorney. (3) An attorney who acts merely as a scrivener in drafting a will, recording a testatrix's wishes without questioning or discussing who she designates as a beneficiary, does not provide meaningful independent advice or counsel as to the disposition of her estate, such as would overcome the presumption of undue influence on the part of her regular attorney with whom she has an intimate relationship. *44*

7. *Lipper v. Weslow.* Undue influence is shown when such control was exercised over the mind of the testator so as to overcome the testator's free agency and free will and to substitute the will of another so as to cause the testator to do what the testator would not otherwise have done but for such control. *47*

8. *Latham v. Father Divine.* Where a testator is prevented from executing a new will in favor of an intended beneficiary by the fraud, duress, or undue influence of a present beneficiary or heir, the property intended to go to the new beneficiary will pass to the present beneficiary subject to a constructive trust in favor of the intended beneficiary. *49*

9. *Schilling v. Herrera.* A party who would have contested a will but was prevented from doing so by another person's fraudulent conduct may bring a claim for intentional interference with an expectancy of inheritance. *51*

In re Wright's Estate

Decedent's daughter (P) v. Executrix (D)

Cal. Sup. Ct., 60 P.2d 434 (1936)

NATURE OF CASE: Executrix's appeal from lower court decision finding that the decedent lacked the required testamentary capacity at the time he created his will.

FACT SUMMARY: Lorenzo Wright created a will with the assistance of a notary public. Two other persons signed Wright's will as witnesses. After Wright's death, the notary public and the witnesses claimed Wright was of unsound mind at the time he created his will.

RULE OF LAW

Testamentary capacity to create a will cannot be destroyed by testimony regarding a testator's few isolated acts, idiosyncrasies or mental irregularities unless they bear directly upon the testamentary act of creating the will itself.

FACTS: Decedent Lorenzo Wright drafted a list of his beneficiaries and then met with Grace Thomas, a notary public, to prepare his will. She prepared his will accordingly. The will bequeathed one house to his daughter, Maud Wright Angell (P), and another house to a friend. He instructed that various personal items be given to relatives. He also instructed that his nephew and some friends should receive one dollar each. James Thomas and G.W. Madden signed the will as witnesses. After Wright's death, Angell (P) contested the will. The notary public, the two witnesses and several other persons testified at trial as to Wright's alleged lack of mental capacity. The notary public testified she thought Wright was of unsound mind because his will was the "funniest" will she had ever seen. James Thomas testified that he believed Wright was of unsound mind. G.W. Madden, the other witness, also testified that he believed Wright had been of unsound mind for some years. Other witnesses testified to Wright's odd behavior during his lifetime. One witness described how Wright presented her with a fish soaked in kerosene and how he offered to buy all of her furniture, even though it was not for sale. Others testified that Wright drank alcohol in excess and often left his house without enough clothing. Another witness testified that Wright would leave his house for days and return without any explanation for his absence. The trial court found Wright was of unsound mind at the time he created his will and denied the will admission to probate. The executrix of the will appealed.

ISSUE: Can testamentary capacity to create a will be destroyed by testimony regarding a testator's few isolated acts, idiosyncrasies or mental irregularities unless they bear directly upon the testamentary act of creating the will itself?

HOLDING AND DECISION: (Seawell, J.) No. Testamentary capacity to create a will cannot be destroyed by testimony regarding a testator's few isolated acts, idiosyncrasies or mental irregularities unless they bear directly upon the testamentary act of creating the will itself. The legal presumption is that a testator was sane at the time the will was created. At trial, the contestant, Angell (P), did not present any medical testimony relating to any injury or medical condition that would affect Wright's mental capacity to create a will. No evidence was submitted that Wright could not transact business for himself or take care of himself personally. Wright drafted his own list of beneficiaries and then went to meet with the notary public to create a formal will. There is no evidence he was not mindful of the property he owned. He specifically bequeathed one house to his daughter and another to a friend. All of the testimony given at trial was trivial in nature and did not establish that Wright lacked the appropriate mental capacity to enter into the will. In addition, it is the duty of the subscribing witnesses to ensure that the testator was of sound mind at the time testator created the will. Any adverse testimony from witnesses to a will who failed to object to the testator's mental capacity at the time will be subject to heightened judicial scrutiny. Because they did not object at the time, their credibility as witnesses that the testator lacked capacity is severely weakened. Accordingly, the trial court improperly found that Wright lacked the capacity to create his will. Reversed.

ANALYSIS

At the time the will is created, a testator must understand the nature and extent of their estate, the recipients of the property and the effects of their disposition of the estate. When challenging the mental capacity of a decedent, a contestant must show the testator lacked the capacity at the precise time the testator created the will. Anecdotal evidence in the form of a past history of mental irregularities is not sufficient. The contestant needs to admit medical records or testimony relating to a medical condition or injury that affected the testator's capacity around the time the testator created the will.

Continued on next page.

Quicknotes

TESTAMENTARY CAPACITY The requisite level of mental capacity required by law at the time a testator executes a testamentary instrument for the document to be valid; this generally requires a finding that the testator understood the nature and extent of the testator's estate, the natural recipients of the testator's property, and the effects of the disposition of their estate.

TESTAMENTARY INCAPACITY Absence of the requisite level of mental capacity required by law at the time a testator executes a testamentary instrument for the document to be valid.

Wilson v. Lane

Caveator (P) v. Executrix (D)

Ga. Sup. Ct., 614 S.E.2d 88 (2005)

NATURE OF CASE: Appeal from judgment notwithstanding the verdict in action challenging testators' testamentary capacity.

FACT SUMMARY: Wilson (P) challenged Greer's testamentary capacity on the grounds that she was elderly, eccentric, and feeble.

RULE OF LAW

Evidence that a testator was eccentric, elderly, and feeble at the time the testator signed the will by itself is not indicative of a lack of testamentary capacity.

FACTS: Lane (D), the executrix for Greer's will, offered the will for probate. Wilson (P) filed a caveat, challenging Greer's testamentary capacity. Wilson (P) presented evidence that Greer had been eccentric, elderly, and feeble at the time she made her will; that she had difficulty engaging in daily activities without help; and that she had some irrational fears. Wilson (P) also presented evidence of a guardianship petition filed for Greer a few months after the will was executed, the testimony of an expert witness, and a letter written by Greer's physician. The expert, however, had never examined Greer, and his testimony was based solely on a cursory review of some of her medical files. He also was equivocal in his testimony that Greer was in some form of the early to middle stages of a dementia like Alzheimer's. Similarly, Greer's physician testified that Greer suffered from senile dementia, but that he was not sure whether she in fact had senile dementia at the time. The evidence also showed that Lane (D) had filed a guardianship petition after the will was executed, but that this was done solely to satisfy the Department of Family and Children Services' concerns regarding Greer's ability to continue living on her own, and thus to allow Greer to remain in her home. On the other hand, Lane (D) and the drafting attorney, as well as numerous other friends and acquaintances, testified that Greer was mentally competent at the time she selected her beneficiaries and had a clear mind at the time she signed the will. A jury held for Wilson (P), but the court granted Lane's (D) motion for judgment notwithstanding the verdict. The state's highest court granted review.

ISSUE: Is evidence that a testator was eccentric, elderly, and feeble at the time the testator signed the will by itself indicative of a lack of testamentary capacity?

HOLDING AND DECISION: (Fletcher, C.J.) No. Evidence that a testator was eccentric, elderly, and feeble at the time the testator signed the will by itself is not indicative of a lack of testamentary capacity. Here, the evidence presented by Lane (D) established a presumption that Greer possessed testamentary capacity. Despite Wilson's (P) evidence, the law does not withhold from the aged, the feeble, the weak-minded, the capricious, or the notionate, the right to make a will, provided such person has a decided and rational desire as to the disposition of their property. Eccentric habits and absurd beliefs by themselves do not establish testamentary incapacity. All that is required to sustain the will is proof that Greer was capable of forming a certain rational desire with respect to the disposition of her assets. The evidence offered by Wilson's (P) expert and by Greer's physician was insufficient to deprive Greer of her right to make a valid will, as none of it showed that she was incapable of forming a rational desire as to the disposition of her property. Regardless of the stigma associated with the term "Alzheimer's," the expert's testimony did not show how Greer would have been unable to form a rational desire regarding the disposition of her assets, and the expert did not explain how having Alzheimer's would affect her testamentary capacity. Similarly, the physician's vague reference to senile dementia cannot eliminate such capacity. Finally, even though Greer was unable to live alone, that fact would have no bearing on her ability to form a rational desire regarding the disposition of her property. Because no evidence was offered to show that at the time the will was executed Greer suffered from a form of dementia sufficient in form or extent to render her unable to form a decided and rational desire regarding the disposition of her assets, the trial court did not err in finding that the evidence demanded a verdict upholding the validity of the will and in reversing the jury's verdict. Affirmed.

DISSENT: (Carley, J.) The jury found that Greer lacked testamentary capacity and the court must decide if the evidence supports the jury's finding. When the totality of the evidence as to Greer's condition during the time period is considered, a jury certainly would be authorized to find that she suffered from serious dementia. Since the evidence supports such a finding, the trial court erred in granting Lane's (D) motion for judgment notwithstanding the verdict.

ANALYSIS

In general, the standard for testamentary capacity—which is a legal standard, not a medical standard—is relatively low. Accordingly, courts have found

Continued on next page.

testamentary capacity even where the testator was suffering from Alzheimer's disease or senile dementia, and even after a guardian or conservator was appointed to manage the testator's affairs.

Quicknotes

CAVEAT A formal warning provided to the court by an interested party urging the court to refrain from certain action.

CONSERVATOR A court-appointed custodian of property belonging to a person found to be unable to manage their property.

EXECUTRIX *(ARCHAIC)* A woman who executes a will.

GUARDIANSHIP A legal relationship whereby one party is responsible for the care and control over another, called the "ward," and the ward's property, resulting from the ward's legal incapacity.

JUDGMENT NOTWITHSTANDING THE VERDICT (JNOV) A judgment entered by the trial judge reversing a jury verdict if the jury's determination has no basis in law or fact.

PROBATE The administration of a decedent's estate.

TESTAMENTARY CAPACITY The requisite level of mental capacity required by law at the time a testator executes a testamentary instrument for the document to be valid; this generally requires a finding that the testator understood the nature and extent of the testator's estate, the natural recipients of the testator's property, and the effects of the disposition of their estate.

TESTATOR One who executes a will.

In re Strittmater's Estate

Cousins of decedent (P) v. Court (D)

N.J. Ct. Err. & App., 53 A.2d 205 (1947)

NATURE OF CASE: Appeal from decree admitting will to probate.

FACT SUMMARY: Strittmater left her estate to the National Women's Party out of an extreme hatred for men.

RULE OF LAW

A will that is the product of an insane delusion will not be probated.

FACTS: Strittmater, upon her death, bequeathed her estate to the National Women's Party rather than to her cousins with whom she had very little to do. The cousins (P) contested the will. Strittmater's personal physician testified that she felt Strittmater had suffered from schizophrenia all her adult life. Strittmater's mental illness was manifested by her angry comments about her deceased parents; her vocal, intense hatred of men; and her fervent support of the women's movement. However, her relationships with her bankers and lawyer were entirely normal. The orphan's court admitted the will to probate, the cousins (P) appealed and the probate was set aside.

ISSUE: Will a will that is the product of an insane delusion be probated?

HOLDING AND DECISION: (Per curiam) No. A will that is the product of an insane delusion will not be probated. The testator must have been sane at the time of the will's execution to enforce the will. Strittmater's extreme hatred of men and "feminism to a neurotic extreme" demonstrated her obvious mental illness. This is true even though she had the capacity to transact ordinary business. While Strittmater gave her money to this organization, to which she belonged for eleven years, she did not involve herself enough in the party to justify her bequest. Strittmater's will was the result of mental illness and, thus, will not be entered into probate. Affirmed.

ANALYSIS

There are three historical rationales for the sanity requirement. First of all, wills should carry out a person's intent; if the will is a product of insanity, it cannot represent the person's wishes. Secondly, an insane person is not a "person" as a recognized legal entity and therefore cannot be allowed to bequeath possessions. Thirdly, mental capacity is required in order to protect the family, which relies on the decedent for economic support.

Quicknotes

PROBATE The administration of a decedent's estate.

TESTATRIX ***(Archaic)*** A woman who executes a will.

Breeden v. Stone

Heirs at law (D) v. Executor (P)

Colo. Sup. Ct., 992 P.2d 1167 (2000)

NATURE OF CASE: Appeal from admittance of will to probate.

FACT SUMMARY: Spicer Breeden executed a holographic will shortly before committing suicide. When the will was admitted to probate, Breeden's relatives (D) challenged Breeden's testamentary capacity due to his excessive drug and alcohol use.

RULE OF LAW

An objector to a will may challenge a testator's capacity based on both or either of the *Cunningham* and insane delusion tests.

FACTS: Spicer Breeden and his friend Peter Schmitz struck and killed another motorist while they were driving drunk and high on cocaine. For two days following the accident, Breeden continued to consume copious amounts of cocaine and alcohol. When the police finally arrived at Breeden's house, he barricaded the door and wrote out a handwritten will leaving his entire estate to a friend named Sydney Stone (P). Breeden then shot his dog and killed himself. When Stone (P) submitted the will to probate, Breeden's relatives (D) objected, claiming that Breeden lacked testamentary capacity because his excessive drug use made him insane. The trial court applied two tests of testamentary capacity, the *Cunningham* test and the insane delusion test. The *Cunningham* test [*Cunningham v. Stender*, 255 P.2d 977, 981-82 (Colo. 1953)], is usually used when objectors claim that there are numerous reasons for testamentary incapacity, such as mental illness and dementia. It asks whether the testator (1) understands the nature of their act; (2) knows the extent of their property; (3) understands the proposed disposition; (4) knows the natural objects of their bounty; and (5) executed a will that represents their wishes. The insane delusion test is used when the testator is generally sane but suffering from a temporary delusion or break with reality when executing the will. The probate court applied both tests and determined that Breeden had testamentary capacity. Breeden's relatives (D) appealed, claiming that the trial court should not have applied both tests and that the trial court improperly merged the two tests.

ISSUE: May an objector to a will challenge a testator's capacity based on both or either of the *Cunningham* and insane delusion tests?

HOLDING AND DECISION: (Rice, J.) Yes. An objector to a will may challenge a testator's capacity based on both or either of the *Cunningham* and insane delusion tests. The trial court correctly applied these two exclusive tests to find that Breeden was of sound mind at the time that he executed his holographic will. Despite evidence showing Breeden's severe drug and alcohol abuse, the court applied the *Cunningham* test and found that the decedent (1) could index the major categories of the property comprising his estate; (2) knew his home and rental address; and (3) identified the devisee by name and provided her current address. In addition, testimony of handwriting experts indicated that Breeden was in command of his motor skills and his handwriting was unremarkable when compared to other samples. Therefore, the trial court found that Breeden met the *Cunningham* test for sound mind. The court then applied the insane delusion test and found that although Breeden was suffering from insane delusions at the time he executed the will, the delusions did not affect or influence the disposition of his property. The court considered testimony that indicated he was not close to his family, and also noted that Breeden did not make provisions for his father or sister in his previous will. In sum, the probate court correctly applied the two exclusive tests for testamentary capacity, and the probate court order reflects that the court thoroughly considered all of the evidence presented by the parties and concluded that (1) the testator met the *Cunningham* test for sound mind and (2) the insane delusions from which Breeden was suffering did not materially affect or influence his testamentary disposition. Affirmed.

ANALYSIS

The Court applied the majority view of the insane delusion test when it found that Breeden had testamentary capacity because his insane delusions did not "materially affect or influence" the will. The minority view asks whether the insane delusion "might have caused or affected" the testamentary disposition.

Quicknotes

CAPACITY The legal or physical ability to act or to understand the consequences of one's actions.

HOLOGRAPHIC WILL A will that is handwritten by the testator.

TESTATOR One who executes a will.

In re Estate of Sharis

[Parties not identified.]

Mass. App. Ct., 990 N.E.2d 98 (2013)

NATURE OF CASE: Appeal from decision invalidating a will on grounds of undue influence and lack of testamentary capacity.

FACT SUMMARY: J. Richard Spinelli contended that there was insufficient evidence of undue influence on his part, or lack of testamentary capacity, to invalidate the will of his grandmother, Alice Sharis (Alice).

RULE OF LAW

Circumstantial evidence may support a finding that a will is the product of undue influence, and therefore invalid, where such evidence supports a finding that a named beneficiary was in a fiduciary relationship to the testator, the testator did not have independent legal counsel, the testator was susceptible to the fiduciary's influence, and the fiduciary's actions were made in secret and without an accounting.

FACTS: J. Richard Spinelli, one of Alice Sharis's (Alice's) grandchildren, lived with Alice and her husband, Peter, for over seven years. Peter, who had Alzheimer's disease, eventually moved into a nursing home and predeceased Alice by 13 months. During this period, Spinelli gained almost complete control over the couple's finances and checking account, and had been granted a durable power of attorney by Alice. Around two years before Alice died, Spinelli had an attorney draft a will for Alice. Alice, who had only a seventh grade education, was unfamiliar with the operation and terminology of wills. The attorney called Alice and had a brief phone conversation with her, but he did not remember the details of the call. However, the attorney never met with Alice, and the attorney's associate drafted the will. All of the associate attorney's communications were by e-mail with Spinelli, and never with Alice. Once the will was drafted and sent to Alice, the attorney conducted a brief, two-minute telephone conversation with her. No attorney reviewed the terms of the will in person with Alice, nor did an attorney attend the execution of the will. The will provided that all of Alice's assets be distributed to her husband, Peter, should he survive her. If not, the house and all of the assets and property contained therein were to go to Spinelli, along with all her stocks and securities. Her savings and checking accounts were distributed equally to her three daughters. The residuary was distributed equally among her three daughters and Spinelli. Neither the attorney nor the associate inquired why Alice would favor Spinelli over her daughters and other grandchildren, and Alice never explained why she would do so. Alice executed the will at the nursing home where Peter was a resident, and the nursing home's staff served as witnesses. Spinelli, who had not informed any other family members that he was acting under a power of attorney, also did not let any other family members know about the will. A couple of months later, Spinelli opened a checking account in his name in trust for Peter and Alice. Between opening the trust account and the date Alice died, Spinelli transferred $71,450 from the checking account to the trust account, and substantial sums were then expended from the trust account. Spinelli could not account for these expenditures. These transfers had the effect of disrupting Alice's bequest of her checking and savings accounts to her daughters. One of the daughters brought an action contesting the will on grounds of lack of testamentary capacity and undue influence, and the trial court, which found that Spinelli stood in a fiduciary relationship to Alice, and lacked credibility on key issues, disallowed the will. The state's intermediate appellate court granted review.

ISSUE: May circumstantial evidence support a finding that a will is the product of undue influence, and therefore invalid, where such evidence supports a finding that a named beneficiary was in a fiduciary relationship to the testator, the testator did not have independent legal counsel, the testator was susceptible to the fiduciary's influence, and the fiduciary's actions were made in secret and without an accounting?

HOLDING AND DECISION: (Sullivan, J.) Yes. Circumstantial evidence may support a finding that a will is the product of undue influence, and therefore invalid, where such evidence supports a finding that a named beneficiary was in a fiduciary relationship to the testator, the testator did not have independent legal counsel, the testator was susceptible to the fiduciary's influence, and the fiduciary's actions were made in secret and without an accounting. A claim of undue influence is composed of four elements: (1) an unnatural disposition has been made (2) by a person susceptible to undue influence to the advantage of someone (3) with an opportunity to exercise undue influence and (4) who in fact has used that opportunity to procure the contested disposition through improper means. Such elements may be proved by circumstantial evidence. Although the burden of proof ordinarily rests with the party contesting the will, a fiduciary, who benefits in a transaction with the person for whom he or she is a fiduciary, bears the burden of establishing that the transaction did not violate their obligations. Here, Spinelli does not contest that he stood in a fiduciary relationship to Alice. Therefore, he has

Continued on next page.

the burden of proving that he did not exert undue influence in the making of Alice's will. Contrary to Spinelli's assertion, Alice was not represented by independent legal counsel. Spinelli selected the attorney, communicated with the drafting attorney by e-mail, filled in certain terms, and transported Alice to Peter's nursing home for the execution of her will. Alice never met the attorney in person. She communicated with him briefly only twice by telephone. The associate who drafted the will never spoke with Alice, but only communicated by e-mail with Spinelli. No attorney reviewed the terms of the will with Alice. Only Spinelli did so. Given that Alice had no prior wills, and that she was unfamiliar with wills or their terminology, and that the attorney could not recall the specifics of his conversation with Alice or any specific advice he offered her with respect to the dispositions in her will, the trial court did not clearly err in finding that Alice lacked the benefit of independent advice of counsel. Additionally, there was an aura of secrecy surrounding the estate planning, as no one in the family, other than Spinelli, was aware that Alice had executed a will before her death or that Spinelli had a power of attorney to conduct Alice's financial affairs. Because it was within the trial judge's purview not to credit Spinelli's credibility regarding whether Alice had asked him to keep the will confidential, and because Spinelli alone was in a position to ensure that there was proof that Alice was fully informed and independently made the bequests at issue, there was no error in the trial judge's finding that Spinelli failed to do so. Further, Alice's advanced age, lack of familiarity with wills, and seventh grade education, coupled with Spinelli's nearly complete control of her finances, among other factors, permitted the inference that she was susceptible to his influence. Spinelli clearly had the opportunity to exercise influence to his benefit. Notwithstanding that Spinelli lived with Alice during the last eight years of her life, the trial judge was not compelled to conclude that the dispositions made in Alice's will were natural. Nor was the trial judge compelled to credit Spinelli's evidence of a particularly close relationship between them, and, in fact, the trial judge credited evidence to the contrary. Even absent direct evidence of self-dealing, these facts alone support the conclusion that Spinelli did not meet his burden to prove that the will was executed without undue influence, since the conduct of a fiduciary prior to the making of a will in which he or she is named as beneficiary may be such as to amount to undue influence, without proof of specific acts of the advisor at the time the will was made. In addition, Spinelli was unable adequately to explain where the money in the trust account went. Spinelli's failure to account fully for these funds was a proper matter of consideration for the judge, and, as to this matter, the trial judge's credibility findings will be left undisturbed. Although there was no direct evidence that Spinelli emptied the trust account for his personal benefit, by depleting the checking account bequeathed to others, Spinelli preserved those assets bequeathed to him. When a testator is enfeebled by age or disease although not reaching to unsoundness of mind, and the relation between the parties is fiduciary or intimate, the transaction ordinarily is subject to careful scrutiny, and neither direct evidence nor evidence of appropriation of assets for personal use before death is required to support an inference of undue influence. For these reasons, the judge's ruling that Alice's will was the result of undue influence by Spinelli was not clearly erroneous, and the trial judge permissibly found that Spinelli failed to meet his burden of proving that Alice, with full knowledge and intent, favored him over her children and other grandchildren without his undue influence. Affirmed.

ANALYSIS

The rationale for shifting the burden to a fiduciary who benefits from a transaction with their principal is that the fiduciary can take precautions to ensure that proof exists that the transaction was fair and that the principal was fully informed, and the fiduciary is in the best position after the transaction to explain and justify it. Thus, the burden to prove the transaction was fair is generally met if the fiduciary shows that the principal made the request with full knowledge and intent, or with the advice of independent legal counsel, one of the functions of which is to provide documentation that the making and execution of a will is voluntary and knowing, thus lending transparency and credibility to the bequest. As this decision illustrates, it is not always enough for an independent attorney to draft a will to render it valid, since the court may consider all the circumstances surrounding the making of the will, and may conclude that notwithstanding that an independent attorney drafted the will, the will was a product of undue influence.

Quicknotes

CIRCUMSTANTIAL EVIDENCE Evidence that, though not directly observed, supports the inference of principal facts.

DURABLE POWER OF ATTORNEY (DPOA) A written document pursuant to which one party confers the authority to act as an agent on their behalf to another party, who is known as the "attorney-in-fact"; that becomes effective immediately or upon the grantor becoming incapacitated; and that terminates immediately upon the grantor's death.

TESTAMENTARY CAPACITY The requisite level of mental capacity required by law at the time a testator executes a testamentary instrument for the document to be valid; this generally requires a finding that the testator understood the nature and extent of the testator's estate, the natural recipients of the testator's property, and the effects of the disposition of their estate.

UNDUE INFLUENCE Improper persuasion that deprives an individual of freedom of choice.

In re Will of Moses

[Parties not identified.]

Miss. Sup. Ct., 227 So. 2d 829 (1969)

NATURE OF CASE: Appeal from judgment denying probate of a will on the grounds of undue influence.

FACT SUMMARY: Holland, Moses's lover and lawyer, contended that he did not exert undue influence over the making of Moses's will, since he did not know that Moses had made the will, and since she had independent legal counsel who drafted the will and did so in a manner that reflected Moses's wishes.

RULE OF LAW

(1) Where an attorney and client have an intimate relationship, a presumption of undue influence arises where the client leaves most of her estate to the attorney, even if the attorney had no knowledge of the will until after the client's death.

(2) The presumption of undue influence that arises when a client leaves most of her estate to her attorney, with whom she has an intimate relationship, may be rebutted by evidence that, in making will, she acted upon independent advice and counsel of a third-party, disinterested attorney.

(3) An attorney who acts merely as a scrivener in drafting a will, recording a testatrix's wishes without questioning or discussing who she designates as a beneficiary, does not provide meaningful independent advice or counsel as to the disposition of her estate, such as would overcome the presumption of undue influence on the part of her regular attorney with whom she has an intimate relationship.

FACTS: Moses was married three times, with each of her husbands predeceasing her. During the second marriage, she struck up a friendship with Holland, a lawyer 15 years her junior. After the death of her third husband, Holland became Moses's lover as well as lawyer, and this relationship continued for several years until Moses's death. During the six or seven years preceding her death, Moses suffered from serious heart trouble, had a breast removed because of cancer, and became an alcoholic. Three years before death, Moses made a will devising almost all of her property to Holland. This will was drafted by a lawyer, Shell, who had no connection with Holland, and who did not tell Holland of the will. According to Shell, when Moses came to his office to arrange for the will, she was not intoxicated and seemed to know exactly what she wanted. Shell ascertained Moses had no husband or children, but they did not discuss Moses's preferring Holland to the exclusion of her blood relatives, nor was there any inquiry or discussion as to a possible client-attorney relationship with Holland. Shell indicated he believed it was Moses's business to which she left her property. During her life, Moses was a property manager and was known to be a good businesswoman. She also was known to have a strong personality and a strong will. Her closest relative was an older sister. The sister attacked the will on the ground of undue influence. The chancellor found undue influence and denied probate, in large part on the basis of the attorney-client relationship, as well as the intimate relationship, between Moses and Holland. The chancellor believed the nature of the relationship gave rise to a presumption of undue influence. The state's highest court granted review.

ISSUE:

(1) Where an attorney and client have an intimate relationship, does a presumption of undue influence arise where the client leaves most of her estate to the attorney, even if the attorney had no knowledge of the will until after the client's death?

(2) May the presumption of undue influence that arises when a client leaves most of her estate to her attorney, with whom she has an intimate relationship, be rebutted by evidence that, in making will, she acted upon independent advice and counsel of a third-party, disinterested attorney?

(3) Does an attorney who acts merely as a scrivener in drafting a will, recording a testatrix's wishes without questioning or discussing who she designates as a beneficiary, provide meaningful independent advice or counsel as to the disposition of her estate, such as would overcome the presumption of undue influence on the part of her regular attorney with whom she has an intimate relationship?

HOLDING AND DECISION: (Smith, J.)

(1) Yes. Where an attorney and client have an intimate relationship, a presumption of undue influence arises where the client leaves most of her estate to the attorney, even if the attorney had no knowledge of the will until after the client's death. The chancellor did not err in finding that the fiduciary relationship between Holland and Moses, coupled with their intimate relationship, created a presumption of undue influence. The presumption of undue influence in the production of a will may arise from antecedent circumstances about which the will's draftsman and witnesses knew nothing. Undue influence will be presumed where the

Continued on next page.

beneficiary has been actively concerned in some way with the preparation or execution of the will—which was not the case here—or where the relationship is coupled with some suspicious circumstances, such as mental infirmity of the testator. Although the sexual morality of the personal relationship between Moses and Holland is not at issue, the intimate nature of their relationship is relevant to the inquiry to the extent that its existence, under the circumstances, warranted an inference of undue influence, extending and augmenting that which flowed from the attorney-client relationship. Thus, for that purpose, it was properly taken into consideration by the chancellor. Affirmed as to this issue.

(2) Yes. The presumption of undue influence that arises when a client leaves most of her estate to her attorney, with whom she has an intimate relationship, may be rebutted by evidence that, in making will, she acted upon independent advice and counsel of a third-party, disinterested attorney. The presumption of undue influence presented by such circumstances may only be rebutted by a clear showing that in making and executing the will, the testatrix acted upon her own volition and upon the fullest deliberation, or upon independent advice and counsel of one wholly devoted to her interest. Affirmed as to this issue.

(3) No. An attorney who acts merely as a scrivener in drafting a will, recording a testatrix's wishes without questioning or discussing who she designates as a beneficiary, does not provide meaningful independent advice or counsel as to the disposition of her estate, such as would overcome the presumption of undue influence on the part of her regular attorney with whom she has an intimate relationship. Shell did not question Moses about her testamentary disposition whereby she gave preference was to be given a nonrelative to the exclusion of her blood relatives. There was no discussion of her relationship with Holland, nor as to whom her legal heirs might be, nor as to their relationship to her, after it was discovered that she had neither a husband nor children. Shell did no more than write down, according to the forms of law, what Moses told him. There was no meaningful independent advice or counsel touching upon these matters, so that Shell's role in writing the will was little more than that of scrivener. Therefore, the chancellor was justified in holding that this did not meet the burden for overcoming the presumption of undue influence. Affirmed as to this issue. Affirmed.

DISSENT: (Robertson, J.) There was no dispute that Moses had a strong will, knew what she wanted, was a good businesswoman, and was of sound mind when she made her will. Also, there was no evidence that Holland was in any way actively concerned with the preparation or execution of the will, or even knew about it. The chancellor's finding of suspicious circumstances had nothing whatsoever to do with the preparation or execution of the will. These were remote antecedent circumstances having to do with the meretricious relationship of the parties, and the fact that at times Moses drank to excess and could be termed an alcoholic, but there was no proof in the record that her use of alcohol affected her will power or her ability to look after her extensive real estate holdings. As to Shell, he did what an attorney drafting a will is supposed to do: he ascertained that Moses was competent to make a will; he satisfied himself that she was acting of her own free will and accord, and that she was disposing of her property exactly as she wished and intended. No more is required. The "suspicious circumstances" raised by the majority had absolutely nothing to do with the preparation or execution of the will. Instead, they had to do with her love life and her drinking habits and propensities. Based on the record, as opposed to speculation about what may have happened, all the tests for making a valid will were met. If full knowledge, deliberate and voluntary action, and independent counsel and advice have not been proved in this case, then they just cannot be proved. Accordingly, Moses's will should be admitted to probate.

ANALYSIS

As this case illustrates, in addition to a confidential relationship, to trigger a presumption of undue influence, one contesting the validity of a will must usually show the existence of "suspicious circumstances." In 1969, when *Moses* was decided, the court found that such circumstances included a sexual relationship between a woman and a significantly younger man. However, 45 years later, the Mississippi Supreme Court held in *Kimbrough v. Estate of Kimbrough,* 134 So. 3d 281 (Miss. 2014), that if a confidential relationship exists, an abuse of relationship must be shown to raise a presumption of undue influence, and the existence of a confidential relationship, standing alone, does not raise a presumption of undue influence. Thus, ostensibly, a sexual relationship that did not constitute an abuse of the fiduciary relationship, would not constitute a "suspicious circumstance." The Restatement (Third) of Property: Wills and Other Donative Transfers § 8.3 cmt. h, lists other "suspicious circumstances:" (1) the extent to which the donor was in a weakened condition, physically, mentally, or both, and therefore susceptible to undue influence; (2) the extent to which the alleged wrongdoer participated in the preparation or procurement of the will or will substitute; (3) whether the donor received independent advice from an attorney or from other competent and disinterested advisors in preparing the will or will substitute; (4) whether the will or will substitute was

Continued on next page.

prepared in secrecy or in haste; (5) whether the donor's attitude toward others had changed by reason of their relationship with the alleged wrongdoer; (6) whether there is a decided discrepancy between a new and previous wills or will substitutes of the donor; (7) whether there was a continuity of purpose running through former wills or will substitutes indicating a settled intent in the disposition of their property; and (8) whether the disposition of the property is such that a reasonable person would regard it as unnatural, unjust, or unfair, for example, whether the disposition abruptly and without apparent reason disinherited a faithful and deserving family member.

Quicknotes

TESTATRIX (*Archaic*) A woman who executes a will.

UNDUE INFLUENCE Improper persuasion that deprives an individual of freedom of choice.

Lipper v. Weslow

Son of decedent (D) v. Disinherited grandchildren of decedent (P)

Tex. Ct. Civ. App., 369 S.W.2d 698 (1963)

NATURE OF CASE: Appeal from refusal to admit will to probate.

FACT SUMMARY: The will of a testatrix was refused probate on the basis that it had been procured by undue influence of her son (D), who was also the lawyer who had prepared the document. The challenge was brought by three grandchildren (P) of the testatrix who had been specifically disinherited by the terms of the will.

RULE OF LAW

Undue influence is shown when such control was exercised over the mind of the testator so as to overcome the testator's free agency and free will and to substitute the will of another so as to cause the testator to do what the testator would not otherwise have done but for such control.

FACTS: Shortly before her death, Mrs. Block executed a will that in large measure left her estate to her two surviving children. The will specifically disinherited three of her grandchildren (P) who were descendants of a son who had died some years before. The will contained a lengthy explanation of her reasons for excluding the grandchildren (P). The basic theme of this portion of the will was that the grandchildren's mother had been unfriendly toward the testatrix and that the grandchildren (P) themselves had shown no interest in the testatrix and had refrained from any contact with her. The will had been prepared by the testatrix's son (D), who was also a lawyer and had maintained close ties with his mother. The disinheritance of the grandchildren (P) had the effect of increasing his share of the estate by redistributing that portion that would otherwise have gone to the grandchildren (P). The grandchildren [the Weslows (P)] challenged the admission of the will to probate, contending that it had been procured through the undue influence of Lipper (D), the lawyer-son. The Weslows (P) contended the disinheritance clause had been inserted because Lipper (D) disliked his deceased brother. Further, the Weslows (P) disputed the factual assertions in the will that they had neglected their grandmother and contended that their attempts at contact with her had somehow been thwarted by Lipper (D). A jury returned a verdict that the will had been procured by undue influence, and the will was refused probate. Lipper (D) then brought this appeal, contending the verdict did not have a factual basis.

ISSUE: Is undue influence shown when such control was exercised over the mind of the testator as to overcome the testator's free agency and free will and to substitute the will of another so as to cause the testator to do what the testator would not otherwise have done but for such control?

HOLDING AND DECISION: (McDonald, C.J.) Yes. Undue influence is shown when such control was exercised over the mind of the testator so as to overcome the testator's free agency and free will and to substitute the will of another so as to cause the testator to do what the testator would not otherwise have done but for such control. The evidence produced at trial showed that although the testatrix was 81 years old at the time this will was executed, she was sound both physically and mentally. The Weslows (P) were able to show opportunity and motive for Lipper (D) to exercise influence over the testatrix in the preparation of her will. There was a factual dispute over whether the recitation of neglect by the Weslows (P) was a true picture of what actually occurred. However, a showing of undue influence requires more than circumstantial evidence of opportunity and motive. There must be a positive showing that such control was exercised over the mind of the testator as to overcome their free will and free agency and to substitute the will of another so as to cause the testator to do what they would not otherwise have done but for such control, the groundwork for such confidential relationship and motive in the form of an unilateral disposition of the testator's estate. But thereafter, the party contending that undue influence existed must bear the burden of proof that the will of the testator was replaced by that of another. The Weslows (P) laid the groundwork but failed to carry the burden of proof thereafter required. The absence of the required proof of actual influence is sufficient to warrant a reversal of the judgment below.

ANALYSIS

A principle ignored by the appellate court was that any bequest to the attorney preparing the will is presumed to have resulted from undue influence. The ABA Model Rules of Professional Conduct strongly recommend that where a client wishes to name their attorney as a beneficiary, the attorney should refer the client to another disinterested attorney for preparation of the will. The clause in the will outlining the reasons for the exclusion of the grandchildren would seem to be entitled to little weight in determining the issue of undue influence. If the will was induced by such influence, then this clause

Continued on next page.

would have been no more valid than any other portion and would become merely a self-serving attempt by the influencer to cover their acts.

Quicknotes

PROBATE The administration of a decedent's estate.

TESTATRIX *(Archaic)* A woman who executes a will.

UNDUE INFLUENCE Improper influence that deprives the individual freedom of choice or substitutes another's choice for the person's own choice.

Latham v. Father Divine

Cousins of decedent (P) v. Beneficiary (D)

N.Y. Ct. App., 85 N.E.2d 168 (1949)

NATURE OF CASE: Suit in equity to impose constructive trust on proceeds from a will.

FACT SUMMARY: The natural heirs of a testatrix sought to gain control of a will distribution made to a religious leader who had been named sole beneficiary. The heirs claimed that the testatrix had been prevented from executing a new will in their favor by the fraud and undue influence of the religious leader.

RULE OF LAW

Where a testator is prevented from executing a new will in favor of an intended beneficiary by the fraud, duress, or undue influence of a present beneficiary or heir, the property intended to go to the new beneficiary will pass to the present beneficiary subject to a constructive trust in favor of the intended beneficiary.

FACTS: Mary Lyon died, leaving a will that devised her entire estate to Father Divine (D), the leader of a religious cult, and to two corporations controlled by him. The will was accepted for probate after a contest filed by two first cousins (P) of the testatrix. Thereafter, the cousins (Latham [P]), who were the testatrix's only close relatives, instituted this suit, claiming that the testatrix had expressed an intention to alter her will so as to bequeath to them property in the amount of $350,000. Latham (P) further alleged that the testatrix had been prevented from doing so by the false representations, undue influence, and physical force of Father Divine (D). Latham (P) requested that a constructive trust in the cousins' favor be imposed on the proceeds of the will to the extent of the property that would otherwise have gone to them if the testatrix had not been prevented from executing the new will. The suit was dismissed for failure to state a cause of action, and Latham (P) appealed that dismissal.

ISSUE: Where a testator is prevented from executing a new will in favor of an intended beneficiary by the fraud, duress, or undue influence of a present beneficiary or heir, will the property intended to go to the new beneficiary pass to the present beneficiary subject to a constructive trust in favor of the intended beneficiary?

HOLDING AND DECISION: (Desmond, J.) Yes. Where a testator is prevented from executing a new will in favor of an intended beneficiary by the fraud, duress, or undue influence of a present beneficiary or heir, the property intended to go to the new beneficiary will pass to the present beneficiary subject to a constructive trust in favor of the intended beneficiary. In reviewing an appeal of a dismissal of a complaint for insufficiency, the allegations of that complaint must be taken as true. If, on that basis, the complaint fails to state a cause of action, then the dismissal must be affirmed. Therefore, we must assume that the allegations of fraud, undue influence, and physical coercion actually occurred. Father Divine (D) states that a showing of the alleged acts cannot empower a court to write a new will for the testatrix. In this contention he is correct. But, where a testator is prevented from executing a new will by the wrongful acts of a present beneficiary or heir to the detriment of an intended beneficiary, and the existing will is otherwise valid, then the existing beneficiary takes their bequest subject to a constructive trust as to that portion that would have gone to the intended beneficiary but for the wrongful acts. A court of equity attempts, to the extent possible, to render complete justice. By imposing a constructive trust to avoid the result of the wrongful prevention of the execution of a new will, the court does not violate the Statute of Frauds or ignore the requirements for a valid will. The will itself is not affected; it is only the property passed under that will. If Latham (P) is able to show that the testatrix intended a different testamentary disposition than is reflected in the probated will, then Father Divine (D) cannot profit by his misconduct. The dismissal is reversed.

ANALYSIS

The constructive trust remedy has also been applied where an impatient beneficiary has killed the testator in order to advance the date of the inheritance. In one instance, a number of beneficiaries were named in a will. The testatrix expressed a desire to change her will, substantially cutting out the presently named beneficiaries. Some of the present beneficiaries succeeded in physically preventing the testatrix from executing the newly drawn will. The result was a trust imposed on the entire proceeds of the will, even though this disinherited some beneficiaries who did not participate in the wrongful acts. The court reasoned that had the testatrix's intent not been thwarted, even the innocent beneficiaries would have lost their bequests. They should not be allowed to profit unjustly by the wrongful acts of the others.

Continued on next page.

Quicknotes

CONSTRUCTIVE TRUST A trust that arises by operation of law whereby the court imposes a trust upon property lawfully held by one party for the benefit of another, as a result of some wrongdoing by the party in possession so as to avoid unjust enrichment.

DURESS Unlawful threats or other coercive behavior by one person that causes another to commit acts they would not otherwise do.

FRAUD A false representation of facts with the intent that another will rely on the misrepresentation to their detriment.

LEGATEE A person who is granted a legacy or bequest pursuant to a will.

UNJUST ENRICHMENT The unlawful acquisition of money or property of another for which both law and equity require restitution be made.

Schilling v. Herrera

Disinherited brother of decedent (P) v. Decedent's caretaker (D)

Fla. Dist. Ct. App., 952 So. 2d 1231 (2007)

NATURE OF CASE: Appeal from dismissal of claim for intentional interference with an expectancy of inheritance.

FACT SUMMARY: Schilling (P) claimed that Herrera (D), who was his sister's caretaker, intentionally interfered with his expectancy of inheritance after Herrera (D) helped Ms. Schilling execute a new will naming Herrera (D) as her sole beneficiary and then fraudulently failed to inform Schilling (P) of Ms. Schilling's death until after probate was discharged.

RULE OF LAW

A party who would have contested a will but was prevented from doing so by another person's fraudulent conduct may bring a claim for intentional interference with an expectancy of inheritance.

FACTS: In 1996, Mignonne Helen Schilling (Ms. Schilling) executed a will, naming her brother, Edward Schilling (Schilling) (P), as her personal representative and sole beneficiary. Over the following years, Ms. Schilling's health declined, and Schilling (P), who lived in New Jersey, traveled to Florida on several occasions to assist his sister. In 2001, Ms. Schilling met Maria Herrera (D), who became Ms. Schilling's caretaker. After several years, Ms. Schilling moved into Herrera's (D) renovated garage, where she paid Herrera (D) rent and fees for her services. Ms. Schilling became entirely dependent on Herrera (D), and in September 2003, Herrara (D) had Ms. Schilling prepare a new will, naming Herrera (D) as her personal representative and sole beneficiary. Ms. Schilling died in August 2004, and Herrera (D) filed a petition for administration with the probate court. Despite numerous phone calls from Schilling (P) in the months following Ms. Schilling's death, Herrara (D) never informed Schilling (P) that his sister had died. Schilling (P) did not find out that his sister was dead until December 6, 2004, and shortly thereafter, the probate court entered a final order of discharge closing Ms. Schilling's estate. Schilling (P) filed suit against Herrera (D) for intentional interference with an expectancy of inheritance, but the trial court dismissed his suit, finding that Herrera (D) had no duty to inform Schilling (P) of his sister's death and that Schilling (P) had not exhausted all of his remedies in the probate court. Schilling (P) appealed.

ISSUE: May a party who would have contested a will but was prevented from doing so by another person's fraudulent conduct bring a claim for intentional interference with an expectancy of inheritance?

HOLDING AND DECISION: (Rothenberg, J.) Yes. A party who would have contested a will but was prevented from doing so by another person's fraudulent conduct may bring a claim for intentional interference with an expectancy of inheritance. To state a cause of action for intentional interference with expectancy of inheritance, the complaint must allege the following elements: (1) the existence of expectancy; (2) intentional interference with the expectancy through tortuous conduct; (3) causation; and (4) damages. In the instant case, the trial court's ruling was based on the fact that Schilling's (P) complaint failed to allege that Herrera (D) breached a legal duty owed to Schilling (P). However, breach of a duty is not one of the elements of the cause of action. We therefore review Schilling's (P) complaint to determine if it sufficiently pleads the cause of action. We conclude that Schilling's (P) complaint states a cause of action because it alleges that Schilling (P) was named as Ms. Schilling's sole beneficiary; that, based on the last will and testament, Schilling (P) expected to inherit Ms. Schilling's estate; that Herrera (D) intentionally interfered with Schilling's (P) expectancy by "convincing" the decedent, while she was ill and completely dependent on Herrera (D), to execute a new will naming Herrera (D) as the sole beneficiary; and that Herrera's (D) fraudulent actions and undue influence prevented Schilling (P) from inheriting his sister's estate. A review of the amended complaint reflects that Schilling (P) has alleged two separate frauds. The first stems from Herrera's (D) undue influence in procuring the will, and the second stems from Herrera's (D) actions in preventing Schilling (P) from contesting the will in probate court. If only the first type of fraud was involved, Schilling's (P) collateral attack on the will would be barred. However, the cause of action may be permitted when "the circumstances surrounding the tortuous conduct effectively preclude adequate relief in the probate court." As the facts in the amended complaint sufficiently allege that Schilling (P) was prevented from contesting the will in the probate court due to Herrera's (D) fraudulent conduct, we find that the trial court erred in finding that Schilling's (P) claim for intentional interference with an expectancy of inheritance was barred. Reversed and remanded.

Continued on next page.

ANALYSIS

Intentional interference with an expectancy of inheritance is not a will contest. Typically, the statute of limitations for the action is the longer statute for tort actions, which does not begin to run until a plaintiff discovers or should have discovered the fraud. However, if a plaintiff challenges the will in a probate action and loses, most states bar the plaintiff from then asserting the tort claim.

Quicknotes

EXPECTANCY The expectation or contingency of obtaining possession of a right or interest in the future.

EXPECTANCY INTEREST The expectation or contingency of obtaining possession of a right or interest in the future.

CHAPTER 5

Wills: Construction

Quick Reference Rules of Law

PAGE

1. *Mahoney v. Grainger.* A will duly executed and allowed by the court must, under the statute of wills, be accepted as the final expression of the intent of the person executing it. 54

2. *In re Estate of Cole.* A court may resort to extrinsic evidence if, after examining the circumstances surrounding the creation of a will, an ambiguity or inconsistency remains. 55

3. *Arnheiter v. Arnheiter.* An erroneous description of a particular devise will not cause the devise to fail where less essential particulars can be eliminated, leaving a resulting description that is clearly accurate. 56

4. *In re Gibbs' Estate.* When minor details of identification in a will are at issue, including middle initials or street addresses, courts should admit extrinsic evidence and should disregard such minor details when the proof establishes that a mistake in identification was actually made. 57

5. *In re Estate of Duke.* An unambiguous will may be reformed to conform to the testator's intent if clear and convincing evidence establishes that the will contains a mistake in the testator's expression of intent at the time the will was drafted, and also establishes the testator's actual specific intent at that time. 58

6. *In re Estate of Russell.* When an uncertainty arises upon the face of a will, it cannot always be determined whether the will is ambiguous or not before the circumstances surrounding the writing of the will are first considered. 61

7. *Gibney v. Hossack.* The phrase "if she survives me" in a devise adequately demonstrates a contrary intention to avoid application of an anti-lapse statute. 62

8. *Dawson v. Yucus.* Where the number of beneficiaries to a gift is certain, and the share each is to receive is also certain and in no way dependent for its amount upon the number who shall survive, it is not a gift to a class but to the individuals. 64

9. *In re Estate of Anton.* The identity rule adeeming bequests not specifically found in an estate will not be applied to cases where specifically devised property is removed from the testator's estate through an act that is involuntary to the testator. 65

Mahoney v. Grainger

[Parties not identified.]

Mass. Sup. Jud. Ct., 186 N.E. 86 (1933)

NATURE OF CASE: Appeal from a decree denying a petition for distribution of a legacy under a will.

FACT SUMMARY: After a trial judge found that a testatrix's sole heir at law was her maternal aunt, ruling that statements of the testatrix were admissible only insofar as they gave evidence of the material circumstances surrounding the testatrix at the time of the execution of the will, her first cousins appealed the ruling, contending they were her heirs at law.

RULE OF LAW

A will duly executed and allowed by the court must, under the statute of wills, be accepted as the final expression of the intent of the person executing it.

FACTS: Sullivan told her attorney she wanted to make a will. She left the bulk of her estate to two first cousins and told the attorney that the rest of the estate should be shared equally by "about twenty-five first cousins." The attorney subsequently drafted the will containing a residuary clause stating in part: "all the rest and residue of my estate, both real and personal property, I give, devise and bequeath to my heirs at law living at the time of my decease." After Sullivan's death, the trial judge found that Sullivan's sole heir at law at the time of her death was her maternal aunt, Frances Greene. The first cousins argued that Sullivan's statement regarding the twenty-five first cousins should be admitted to prove her testamentary intention. However, the trial judge ruled that the statements were not admissible to prove intention and dismissed the cousins' petition. They appealed.

ISSUE: Must a will duly executed and allowed by the court, under the statute of wills, be accepted as the final expression of the intent of the person executing it?

HOLDING AND DECISION: (Rugg, C.J.) Yes. A will duly executed and allowed by the court must, under the statute of wills, be accepted as the final expression of the intent of the person executing it. It is only where testamentary language is not clear in its application to facts that evidence may be introduced in order to clarify the language. In this case, there is no doubt as to Sullivan's heirs at law. The aunt alone falls within that description. The cousins are excluded. The circumstance that the plural word "heirs" was used does not prevent one individual from taking the entire gift. Decree affirmed.

ANALYSIS

Most courts subscribe to the rule that when an instrument has been proved and allowed as a will, oral testimony as to the meaning and purpose of a testator cannot be used to disturb the plain meaning of a will. The fact that a will does not conform to the instructions given to the draftsman who prepared it, by reason of mistake or otherwise, does not authorize a court to reform or alter the will or remold it by amendments. Where no doubt exists as to the property bequeathed or the identity of the beneficiary, there is no room for extrinsic evidence.

Quicknotes

EXTRINSIC EVIDENCE Evidence that is not contained within the text of a document or contract but that is derived from the parties' statements or the circumstances under which the agreement was made.

RESIDUARY CLAUSE (OF WILL) A clause contained in a will disposing of the assets remaining following distribution of the estate.

TESTATRIX ***(Archaic)*** A woman who executes a will.

In re Estate of Cole

Decedent's personal representative (P) v. Decedent's friend (D)

Minn. Ct. App., 621 N.W.2d 816 (2001)

NATURE OF CASE: Defendant's appeal from lower court decision finding that decedent intended to bequeath the defendant $25,000 and not $200,000.

FACT SUMMARY: Decedent Ruth Cole's will stated that she bequeathed to the defendant Veta Vining (D) "the sum of two hundred thousand dollars ($25,000)." The trial court found that Ms. Cole intended to bequeath Vining (D) $25,000.

RULE OF LAW

A court may resort to extrinsic evidence if, after examining the circumstances surrounding the creation of a will, an ambiguity or inconsistency remains.

FACTS: Decedent Ruth Cole's will stated that she bequeathed the defendant Veta Vining (D) "the sum of two hundred thousand dollars ($25,000)." Cole's personal representative (P) petitioned the court to interpret the gift as $25,000 whereas Vining (D) argued Cole's intent was to provide her with $200,000. At trial, the attorney who drafted the will testified he cut and pasted another provision from the will where Cole actually did provide a gift of $200,000. For the gift to Vining (D), the attorney changed the figures to $25,000 but failed to change the wording of the gift. The trial court determined that Cole intended to give Vining (D) $25,000 and granted summary judgment to Cole's personal representative (P). Vining (D) appealed.

ISSUE: May a court resort to extrinsic evidence if, after examining the circumstances surrounding the creation of a will, an ambiguity or inconsistency remains?

HOLDING AND DECISION: (Crippen, J.) Yes. A court may resort to extrinsic evidence if, after examining the circumstances surrounding the creation of a will, an ambiguity or inconsistency remains. Historically, courts have examined inconsistencies in the will depending on whether they were latent or patent ambiguities. Extrinsic evidence can be allowed in to determine latent ambiguities. Such ambiguities are provisions that could apply to one or more persons. Patent ambiguities are inconsistencies readily apparent on the face of the document. In those situations, extrinsic evidence is not admissible and the provision will usually be found void for uncertainly. The common trend now is to do away with the distinction between latent and patent ambiguities. A reviewing court should examine the circumstances surrounding the gift in question first. If the ambiguity persists, whether latent or patent, extrinsic evidence may be allowed to assist with the determination of the testator's intent. Here, the court properly allowed the testimony of the drafting attorney which was undisputed by Vining (D). Affirmed.

ANALYSIS

The decision aptly summarizes the trend regarding the admissibility of evidence for ambiguities in certain provisions of the will. Some states still prohibit introduction of evidence for patent ambiguities. The historical rationale is that the words of the testator were paramount and courts were reluctant to rewrite any section of the will with the use of outside evidence.

Quicknotes

EXTRINSIC EVIDENCE Evidence that is not contained within the text of a document or contract, but which is derived from the parties' statements or the circumstances under which the agreement was made.

Arnheiter v. Arnheiter

[Parties not identified.]

N.J. Ch., 125 A.2d 914 (1956)

NATURE OF CASE: Application to correct mistake in probated will.

FACT SUMMARY: Executrix (P) of Guterl's will applied to the court to correct an obvious mistake in the will by changing the street number of property devised to correctly identify property owned by Guterl.

RULE OF LAW

An erroneous description of a particular devise will not cause the devise to fail where less essential particulars can be eliminated, leaving a resulting description that is clearly accurate.

FACTS: Upon Guterl's death, her will was duly probated. The will provided that the executrix (P) was to sell Guterl's half interest in the property known as "304" Harrison Avenue, and to use the proceeds to establish trusts for her nieces. At the time of the execution of her will and at her death, Guterl owned a half interest in "317" Harrison Avenue, not "304" Harrison Avenue. This was the only property on Harrison Avenue in which Guterl held any interest. The executrix (P) applied to the court to correct the will, changing "304" to "317."

ISSUE: Will an erroneous description of a particular devise cause a devise to fail where less essential particulars can be eliminated, leaving a resulting description that is clearly accurate?

HOLDING AND DECISION: (Sullivan, J.) No. An erroneous description of a particular devise will not cause the devise to fail where less essential particulars can be eliminated, leaving a resulting description that is clearly accurate. The court is powerless to reform the will in the manner requested by the executrix (P), because reformation is not available to change a testamentary instrument. But where there is an obvious mistake, the court may delete particulars from the description of a particular devise so long as the resulting description fits. Here, the mistake was clear: Guterl owned no interest in "304" Harrison Avenue. By disregarding the street number, the rest of the description is sufficient to identify the property described, as her interest in "317" Harrison Avenue, and the will should be so construed. Judgment entered construing decedent's will.

ANALYSIS

This is the doctrine of "*Falsa Demonstratio Non Nocet,*" which allows courts to prevent devises from failing. The key in applying the doctrine is that after the "false" or less important particular is dropped from the description, whether the object or subject of the devise can be identified with sufficient certainty. If not, the devise will still fail.

Quicknotes

EXECUTRIX ***(Archaic)*** A woman who executes a will.

In re Gibbs' Estate

Former employee of decedent (P) v. Named beneficiary (D)

Wis. Sup. Ct., 111 N.W.2d 413 (1961)

NATURE OF CASE: Defendant's appeal from lower court decision finding that decedents intended to bequeath one percent of their estate to a man with the same first and last name but with a different middle initial.

FACT SUMMARY: Decedents George and Lena Gibbs stated in their will that Robert J. Krause should receive one percent of their estate. Robert W. Krause, a long-time employee and family friend of the Gibbses, contested the will and argued the Gibbses intended to make the bequest to him.

RULE OF LAW

When minor details of identification in a will are at issue, including middle initials or street addresses, courts should admit extrinsic evidence and should disregard such minor details when the proof establishes that a mistake in identification was actually made.

FACTS: In wills executed in the years before their deaths, both George Gibbs and Lena Gibbs bequeathed one percent of their combined estate as follows: "To Robert J. Krause, now of 4708 North 46th Street, Milwaukee, Wisconsin." A man with that exact name lived at that address. However, when the Gibbs' wills were probated, Robert W. Krause (P) contested the provision. He argued that he was an employee of George Gibbs for thirty years at the Gibbs Steel Plant. Robert W. (P) also provided testimony that he visited the Gibbs' home often and even did work around the house. The Gibbs' housekeeper also testified that Robert W. (P) was a friend of the family by virtue of his long service at the steel plant and his many visits to the home. The will also included sequential one percent bequest to three other long-time employees of the steel mill. Robert J. Krause (D) actually lived at 4708 North 46th Street. However, his only connection to the Gibbs family was a taxi ride he allegedly gave to Mrs. Gibbs in 1955. The lower court concluded the Gibbses made a mistake of identification in the will and ordered that the one percent bequest go to Robert W. (P). Robert J. (D) appealed.

ISSUE: When minor details of identification in a will are at issue, including middle initials or street addresses, should courts admit extrinsic evidence and disregard such minor details when the proof establishes that a mistake in identification was actually made?

HOLDING AND DECISION: (Fairchild, J.) Yes. When minor details of identification in a will are at issue, including middle initials or street addresses, courts should admit extrinsic evidence and should disregard such minor details when the proof establishes that a mistake in identification was actually made. At common law, no reformation of this will would be possible. The terms of the one percent provision, without reference to any extrinsic evidence, apply to Robert J. Krause (D) and no one else. There is no ambiguity in the language. Typically, only when there is ambiguity in the language will outside evidence be admitted to interpret a will. When there is no ambiguity, extrinsic evidence is typically barred. The rationale for the strict rule was to prohibit plausible claims of mistaken identity by disappointed heirs made after a testator is no longer present to refute such claims. However, courts have relaxed the prohibition on extrinsic evidence somewhat. Details such as middle initials and addresses should not be accorded the same level of sanctity as full names so as to frustrate the testator's intent. When circumstances tend to show a mistake was made, courts should allow contestants to admit evidence to prove that in fact the testator made a mistake in the will. Here, the evidence was clear that the Gibbses intended to give the one percent gift to their long-time friend and employee, Robert W. Krause (P). Affirmed.

ANALYSIS

While the modern trend is to admit extrinsic evidence when there is an ambiguity in the contract, not all courts would have reached the same conclusion as the court did here. Here, the will was not ambiguous. Many courts would refuse to reform the will based on the long held doctrine that extrinsic evidence is only allowed if there is a latent ambiguity in the language. In addition, this decision was criticized because it did not specifically define "minor details of identification" and many commentators felt the decision provided courts with unlimited ability to reform wills as they saw fit.

Quicknotes

EXTRINSIC EVIDENCE Evidence that is not contained within the text of a document or contract, but which is derived from the parties' statements or the circumstances under which the agreement was made.

LATENT AMBIGUITY Language capable of more than one interpretation that seems clear on its face, but the introduction of extrinsic evidence proves it to have a different meaning.

In re Estate of Duke

[Parties not identified.]

Cal. Sup. Ct., 352 P.3d 863 (2015)

NATURE OF CASE: Appeal from affirmance of grant of summary judgment to will contestants on ground that will was unambiguous and, therefore, not susceptible to reformation.

FACT SUMMARY: Irving Duke's (Duke's) (D) will provided if he and his wife, Beatrice, died at "the same moment," his estate would pass equally to two charities, City of Hope (COH) and the Jewish National Fund (JNF). However, Beatrice predeceased him. The charities sought to probate the will, but Duke's intestate heirs, the Radins, challenged the admittance of the will to probate, claiming that they should inherit the estate, since the will was unambiguous and had not provided for the contingency of Beatrice predeceasing Duke. The charities contended that notwithstanding that the will was unambiguous, it was Duke's manifest intent that they receive Duke's estate upon his death, so that extrinsic evidence should be allowed to reform the will in accord with that intent.

RULE OF LAW

An unambiguous will may be reformed to conform to the testator's intent if clear and convincing evidence establishes that the will contains a mistake in the testator's expression of intent at the time the will was drafted, and also establishes the testator's actual specific intent at that time.

FACTS: Irving Duke (Duke), who was 14 years older than his wife, Beatrice, prepared a holographic will that left all of his property to "my beloved wife." The will provided that "[s]hould my wife . . . and I die at the same moment . . . ," the entire estate was to be divided equally between two charities, City of Hope (COH) and the Jewish National Fund (JNF). The will did not provide for the contingency of Beatrice predeceasing him. Beatrice died 18 years after the will was made, predeceasing Duke, who did not die until five years later. COH and JNF petitioned for probate and for letters of administration. The Radins, sons of Duke's sister, who had also predeceased Duke, filed a petition for determination of entitlement to estate, alleging that they were entitled to the distribution of Duke's estate as his sole intestate heirs. The Radins, who did not challenge the validity of the will, moved for summary judgment, asserting that the estate had to pass to Duke's closest surviving intestate heirs, the Radins, because he did not predecease Beatrice, nor did he and Beatrice "die at the same moment," and there was no provision in the will for disposition of the estate in the event Duke survived Beatrice. In opposition to the motion, COH and JNF offered extrinsic evidence to prove that Duke intended the will to provide that in the event Beatrice was not alive to inherit his estate when he died, the estate would be distributed to COH and JNF. The probate court concluded that the will was not ambiguous, and, on that ground, it declined to consider extrinsic evidence of Duke's intent, and granted summary judgment for the Radins. The state's intermediate appellate court affirmed, and the state's highest court granted review.

ISSUE: May an unambiguous will be reformed to conform to the testator's intent if clear and convincing evidence establishes that the will contains a mistake in the testator's expression of intent at the time the will was drafted, and also establishes the testator's actual specific intent at that time?

HOLDING AND DECISION: (Cantil-Sakauye, C.J.) Yes. An unambiguous will may be reformed to conform to the testator's intent if clear and convincing evidence establishes that the will contains a mistake in the testator's expression of intent at the time the will was drafted, and also establishes the testator's actual specific intent at that time. The common law has categorically barred the reformation of an unambiguous will, and state law hitherto has only permitted extrinsic evidence to reform an ambiguous will. However, state law also permits the admission of extrinsic evidence to correct errors in donative documents other than wills, even when the donor is deceased. Extrinsic evidence is also admissible to aid in the construction of a will, and in some cases, the resulting "construction" has essentially reformed the will. Extrinsic evidence is also admissible to determine whether a document was intended to be a will, and to prove the contents of a will that has been lost or destroyed. Extrinsic evidence is also admitted in myriad circumstances to determine a testator's intent. Because extrinsic evidence is not inherently more reliable when admitted for these various purposes than when admitted to correct an error in a will, concerns about the reliability of evidence do not justify a categorical bar on reformation of wills. Evidentiary concerns also do not justify such a bar. Cases arising under the statute of wills always involve a testator who is deceased and therefore cannot explain their intentions. It already has been recognized, however, in the context of inheritance rights, that imposing a burden of proof by clear and convincing evidence is a means to address evidentiary concerns related to the circumstances that the principal witness is deceased and statutory formalities were not followed. Therefore, the

Continued on next page.

fact that the testator will always be unavailable to testify does not warrant a categorical bar on the admission of extrinsic evidence to reform a will. In cases in which clear and convincing evidence establishes both a mistake in the drafting of the will and the testator's actual and specific intent at the time the will was drafted, it is plain that denying reformation would defeat the testator's intent and result in unjust enrichment of unintended beneficiaries. Given that the paramount concern in construing a will is to determine the subjective intent of the testator, only significant countervailing considerations can justify a rule categorically denying reformation. One countervailing consideration is that the will's maker will always be dead and unavailable in these situations. However, the death of a principal witness has not been viewed as a reason to deny reformation in other contexts. Another concern is that anyone could claim to be an unintended beneficiary. However, an appropriately tailored reformation remedy will alleviate concerns regarding unintended beneficiaries, since it is unlikely that there will be many persons who have a connection to a testator and can produce clear and convincing evidence both of a mistake in the drafting of the will at the time the will was written and of the testator's specific intentions concerning the disposition of property. It is also asserted that allowing reformation will result in a significant increase in probate litigation and expenses. Claimants have long been entitled, however, to present extrinsic evidence to establish that a will is ambiguous despite the fact that it appears to be unambiguous. Therefore, probate courts already receive extrinsic evidence of testator intent from claimants attempting to reform a will through the doctrine of ambiguity. The task of deciding whether the extrinsic evidence establishes by clear and convincing evidence that a mistake was made in the drafting of the will is a relatively small additional burden, because the court is already evaluating the evidence's probative value to determine the existence of an ambiguity. To the extent additional claims are made that are based on a theory of mistake rather than a theory of ambiguity, the heightened evidentiary standard will help the probate court to filter out weak claims. For these and other reasons, the categorical bar on permitting extrinsic evidence in cases involving wills that have been determined to be unambiguous, in the appropriate circumstances, is not justified. This is especially true because the interest in ensuring certainty, predictability, and stability has been undermined by the inconsistent application of the principles applicable to the construction of wills, since, in the course of applying the doctrine that an ambiguous will may be clarified through the admission of extrinsic evidence, courts have essentially reformed wills. Allowing reformation of a will upon a clear and convincing showing of a mistake in expression and the testator's actual and specific intent helps ensure that the testator's affairs are settled as intended. Additionally, because the newly announced rule will be relevant only in the context of litigation, in limited circumstances, adoption of the doctrine will not diminish the principles of law that encourage the preparation of well-drafted, properly executed wills. Finally, allowing reformation in these circumstances is consistent with the legislature's efforts to apply the same rules of construction to all donative documents, and will promote fairness in the treatment of estates, regardless of the tools used for estate planning. Allowing reformation of trusts and other instruments, but never of wills, appears to favor those with the means to establish estate plans that avoid probate proceedings, and to deny a remedy with respect to the estates of individuals who effect their plans through traditional testamentary documents. Denying reformation in these circumstances seems particularly harsh with respect to individuals who write wills without the assistance of counsel, and are more likely to overlook flaws in the expression of their intent. Here, COH and JNF contend that Duke actually intended at the time he wrote his will to provide that his estate would pass to COH and JNF in the event Beatrice was not alive to inherit his estate when he died, but that his intent was inartfully expressed in his will and thus there is a mistake in the will that should be reformed to reflect his intent when the will was drafted. Their contention, if proved by clear and convincing evidence, would support reformation of the will to reflect Duke's actual intent. If his only intent at the time he wrote his will was to address the disposition of his estate in the circumstances in which he died before Beatrice or they died simultaneously, his will accurately reflects his intent. In that circumstance, his mistake, if any, would be in failing subsequently to modify the will after Beatrice died, and that mistake would not be related to the will he wrote and that COH and JNF seek to have reformed. Because the charities have articulated a valid theory that will support reformation if established by clear and convincing evidence, the probate court, in accordance with the rule set forth in this decision, should consider such extrinsic evidence. Reversed and remanded.

ANALYSIS

To date, only a few states allow reformation of wills. However, both the Restatement (Third) of Property and the Uniform Probate Code (UPC) now support the remedy. The Restatement's reformation provision appeared in the tentative draft of March 1995, and in the final draft issued in 2003. The UPC's provision authorizing the reformation of wills was added in 2008, and several states have adopted that provision. In addition, Washington, which has not adopted the UPC, has provided by statute that an unambiguous will "may be reformed . . . to conform the terms to the intention of the testator" upon

Continued on next page.

clear and convincing evidence of a mistake. (Wash. Rev. Code § 11.96A.125 (2011).) In Connecticut, extrinsic evidence is admissible to prove a scrivener's error in a will, and a correction will be made upon a clear and convincing showing of error. Courts in New York and New Jersey have also applied a more liberal approach to correcting flaws in wills. Thus, it seems that adoption of this remedy is slowly gaining traction, and overturning decades of precedent in favor of a more nuanced approach to reformation.

Quicknotes

CLEAR AND CONVINCING EVIDENCE An evidentiary standard requiring a demonstration that the fact sought to be proven is reasonably certain.

EXTRINSIC EVIDENCE Evidence that is not contained within the text of a document or contract, but which is derived from the parties' statements or the circumstances under which the agreement was made.

REFORMATION A correction of a written instrument ordered by a court to cause it to reflect the true intentions of the parties.

In re Estate of Russell

[Parties not identified.]

Cal. Sup. Ct., 444 P.2d 353 (1968)

NATURE OF CASE: Appeal from a determination of heirship.

FACT SUMMARY: The testator left her $10 gold piece and diamonds to Hembree, her only heir-at-law, and the residue of her estate to Charles Quinn and Roxy Russell, the latter being her dog, who predeceased her.

RULE OF LAW

When an uncertainty arises upon the face of a will, it cannot always be determined whether the will is ambiguous or not before the circumstances surrounding the writing of the will are first considered.

FACTS: The testatrix left her $10 gold piece to her sister, Hembree, who was her only heir-at-law, and the residue of her estate to Charles Quinn and Roxy Russell. Charles was a longtime friend and confidante, while Roxy was the testatrix's dog. Roxy predeceased the testatrix but was alive at the time of execution of the will. Extrinsic evidence was introduced to establish Roxy's identity. The trial court found that it was the testatrix's intention that Charles was to receive the entire residue and that the gift to Roxy was merely precatory in nature. It further found that there was no lapse of the gift to Charles, but that the gift was to maintain Roxy. Hembree appealed, arguing that the gift of one-half of the residue to a dog was clear and unambiguous; that it was void and passed to her under the laws of intestate succession; and that the admission of extrinsic evidence did not cure the invalidity of the gift.

ISSUE: When an uncertainty arises upon the face of a will, can it always be determined whether the will is ambiguous or not before the circumstances surrounding its writing are first considered?

HOLDING AND DECISION: (Sullivan, J.) No. When an uncertainty arises upon the face of a will, it cannot always be determined whether the will is ambiguous or not before the circumstances surrounding the writing of the will are first considered. The exclusion of extrinsic evidence regarding surrounding circumstances merely because no ambiguity appears can easily lead to giving the will a meaning never intended. California probate code § 105 provides that if, after the admission of extrinsic evidence, the will is not susceptible to two or more meanings, then no ambiguity exists. The statute simply delineates the manner of ascertaining testator's intention. Here, the trial court's conclusion was unreasonable. No words gave the residuary all to Charles or appeared to be merely precatory in nature. A distribution in equal shares to two persons cannot be said to be for one to use whatever portion is necessary in behalf of the other. No extrinsic evidence should have been admitted that would lead to a meaning to which the will was not reasonably susceptible. As for the gift to Roxy, it was clearly void so it lapsed and passed to the heirs-at-law by intestacy. Reversed.

ANALYSIS

Few definite guidelines can be given as to interpretation of wills. Rules and "trends" are conflicting. The rules of the case above apply not only to wills but to contracts and deeds also. They are important in evidence cases as well. What evidence to admit is usually the tough question; the student can only consider the appropriate statutory provisions and the various theories presented in the cases and resolve the problem in their own mind.

Quicknotes

EXTRINSIC EVIDENCE Evidence that is not contained within the text of a document or contract but which is derived from the parties' statements or the circumstances under which the agreement was made.

RESIDUE That property which remains following the distribution of the assets of the testator's estate.

TESTATRIX *(Archaic)* A woman who executes a will.

Gibney v. Hossack

Devisee (P) v. Decedent's estate (D)

230 N.E.3d 1009 (Mass. 2024)

NATURE OF CASE: Appeal of order granting summary judgment in favor of residuary estate.

FACT SUMMARY: Heather Hossack's (Heather's) will was interpreted as intending to modify Massachusetts' default rules regarding anti-lapse, and, accordingly, a devise intended for her predeceased mother went to the residuary estate. Heather's brother, John, challenged this ruling, contending that the state's anti-lapse statute required that the mother's lapsed devise fall to him, not the residuary estate, and Gibney (P), the residuary estate's beneficiary, sued, claiming that Heather's will intended to avoid the application of the anti-lapse statute.

RULE OF LAW

The phrase "if she survives me" in a devise adequately demonstrates a contrary intention to avoid application of an anti-lapse statute.

FACTS: Heather Hossack died at age 48. She was unmarried and did not have children, though Heather had been in a long-term relationship with a partner, Donald Etchison. Thomas Gibney (P) was a neighbor and friend and Heather's primary health care proxy. Three years prior to her death, Heather executed a will devising some cash assets to her mother, Ethel Wyman (Wyman), and others to her brother, John, contingent upon each of them independently surviving her.

The will contained a survival requirement that stated, "No beneficiary shall be considered to have survived me and to be entitled to any of my estate unless such beneficiary survives me for at least NINETY (90) days."

Heather left her tangible personal property to Etchison, devised "per stirpes." The will stated that Gibney was to receive the residuary estate, also "per stirpes." Counsel for Heather's estate (D) informed John that because Wyman had not survived Heather, the devise to Wyman lapsed and the cash accounts devised to her would fall to the residuary estate. John challenged this interpretation, arguing that the anti-lapse statute in Massachusetts required the failed devise to fall to him instead of the residuary estate. Gibney (P), as the named beneficiary of the residual estate, filed a complaint contending that Heather intended to avoid application of the anti-lapse statute. The judge granted summary judgment in Gibney's (P) favor. John appealed, arguing that summary judgment was not appropriate because there was still a material fact in dispute: Heather's intent for the devise if Wyman did not survive her. The state's highest court took review of the case.

ISSUE: Does the phrase "if she survives me" in a devise adequately demonstrate a contrary intention to avoid application of an anti-lapse statute?

HOLDING AND DECISION: (Wendlandt, J.) Yes. The phrase "if she survives me" in a devise adequately demonstrates a contrary intention to avoid application of an anti-lapse statute. Construing a will requires an understanding of the testator's intent for the instrument as a whole, attributing due weight to all of its language and considering it in light of the circumstances known to the testator at the time of execution. The Massachusetts Uniform Probate Code (MUPC) creates default rules of construction that will apply in the absence of a contrary instruction shown by the terms of the will. One of these default rules covers anti-lapse, stating that if a devisee fails to survive the testator, the issue of the deceased devisee will take in their place. The anti-lapse statute aims to protect a typical testator who does not intend to disinherit a line of descent.

Notably, when Massachusetts enacted the MUPC, it omitted language from the Uniform Probate Code that followed this provision on anti-lapse, stating that "words of survivorship, such as a devise to an individual 'if [they] survive[] me,' ... are not, in the absence of additional evidence, a sufficient indication of an intent contrary to the application of [the anti-lapse statute]." This legislative omission is interpreted as purposeful.

However, Heather specifically contemplated that her devisee might predecease her and provided in the will that the devise was contingent upon the devisee's survival. This intent seems especially clear when Heather's devises for John and Wyman require them to survive her, but the devises to Etchison and Gibney (P) are per stirpes, meaning they would pass to the descendants of each. Because Heather's will stated a specific intent regarding lapse, that controls over the MUPC's default rule on anti-lapse. Accordingly, the devise to Wyman lapses and falls to the residuary estate devised to Gibney (P). Affirmed.

ANALYSIS

The 2010 Uniform Probate Code has been enacted in 15 states, though new amendments to the act, completed by the Uniform Law Commission in 2019, have yet to be enacted in any states. These amendments created a new formula for intestate shares in blended

Continued on next page.

and non-traditional families, updated terminology, and added in the concept of *de facto* parentage.

Quicknotes

ANTI-LAPSE STATUTE State statute providing for the substitution of a recipient of a devise made pursuant to a testamentary instrument, if the beneficiary of the gift predeceases the testator and no alternative disposition is made.

DEVISE The conferring of a gift of real or personal property by means of a testamentary instrument.

PER STIRPES "By representation"; used primarily in the law of wills to describe the method of distribution where a person, generally because of death, is unable to take that which is left to them by the will of another, and, therefore, their heirs divide such property between them rather than take under the will individually.

RESIDUARY ESTATE That portion of the estate that remains after all of the estate has been distributed through the satisfaction of all claims.

Dawson v. Yucus

Beneficiary (P) v. Executrix (D)

Ill. App. Ct., 239 N.E.2d 305 (1968)

NATURE OF CASE: Appeal from a judgment for defendants in an action to construe a will.

FACT SUMMARY: Wilson (P), the remaining beneficiary of a will, argued that the gift was made to a class, and therefore, as survivor of the class, he was entitled to the entire interest bequeathed to the class.

RULE OF LAW

Where the number of beneficiaries to a gift is certain, and the share each is to receive is also certain and in no way dependent for its amount upon the number who shall survive, it is not a gift to a class but to the individuals.

FACTS: Nelle Stewart left a duly executed will containing ten clauses. The second clause gave the one-fifth interest in farm lands that Stewart inherited from her husband to two of his nephews, Stewart Wilson and Gene Burtle. Each was to receive one-half of Stewart's one-fifth interest. After the will was admitted to probate, Wilson (P) filed suit against the executrix, Yucus (D), to construe the will, alleging that the devise was a class gift, that Burtle had died after the date of execution of the will but before the testatrix, and that Wilson (P), as the survivor of the class, was entitled to the entire one-fifth interest in the farm. Burtle's two children, Dawson (P) and Burtle (P), were subsequently substituted as plaintiffs. The trial court held that clause two did not create a class gift, and therefore the gift to Burtle lapsed and passed into the residue of the estate upon his death. Dawson (P) and Burtle (P) appealed.

ISSUE: Where the number of beneficiaries to a gift is certain, and the share each is to receive is also certain and in no way dependent for its amount upon the number who shall survive, is it a gift to a class?

HOLDING AND DECISION: (Jones, J.) No. Where the number of beneficiaries to a gift is certain, and the share each is to receive is also certain and in no way dependent for its amount upon the number who shall survive, it is not a gift to a class but to the individuals. In this case, Stewart named the individuals, giving them each a specified portion of her interest in the farm, thus making certain the number of beneficiaries and the share each was to receive. The shares in no way depend upon the number who shall survive Stewart's death. She did, however, create a survivorship gift of the residue of her estate, thus indicating she knew how to manifest such intent. Hence, the language of clause two, phrased differently, was intended to create a gift to individuals distributively. Affirmed.

ANALYSIS

A testator is deemed to be "group minded," that is, intends to create a class gift, if they use a generic class label such as "to my nephews" in devising their property. Stewart stated in her bequest in clause two that she believed the farm lands should go back to her late husband's "side of the house." Wilson (P) argued unsuccessfully that this phrase, together with the extrinsic evidence admitted by the court as to Stewart's intentions, clearly required class gift construction.

Quicknotes

CLASS GIFT A gift to a group of unspecified persons whose number, identity, and share of the gift will be determined sometime in the future.

EXTRINSIC EVIDENCE Evidence that is not contained within the text of a document or contract but which is derived from the parties' statements or the circumstances under which the agreement was made.

REMAINDER An interest in land that remains after the termination of the immediately preceding estate.

RESIDUE That property that remains following the distribution of the assets of the testator's estate.

In re Estate of Anton

Beneficiary (P) v. Executor (D)

Iowa Sup. Ct., 731 N.W.2d 19 (2007)

NATURE OF CASE: Appeal of order denying claim against an estate.

FACT SUMMARY: Hester Mary Lewis Anton (Anton) executed a will leaving one-half of her interest in a piece of property to her stepdaughter Gretchen Coy (Coy) (P). Anton's daughter, acting as her mother's agent under a durable power of attorney, sold the property in 2003 to pay for Anton's nursing home care. After Anton died, Coy (P) filed a claim against the estate (D) to recover the value of her share of the property.

RULE OF LAW

The identity rule adeeming bequests not specifically found in an estate will not be applied to cases where specifically devised property is removed from the testator's estate through an act that is involuntary to the testator.

FACTS: In 1981, Anton executed a will leaving one-half of her interest in her duplex to her stepdaughter Coy (P). Anton was injured in a car accident in 1996 and spent the rest of her life living in several nursing homes, where she was also treated for Huntington's Chorea, a progressive neurological disorder. After the accident, Anton executed a valid durable power of attorney naming her daughter Nancy Ezarski (Ezarski) as her attorney-in-fact. Ezarski managed her mother's financial affairs from 1986 until Anton died in 2003, and gradually sold off Anton's assets to pay for her nursing home care. By 2003, Anton was suffering from what one social services progress report referred to as advanced dementia, and was apparently not competent to handle her financial affairs. Ezarski, having run out of assets to sell, finally sold the duplex and used approximately $29,000 out of the $133,263 net proceeds from the sale to pay for Anton's care up until Anton's death. When Anton's will was submitted for probate, Coy (P) filed a claim against the estate (D), claiming that she was entitled to one-half of the net proceeds from the sale of the duplex. The estate (D) claimed that Coy (P) was not entitled to any of the funds because the identity theory of ademption extinguished any specific bequests not in Anton's estate. The trial court denied the claim and the court of appeals upheld the denial. Coy (P) appealed to the Iowa Supreme Court.

ISSUE: Will the identity rule adeeming bequests not specifically found in an estate be applied to cases where specifically devised property is removed from the testator's estate through an act that is involuntary to the testator?

HOLDING AND DECISION: (Appel, J.) No. The identity rule adeeming bequests not specifically found in an estate will not be applied to cases where specifically devised property is removed from the testator's estate through an act that is involuntary to the testator. Our cases hold that the identity rule will not be rigidly applied in all cases. This includes cases where the property is sold by a guardian, or conservator, or is destroyed contemporaneously with the death of the testator. The rationale of our cases is that ademption occurs where a testator had knowledge of a transaction involving a specific devise, realizes the effect of the transaction on their estate plan, and has an opportunity to revise the will. Where these elements are not present, no ademption occurs. The focus of the analysis is on the testator and whether the testator has made a deliberate decision not to revise the will, and not on the nature of the agency causing the involuntary act. If Anton was aware of the transaction, was aware of the impact the transaction had on her estate plan, and did not change her will, ademption would, of course, occur. Here, however, Anton only had a general knowledge that assets would need to be sold for her support at some time in the future. Therefore, ademption does not apply. Reversed and remanded.

ANALYSIS

The Iowa Supreme Court refused to award Coy (P) one-half of the net proceeds from the sale, but instead ordered the trial court to award Coy (P) one-half of the proceeds remaining from the sale after Anton's cost of care was deducted. This is in keeping with most modern statutes; however, some states still award the full value of the property regardless of what happened to the funds between the time of the sale and the testator's death.

Quicknotes

ADEMPTION Revocation of a specific devise or bequest made pursuant to a testamentary instrument if the particular property is not part of the decedent's estate at the time of death.

BEQUEST A transfer of property that is accomplished by means of a testamentary instrument.

DEVISE The conferring of a gift of real or personal property by means of a testamentary instrument.

DURABLE POWER OF ATTORNEY (DPOA) A written document pursuant to which one party confers the authority to act as an agent on their behalf to another party, who is known as the "attorney-in-fact"; that becomes effective immediately or upon the grantor becoming incapacitated; and that terminates immediately upon the grantor's death.

CHAPTER 6

Trusts: Characteristics and Creation

Quick Reference Rules of Law

PAGE

1. *Jimenez v. Lee.* Where funds are held in trust for a specific purpose, the trustee will be liable for all expenditures not related to that purpose. *68*

2. *Hebrew University Assn. v. Nye.* An imperfect gift due to lack of delivery may not be turned into a trust without an express manifestation of intent. *69*

3. *Hebrew University Assn. v. Nye.* Constructive delivery of a gift through an informal document is permitted if accompanied by acts and declarations showing an intention to complete the gift. *70*

4. *Unthank v. Rippstein.* A mere promise to give periodic gifts in the future will not support a finding that a trust has been established. *71*

5. *Clark v. Campbell.* Where the beneficiaries of a noncharitable trust cannot adequately be determined, the trust fails. *72*

6. *In re Searight's Estate.* An "honorary trust" is valid where it is for a legal purpose and the trustee accepts the testator's wishes, even though there is no beneficiary who can enforce the trust. *73*

7. *In re Estate of Fournier.* An enforceable oral trust is created where clear and convincing evidence shows that the settlor intended to create it. *74*

8. *Olliffe v. Wells.* Where a will on its face gives legal title but not any beneficial interest to a devisee, and there is no express trust indicated, a resulting trust will arise in favor of heirs or next of kin. *75*

Jimenez v. Lee

Trustee's daughter (P) v. Trustee (D)

Or. Sup. Ct., 547 P.2d 126 (1976)

NATURE OF CASE: Action for an accounting.

FACT SUMMARY: Jimenez (P) sought an accounting from her father, Lee (D), for his use of trust funds to satisfy his legal support obligations to her.

RULE OF LAW

Where funds are held in trust for a specific purpose, the trustee will be liable for all expenditures not related to that purpose.

FACTS: Jimenez's (P) grandmother purchased a $1,000 savings bond shortly after Jimenez's (P) birth in the joint names of Jimenez (P) and/or her father, Lee (D). The bond was for Jimenez's (P) educational needs. Another $500 bond was purchased by a third party for Jimenez's (P) education. Lee (D) subsequently cashed the bonds in and invested the proceeds in common stock, which Lee (D) held as custodian for Jimenez (P) under the Uniform Gift to Minors Act. Lee (D) had held these funds as trustee and could use them only for a proper trust purpose, Jimenez's (P) education. Jimenez (P) sought an accounting. Lee (D) alleged that no trust existed and that all funds had been used for Jimenez's (P) benefit. The trial court dismissed Jimenez's (P) complaint.

ISSUE: Where funds are held in trust for a specific purpose, will the trustee be liable for all expenditures not related to that purpose?

HOLDING AND DECISION: (O'Connell, C.J.) Yes. Where funds are held in trust for a specific purpose, the trustee will be liable for all expenditures not related to that purpose. A trustee may only use trust funds in a manner authorized under the trust. A trustee may not expand their powers to include unauthorized uses. The evidence indicates that the bonds were to be used for Jimenez's (P) education and were held in trust by Lee (D) for this purpose. The evidence clearly establishes that Lee (D) could not expand his powers by using the bonds to purchase stock, with Lee (D) acting as custodian under the Uniform Gift to Minors Act. The stock is directly traceable to the bonds, and the trust is impressed on the stock. As trustee, Lee (D) was obligated to keep exact records of all expenditures made for Jimenez's (P) education. Failure to keep accurate records can result in a surcharge to the trustee for unaccounted sums. The trustee is liable for expenditures not related to the purpose of the trust. Reversed and remanded.

ANALYSIS

Jimenez is important for a number of reasons. First, it points out the importance of keeping adequate records of expenditures. Even if a trustee has acted entirely properly, they will be liable for any unaccounted-for funds. *White v. Rankin*, 46 N.Y.S. 228 (1897). Next, *Jimenez* indicates that the trustee must be able to establish that all expenditures are within the areas permitted under the trust instrument. Bogart on *Trusts and Trustees* § 972(1) (1962).

Quicknotes

TRUSTEE A person who is entrusted to keep or administer property for the benefit of another.

Hebrew University Assn. v. Nye

[Parties not identified.]

Conn. Sup. Ct., 169 A.2d 641 (1961)

NATURE OF CASE: Appeal from judgment in action over property ownership.

FACT SUMMARY: Yahuda owned an extensive library that she promised to give to a university in Jerusalem but never delivered before her death.

RULE OF LAW

An imperfect gift due to lack of delivery may not be turned into a trust without an express manifestation of intent.

FACTS: Yahuda became the owner of a collection of rare manuscripts on the death of her husband. In January 1953, Yahuda went to Israel and had discussions about the library with the university officers and announced her gift of the manuscripts to them at a luncheon. Thereafter, Yahuda told everyone that she had given the library of books to the university, and she refused offers to sell. In 1954, Yahuda began arranging and cataloguing the materials for shipment to Israel. However, before her tasks were finished and the books delivered, Yahuda died. Yahuda's will left her estate to another charitable institution. The university filed suit, claiming that it was entitled to the library because it was the rightful owner. The trial court ruled for the university on the basis that Yahuda had created a trust with regard to the library in favor of the university. The decision was appealed.

ISSUE: May an imperfect gift due to lack of delivery be turned into a trust without an express manifestation of intent?

HOLDING AND DECISION: (King, J.) No. An imperfect gift due to lack of delivery may not be turned into a trust without an express manifestation of intent. If an intended gift fails because there was not actual or constructive delivery, the intent can be carried out in equity under the fiction that the donor presumed to constitute themself as trustee to make the delivery. However, this is not true unless there is an express trust, which may be oral, created by the donor. In the present case, there are no facts suggesting that Yahuda ever intended to impose on herself the duties of a trustee with regard to the library. The only evidence is that she had a donative intent but failed to make the delivery. There simply is no evidence to support the trial court's conclusion that she established a trust in favor of the university. Reversed and remanded for a new trial so that the university can present another theory of ownership.

ANALYSIS

Other jurisdictions may have reached a different conclusion on these facts. The Connecticut opinion here represents a strict and narrow view of what is required to show that a donor considers themself to be a trustee. While the court seemed to realize that Yahuda had clearly intended the university to receive the library, they seemed concerned that it was subverting the rules on gifts and trusts to fit it in.

Quicknotes

DONOR A person who gives real or personal property or value.

TRUSTEE A person who is entrusted to keep or administer property for the benefit of another.

Hebrew University Assn. v. Nye

[Parties not identified.]

Conn. Super. Ct., 223 A.2d 397 (1966)

NATURE OF CASE: Action to resolve ownership of decedent's property.

FACT SUMMARY: The ownership of Yahuda's rare book collection was disputed because she intended to give it as a gift but died before delivering it.

RULE OF LAW

Constructive delivery of a gift through an informal document is permitted if accompanied by acts and declarations showing an intention to complete the gift.

FACTS: Yahuda became the owner of a collection of rare manuscripts on the death of her husband. In January 1953, Yahuda went to Israel and had discussions about the library with the university officers and announced her gift of it to them at a luncheon. Thereafter, Yahuda told everyone that she had given the library of books to the university, and she refused offers to sell. In 1954, Yahuda began arranging and cataloguing the materials for shipment to Israel. However, before her tasks were finished and the books delivered, Yahuda died. Her will left her estate to another charitable institution. The university filed suit, claiming that it was entitled to the library because it was the rightful owner. The trial court ruled for the university on the basis that Yahuda had created a trust with regard to the library in favor of the university. After the Supreme Court reversed, the case was remanded so that the university could present alternative theories.

ISSUE: Is constructive delivery of a gift through an informal document permitted if accompanied by acts and declarations showing an intention to complete the gift?

HOLDING AND DECISION: (Parskey, J.) Yes. Constructive delivery of a gift through an informal document is permitted if accompanied by acts and declarations showing an intention to complete the gift. Constructive delivery must be the reasonable equivalent of actual delivery depending on the nature of the property and the circumstances. In the present case, Yahuda clearly indicated her intent to give the library of rare books to the university. She was preparing it for actual delivery when she died, and she had already given the university a memorandum containing a list of the contents of the library. If this memorandum was a formal document the gift would have been unquestionably valid. But the lack of formalism is not fatal here, especially given the other facts that show a clear intention to provide the gift to the university. While the court realizes that the facts here stretch the concept of constructive delivery, courts of equity must do their best to effectuate the wishes of the decedent. Thus, the university is entitled to the possession of Yahuda's library.

ANALYSIS

The result reached here seems to be the fairest one possible. However, even the court was a bit apprehensive at stretching the rules to make sure that Yahuda's intent was carried out. They acknowledged that loose rules could give rise to fraudulent claims.

Quicknotes

CONSTRUCTIVE DELIVERY The transfer of title or possession of property by means other than actual delivery indicative of the parties' intent to effect a transfer.

Unthank v. Rippstein

Promisee (P) v. Executor (D)

Tex. Sup. Ct., 386 S.W.2d 134 (1964)

NATURE OF CASE: Action to declare a trust.

FACT SUMMARY: Craft sent a letter to Rippstein (P) promising to give her $200 per month.

RULE OF LAW

A mere promise to give periodic gifts in the future will not support a finding that a trust has been established.

FACTS: Craft sent Rippstein (P) a letter a few days before his death, promising to give her $200 per month. The letter stated that Craft's estate would be liable for such payments if he died. Rippstein (P) alleged that the letter created an enforceable trust. Unthank (D), the executor of Craft's will, alleged this was an unenforceable gift or a voluntary trust that was unenforceable for lack of consideration.

ISSUE: Will a mere promise to give periodic gifts in the future support a finding that a trust has been established?

HOLDING AND DECISION: (Steakley, J.) No. A mere promise to give periodic gifts in the future will not support a finding that a trust has been established. A gift or voluntary trust is merely a promise, without consideration to make payments in the future. As such, it is unenforceable under the rules governing gifts. It is not a trust since there is no res and no intention expressed to hold all of the alleged trustor's property liable for payment. Upon the death of the promisor, the promise cannot be enforced against the estate since the gift of payments after death is a will substitute lacking the requisite testamentary requirements. The gift is unenforceable. Court of Civil Appeals reversed and trial court affirmed.

ANALYSIS

Before a trust may be found to be enforceable, the equitable title must sufficiently rest in the beneficiary so as to allow them to maintain an action for the conversion of the trust property. *Flick v. Baldwin*, 141 Tex. 340. Where there is no specific trust res to which the trust is to attach, the beneficiary has no beneficial interest in any particular property. Additionally, of course, the absence of trust res would in and of itself, cause the trust to fail in most instances.

Quicknotes

HOLOGRAPHIC CODICIL A handwritten provision added to a testamentary instrument.

RES Thing; subject matter of a dispute to establish rights therein.

TRUST The holding of property by one party for the benefit of another.

TRUST CORPUS The aggregate body of assets placed into a trust.

VOLUNTARY TRUST A trust established by a settlor voluntarily, as opposed to by operation of law, with the intent to make a gift of the trust property for the benefit of another.

Clark v. Campbell

[Parties not identified.]

N.H. Sup. Ct., 133 A. 166 (1926)

NATURE OF CASE: Will contest.

FACT SUMMARY: The trustees of the estate were directed to give decedent's personal effects to the friends they knew she wished to receive them.

RULE OF LAW

Where the beneficiaries of a noncharitable trust cannot adequately be determined, the trust fails.

FACTS: Decedent left her personal property to her trustees in trust to "make disposal by way of memento ... to such of my friends as they, my trustees, shall select." Decedent further stated that her trustees were familiar with her friends and her wishes. Heirs alleged that the trust was void for lack of definite beneficiaries or ascertainable standards to identify them.

ISSUE: Where the beneficiaries of a noncharitable trust cannot adequately be determined, will a trust fail?

HOLDING AND DECISION: (Snow, J.) Yes. Where the beneficiaries of a noncharitable trust cannot adequately be determined, the trust fails. "Friends" is too indefinite a class of beneficiaries. Appointment of property by the trustee could not be opposed, in most cases, since the permissible class is too vague for the court to determine whether the distribution was proper. The trust therefore fails, and the trustee holds for the taker under the will. Case discharged.

ANALYSIS

The Attorney General of the state administers charitable trusts and can protect against trustee abuses. Therefore, charitable trusts will not fail for lack of a definite beneficiary. *Harrington v. Pier*, 105 Wis. 485 (1900). Personal wishes conveyed to the trustee by the testator are not sufficient to render an otherwise indefinite description of beneficiaries definite. *Olliffe v. Wells*, 130 Mass. 221 (1881).

Quicknotes

CESTUI QUE TRUST Beneficiary; the party for whose benefit a trust is established.

UNJUST ENRICHMENT The unlawful acquisition of money or property of another for which both law and equity require restitution to be made.

In re Searight's Estate

Department of Taxation (P) v. Executor (D)

Ohio Ct. App., 95 N.E.2d 779 (1950)

NATURE OF CASE: Appeal from probate decision.

FACT SUMMARY: The testator, by will, left $1,000 to his executor (D) to pay another to care for his dog for the rest of the dog's life, and the probate court found it was a valid honorary trust.

RULE OF LAW

An "honorary trust" is valid where it is for a legal purpose and the trustee accepts the testator's wishes, even though there is no beneficiary who can enforce the trust.

FACTS: The testator, by will, left $1,000 to his executor (D) to pay Florence Hand $0.75 per day to care for his dog for the rest of the dog's life. The probate court found that it was a valid "honorary trust."

ISSUE: Is an "honorary trust" valid where it is for a legal purpose and the trustee accepts the testator's wishes, even though there is no beneficiary who can enforce the trust?

HOLDING AND DECISION: (Hunsicker, J.) Yes. An "honorary trust" is valid where it is for a legal purpose and the trustee accepts the testator's wishes, even though there is no beneficiary who can enforce the trust. Normally, attempts to create a trust where there is no ascertainable beneficiary will fail, but an exception permits an "honorary trust" to survive. The requirements are that the trust have some legal purpose and that the trustee accepts the wishes of the testator. Here, the testator attempted to further no illegal purpose but rather a worthy one; and Florence accepted the dog and the responsibilities of care. The transfer into trust does not violate the rule against perpetuities since there is only $1,000 plus accumulated interest involved, which, at $0.75 per day, would be exhausted within five years. [The rule against perpetuities requires the transfer to vest within a life or lives in being plus 21 years.] The Probate Court is affirmed.

ANALYSIS

Most jurisdictions do not recognize "honorary trusts." But no jurisdiction recognizes such a trust where the testator "requests" or "hopes" that the trustee will perform the stated tasks in the purported trust instrument. This would be an aleatory suggestion, which the trustee could ignore while keeping the transfer into trust for their own benefit. It would then be void due to no affirmative trust intent.

Quicknotes

CHARITABLE TRUST A trust that is established for the benefit of a class of persons or for the public in general.

RULE AGAINST PERPETUITIES The doctrine that a future interest that is incapable of vesting within 21 years of lives in being at the time it is created is immediately void.

In re Estate of Fournier

[Parties not identified.]

Me. Sup. Jud. Ct., 902 A.2d 852 (2006)

NATURE OF CASE: Appeal from denial of petition seeking declaratory judgment that an oral trust had been created for an individual.

FACT SUMMARY: Fournier asked a couple to hold $400,000 for him and to turn the money over to his sister, Fogarty (P), when he died since Fogarty (P) needed the money more than his other sister, Flanigan (D). Fogarty (P), the personal representative of Fournier's estate, contended that Fournier had created an oral trust with the couple and that she was the personal beneficiary of that trust.

RULE OF LAW

An enforceable oral trust is created where clear and convincing evidence shows that the settlor intended to create it.

FACTS: Fournier asked a couple who were his trusted friends to hold $400,000 for him and to turn the money over to his sister, Fogarty (P), when he died since Fogarty (P) needed the money more than his other sister, Flanigan (D). Fournier told Flanigan (D) and her daughter about the money. He also gave Fogarty (P) $100,000 during his life. After Fournier died, Fogarty (P) became the personal representative of Fournier's estate. She met with the couple, who turned the $400,000 over to her. Fogarty (P) petitioned for a declaratory judgment to establish that during his lifetime Fournier had created an oral trust for her benefit. The probate court denied her petition because it concluded that by telling Flanigan (D) and her daughter about the money, Fournier had sought to pass the money through his estate, and that by giving Fogarty the $100,000 gift, he decreased her financial need, potentially obviating the need for a trust for her benefit. The state's highest court granted review.

ISSUE: Is an enforceable oral trust created where clear and convincing evidence shows that the settlor intended to create it?

HOLDING AND DECISION: (Dana, J.) Yes. An enforceable oral trust is created where clear and convincing evidence shows that the settlor intended to create it. The creation of an oral trust must be established by clear and convincing evidence. Here, the evidence, primarily in the form of testimony from the couple, clearly and convincingly showed that Fournier intended Fogarty (P) to get the money in her individual capacity, not as the estate's personal representative. It also showed that he did not want Flanigan (D) to get the money. Accordingly, the probate court clearly erred in determining that Fournier wanted the money to pass through his estate. Thus, Fournier created an oral trust in which the couple was to hold the money during his lifetime and turn it over to Fogarty (P) personally after his death. Vacated and remanded.

ANALYSIS

Oral trusts are valid in all but a few states and, as in this case, may be proved by oral testimony.

Quicknotes

TRUST The holding of property by one party for the benefit of another.

Olliffe v. Wells

Family of deceased (P) v. Executor (D)

Mass. Sup. Jud. Ct., 130 Mass. 221 (1881)

NATURE OF CASE: Action to have legacy of estate residue declared lapsed and to have property distributed among heirs at law and next of kin.

FACT SUMMARY: Testatrix devised residue of estate to the executor with an instruction to distribute it, according to his discretion, so as to carry out the testatrix's pre-expressed wishes.

RULE OF LAW

Where a will on its face gives legal title but not any beneficial interest to a devisee, and there is no express trust indicated, a resulting trust will arise in favor of heirs or next of kin.

FACTS: Testatrix left a will, and after giving various legacies, she devised to Wells (D), the named executor, the residue of the estate, which the executor (D) was empowered to distribute in such manner as in his discretion was best calculated to carry out the wishes of the testatrix as expressed to him. In an action by the heirs (P) and next of kin (P) of the testatrix to have the executor (D) distribute the residue to them, the executor (D) claimed that prior to her death the testatrix orally instructed him to give the residue to charities.

ISSUE: Where a will on its face gives legal title but not any beneficial interest to a devisee, and there is no express trust indicated, will a resulting trust arise in favor of heirs or next of kin?

HOLDING AND DECISION: (Gray, C.J.) Yes. Where a will on its face gives legal title but not any beneficial interest to a devisee, and there is no express trust indicated, a resulting trust will arise in favor of heirs or next of kin. The purported trust in favor of the charities did not appear on the face of the will; therefore, it cannot be established by extrinsic evidence. Thus, the executor (D) only has discretion in the manner of distribution; the executor cannot choose the beneficiaries. Since the trust cannot be carried out, the bequest falls within the residue of the estate and goes to the heirs (P) and next of kin (P). If the charities had been expressly named, they could have enforced the trust against the executor (D), who received only a legal title, and no beneficial interest, in the devise. Decision for plaintiffs.

ANALYSIS

Where a testamentary trust fails for any reason, the assets that were to be a part of that trust must still be distributed. In some instances the testator's will may provide for the distribution of such assets. But if no contingent provision was prepared, the assets must pass intestate. This has resulted, in some cases, in the assets going to heirs or next of kin specifically excluded by the testator. A testator's statement in their will that certain individuals are not to share in the estate does not constitute a testamentary scheme.

Quicknotes

DEVISEE A person upon whom a gift of real or personal property is conferred by means of a testamentary instrument.

EXTRINSIC EVIDENCE Evidence that is not contained within the text of a document or contract but that is derived from the parties' statements or the circumstances under which the agreement was made.

RESIDUARY ESTATE That portion of the estate that remains after all the estate has been distributed through the satisfaction of all claims and is conditional upon something remaining after the claims on the testator's estate are satisfied.

RESULTING TRUST An equitable trust that is established from the inferred intent of the parties to create a trust.

TESTATRIX (*Archaic*) A female who executes a will.

CHAPTER 7

Nonprobate Transfers and Planning for Incapacity

Quick Reference Rules of Law

PAGE

1. *Fulp v. Gilliland.* While a trust is revocable, its trustee owes a duty only to the settlor, and not to remainder beneficiaries. *78*

2. *In re Omega Trust.* Emails between a trust settlor and the settlor's attorneys may constitute a valid amendment to a trust, notwithstanding that the settlor dies before fulfilling the trust's requirements for amendments, provided the emails evince a clear and convincing intent by the settlor to amend the trust according to the amendment terms set forth in the emails. *80*

3. *State Street Bank and Trust Co. v. Reiser.* Where a person places property in trust and reserves the right to amend and revoke and direct disposition of principal and income, the settlor's creditors, after the settlor's death, may reach all assets of the trust subjected to those powers. *82*

4. *Clymer v. Mayo.* A state statute that terminates a spouse's interest in the other spouse's will when the couple divorces also applies to a revocable pour-over trust that is funded entirely by the will of the deceased spouse. *83*

5. *Cook v. Equitable Life Assurance Society.* An attempt to change the beneficiary of a life insurance policy by will or other testamentary instrument will be ineffectual because that type of modification fails to follow the prescribed method as stated in the insurance policy. *84*

6. *Nunnenman v. Estate of Grubbs.* A change in the beneficiary of a life insurance policy or individual retirement account may be accomplished via a will so long as the language of the will specifically identifies the insurance policy or individual retirement account involved and evidences the testator's clear intent to change the beneficiary. *85*

7. *Egelhoff v. Egelhoff.* The Employee Retirement Income Security Act of 1974 preempts a state statute that provides for the automatic revocation of a spouse as the designated beneficiary of a nonprobate asset upon the couple's divorce. *86*

8. *Varela v. Bernachea.* A gift is presumed when a joint bank account is established with the funds from one person, and the presumption can be overcome only through clear and convincing evidence to the contrary. *87*

9. *In re Estate of Kurrelmeyer.* A durable power of attorney that authorizes the attorney-in-fact to "execute and deliver any assignments, stock powers, deeds or trust instruments" allows the attorney-in-fact to create and fund a revocable living trust, the creation of which is not an invalid usurpation of the principal's will. *88*

Fulp v. Gilliland

Purchaser of property held in a revocable trust (P) v. Successor trustee (D)

Ind. Sup. Ct., 998 N.E.2d 204 (2013)

NATURE OF CASE: Appeal from decision that the settlor/trustee of a revocable trust did not owe a fiduciary duty to the trust's remainder beneficiaries.

FACT SUMMARY: Ruth Fulp (Ruth), who had placed her farm in a revocable trust, agreed to sell the farm to her son, Harold Jr. (P), for less than fair market value. Her daughter, Nancy Gilliland (Nancy) (D), a remainder beneficiary of the trust, contended that Ruth, as trustee, owed the remainder beneficiaries a fiduciary duty, so that the sale was unenforceable.

RULE OF LAW

While a trust is revocable, its trustee owes a duty only to the settlor, and not to remainder beneficiaries.

FACTS: Ruth Fulp (Ruth) placed her family farm in a revocable trust, the remainder beneficiaries of which were her three children—Harold Jr. (P), Nancy Gilliland (Nancy) (D), and Terry. Under the trust documents, as trustee, she was required to act in the best interests of the remainder beneficiaries. Eventually, she moved into an old-age home, and sought to sell the farm so she could pay her living expenses there. However, she wanted to keep the farm in the family, so she approached Harold Jr. (P), who was interested in purchasing the farm, but at a large discount ($450,000) from fair market value ($1 million). Ruth entered into a purchase agreement to sell the farm to Harold Jr. (P) at the discounted price. Nancy (D) objected, wanting her share of the farm. Harold Jr. (P) brought suit, seeking specific performance of the purchase agreement. Nancy (D), as the successor trustee, argued that the agreement could not be enforced, since Ruth owed the remainder beneficiaries a fiduciary duty to sell the farm at fair market value. The trial court ruled that Ruth breached her fiduciary duty to the children by selling the farm at a low price. The state's intermediate appellate court agreed with the trial court that if Ruth had sold the farm as trustee, she would have breached a fiduciary duty to her children, but it also recognized that if Ruth had such a duty, her conflicting rights and duties as trustee would essentially render the trust irrevocable. To avoid that untenable result, the appellate court instead concluded that Ruth sold the farm as settlor, so that the purchase agreement "in effect" amended the trust. Nancy (D) appealed, and the state's highest court granted review.

ISSUE: While a trust is revocable, does its trustee owe a duty only to the settlor, and not to remainder beneficiaries?

HOLDING AND DECISION: (Rush, J.) Yes. While a trust is revocable, its trustee owes a duty only to the settlor, and not to remainder beneficiaries. The issue presented is one of first impression in this state. Resolution of the issue requires a determination of Ruth's duties under the terms of the trust and the state's trust code. The primary purpose in interpreting the trust is to implement Ruth's intent as settlor, and two provisions of the trust show she intended to owe a duty only to herself. First, Ruth could revoke the trust for any reason at any time, which shows that she intended to control the farm and treat it as her own property. Second, the trust was for Ruth's "use and benefit"—including the right to use all trust assets. The children's interest in the trust was purely secondary and would arise only if Ruth chose not to divest them and if she chose not to use all of the assets. So as trustee, Ruth's fiduciary duty was to herself, as settlor and primary beneficiary. If, as Nancy (D) contends, Ruth owed a fiduciary duty to her children, Ruth would have conflicting duties, thus effectively rendering the trust irrevocable and defeating Ruth's intent in creating a revocable trust. Article V of the trust provided that the trustee owed the remainder beneficiaries fiduciary duties, unless the terms of the trust provided otherwise. Article V would conflict with other rights and duties given to Ruth while the trust was revocable and she was still the primary beneficiary. For example, Ruth could not have a duty to administer the trust solely in the interest of the beneficiaries, when she was permitted to remove any beneficiary at any time. Additionally, she could not have any duty to preserve the trust's assets, when she had the right to consume them. By contrast, no such conflict existed in applying Article V to a successor trustee once the trust became irrevocable and Ruth was no longer the primary beneficiary—at that time, the successor trustee could readily administer the trust for the beneficiaries, treat them impartially, and preserve the trust property. Accordingly, Ruth as trustee owed a duty only to herself. As the primary beneficiary, she was entitled to use the trust assets for her own benefit—and here, selling the farm benefitted her by providing her with money for her care while keeping the farm in the family. Thus, Ruth's actions did not violate the trust. The state's trust code was amended after Ruth created her trust to declare the same rule announced here—that while a trust is revocable, the trustee owes duties only to the settlor. Trust

Continued on next page.

code amendments apply retroactively unless they would "adversely affect a right given to any beneficiary . . . [or] relieve any person from any duty or liability imposed by the terms of the trust or under prior law." Because the code reflects Ruth's intent, and does not adversely affect the rights of any of the beneficiary children because their rights were subject to Ruth's right as settlor to revoke the trust, it may be applied retroactively. Similarly, the law does not relieve any person of a duty because while the trust was revocable, Ruth owed a duty only to herself. Therefore, under both the terms of the trust and under state statute, Ruth owed no duty to her remainder beneficiary children. The judgment of the trial court is therefore reversed and remanded, with instructions to grant specific performance of the purchase agreement.

ANALYSIS

The Uniform Trust Code takes a position similar to the one taken in this decision: "While a trust is revocable . . . , rights of the beneficiaries are subject to the control of, and the duties of the trustee are owed exclusively to, the settlor." Uniform Trust Code § 603(a) (amended 2010). Courts in states that have enacted the Uniform Trust Code have easily concluded that trustees exclusively owe a duty to settlors, and other states that have considered the issue have come to the same conclusion.

Quicknotes

FIDUCIARY DUTY A legal obligation to act for the benefit of another, including subordinating one's personal interests to that of the other person.

IRREVOCABLE TRUST A trust that is not capable of being revoked after it is established.

REMAINDER BENEFICIARY A person who is to receive property that is held in trust after the termination of a preceding income interest.

REVOCABLE TRUST A trust where trustor reserves the right to revoke the trust.

SETTLOR The grantor or donor of property that is to be held in trust for the benefit of another.

In re Omega Trust

Alleged beneficiary (P) v. Special trustee (D)

N.H. Sup. Ct., 281 A.3d 1281 (2022)

NATURE OF CASE: Appeal of order dismissing petition to validate a purported amendment to a trust.

FACT SUMMARY: The beneficiary of an amended trust maintained that the grantor's most recent amendments to the trust were effective, notwithstanding that they had not been signed and the trustee had not been given notice of them, as required by the trust, on the basis that emails between the grantor and his attorneys immediately preceding his death substantially complied with the trust terms and manifested his clear and unequivocal intent to amend the trust in accordance with the proposed amendments contained in the emails.

RULE OF LAW

Emails between a trust settlor and the settlor's attorneys may constitute a valid amendment to a trust, notwithstanding that the settlor dies before fulfilling the trust's requirements for amendments, provided the emails evince a clear and convincing intent by the settlor to amend the trust according to the amendment terms set forth in the emails.

FACTS: In July 2016, the grantor of the Omega Trust (the "trust") informed the Trust Protector that he was in poor health and asked for her help in creating a third amendment to the trust. Additionally, he informed the trustee that he was making changes and contacting his attorney to make amendments. That August, the grantor exchanged various emails about updating his estate plan; the final emails exchanged between the grantor and his attorney memorialized that the firm would prepare the revised documents. The grantor died before he signed the amendment.

David Apostoloff (P) petitioned the court to declare that the third amendment was valid even though it had not been signed, and the trustee not notified, as required by the trust terms. The trust's special trustee (D) filed a motion to dismiss, which the court granted on the basis that the emails exchanged between the grantor and his attorneys did not substantially comply with the trust's terms, which required both the grantor's signature and notice to the trustee (D) with acknowledgement before an amendment could take effect. The court also concluded that because the attorney had stated that the appropriate documents "will" be drafted, it demonstrated that the grantor was still making corrections to the documents and waiting to see the final version when he died. Apostoloff (P) appealed, arguing that the grantor had clearly intended to amend the trust per the terms contained in the emails.

ISSUE: May emails between a trust settlor and the settlor's attorneys constitute a valid amendment to a trust, notwithstanding that the settlor dies before fulfilling the trust's requirements for amendments, provided the emails evince a clear and convincing intent by the settlor to amend the trust according to the amendment terms set forth in the emails?

HOLDING AND DECISION: (Hantz Marconi, J.) Yes. Emails between a trust settlor and the settlor's attorneys may constitute a valid amendment to a trust, notwithstanding that the settlor dies before fulfilling the trust's requirements for amendments, provided the emails evince a clear and convincing intent by the settlor to amend the trust according to the amendment terms set forth in the emails. New Hampshire's version of the Uniform Trust Code states that a settlor may amend a revocable trust through "substantial compliance with a method provided in the terms of the trust" or by "any other method manifesting clear and convincing evidence of the settlor's intent if the terms of the trust do not provide a method or do not expressly prohibit methods other than methods provided in the terms of the trust." Nothing in the trust's terms demonstrate that the amendment process it provides—requiring notice with the trustee and execution by the grantor—is exclusive. Accordingly, under both the Restatement (Third) of Trusts and New Hampshire's statute, any method could be used to amend the trust if there is clear and convincing evidence that the amendment was the settlor's intent. At a minimum, Apostoloff (P) demonstrated an adequate claim that the amendment may be valid to survive a motion to dismiss. Reversed and remanded.

ANALYSIS

On remand, the trial court still found that there was not clear and convincing evidence that the settlor intended for the emails to constitute an amendment, and the New Hampshire Supreme Court agreed. The Court considered testimony from multiple witnesses who stated that it was common for the settlor to engage in multiple rounds of substantive edits before the documents would have been finalized and agreed with the trial court's finding that the emails did not adequately demonstrate that the settlor had a final plan.

Continued on next page.

Quicknotes

CLEAR AND CONVINCING EVIDENCE An evidentiary standard requiring a demonstration that the fact sought to be proven is reasonably certain.

SETTLOR The grantor or donor of property that is to be held in trust for the benefit of another.

TRUST PROTECTOR Any person, other than a trustee, who under the terms of a trust, an agreement of qualified beneficiaries, or a court order has a power or duty with respect to a trust, including, without limitation, one or more statutory enumerated powers.

TRUSTEE A person or entity entrusted to execute a trust and keep or administer the assets of the trust for the benefit of trust beneficiaries.

State Street Bank & Trust Co. v. Reiser

Lending bank (P) v. Estate of decedent (D)

Mass. App. Ct., 389 N.E.2d 768 (1979)

NATURE OF CASE: Appeal from order upholding an inter vivos trust.

FACT SUMMARY: After Dunnebier created an inter vivos trust funded with the capital stock of five closely held corporations that owned certain real estate regarded by State Street Bank (the Bank) (P) as evidence of Dunnebier's solvency, the Bank (P) made an unsecured loan to him without knowledge of the trust and sought to recover assets of the trust after Dunnebier's death for repayment.

RULE OF LAW

Where a person places property in trust and reserves the right to amend and revoke and direct disposition of principal and income, the settlor's creditors, after the settlor's death, may reach all assets of the trust subjected to those powers.

FACTS: Dunnebier held the majority of the capital stock of five closely held corporations that in turn owned real estate development projects and interests. Dunnebier approached State Street Bank (the Bank) (P) for a loan of $75,000 and showed its officer certain of the projects under construction. Regarding these projects as evidence of Dunnebier's solvency, an unsecured loan was approved for that amount, though the Bank (P) was unaware of the fact that Dunnebier had placed his stock in an inter vivos trust. The trust provided that Dunnebier was to have the right to amend or revoke the trust and to direct the disposition of all principal and income during his life. The trial court upheld the trust, insulating the assets from the Bank's (P) claim for the unpaid portion of the debt remaining after Dunnebier's death. The Bank (P) appealed.

ISSUE: Where a person places property in trust and reserves the right to amend and revoke and direct disposition of principal and income, may the settlor's creditors, after the settlor's death, reach all assets of the trust subjected to those powers?

HOLDING AND DECISION: (Kass, J.) Yes. Where a person places property in trust and reserves the right to amend and revoke and direct disposition of principal and income, the settlor's creditors, after the settlor's death, may reach all assets of the trust subjected to those powers. When a person creates a discretionary trust, such as one where virtually all powers to administer the property remain in the settlor, their creditors can reach the assets under the settlor's power during the settlor's lifetime. After death, all power goes either to beneficiaries or to the trustee. However, since the right to use principal and income rested in the settlor, they could have used it to pay debts and may have been forced to do so. The Internal Revenue Code provides that where substantial control resides in the settlor of an inter vivos trust, ownership for tax purposes resides in them after death. By analogy, creditors may reach the assets of a trust subject to a settlor's rights to amend and revoke and direct disposition and death of the settlor does not terminate this right. Reversed.

ANALYSIS

The loan here was unsecured. State Stree Bank (P) held no interest in the real estate shown to it by Dunnebier, however, it relied upon the existence of these assets for future collection purposes. Dunnebier's death was unexpected, and it was not unreasonable in fact to speculate that he would have used his power to invade the corpus or to apply interest in such a way as to pay State Stree Bank (P). Where a settlor retains so much control as to make a trust "discretionary," however, these points need not even be considered. The settlor has not given up control enough to insulate the assets from his creditors.

Quicknotes

CLOSELY HELD CORPORATION A corporation whose shares (or at least voting shares) are held by a closely knit group of shareholders or a single person.

CORPUS The principal property comprising a trust, not including interest or income.

DISCRETIONARY TRUST A trust pursuant to which the trustee is authorized to make decisions regarding the investment of the trust funds and the distribution of such funds to beneficiaries.

INTER VIVOS TRUST Property that is held by one person for the benefit of another and that is created by an instrument that takes effect during the life of the grantor.

Clymer v. Mayo

Administrator of estate (P) v. Decedent's husband (D)

Mass. Sup. Jud. Ct., 473 N.E.2d 1084 (1985)

NATURE OF CASE: Appeal from lower court decision finding that a couple's divorce revoked a husband's interest in his former wife's will but not his interest in her revocable trust.

FACT SUMMARY: Decedent Clara Mayo created a will and a revocable trust that was to be funded from the residuary of her will upon her death. Her husband, James Mayo (D), was the primary beneficiary of the will and the trust. The couple divorced in 1978 and Clara Mayo passed away in 1981.

RULE OF LAW

A state statute that terminates a spouse's interest in the other spouse's will when the couple divorces also applies to a revocable pour-over trust that is funded entirely by the will of the deceased spouse.

FACTS: Decedent Clara Mayo created a will and revocable trust in 1973. Her husband, James Mayo (D), was the primary beneficiary of the will and her trust. The revocable trust was unfunded and would only be funded upon Clara's death. The will provided that upon her death, the residuary of the estate would pour over into the trust for James Mayo's (D) benefit. The couple divorced in 1978. Clara died in 1981. Litigation ensued among the administrator of the estate, Clymer (P), and Mayo (D), as well as other beneficiaries in the will. The issue at trial was whether the state statute that revoked James Mayo's (D) interest in Clara's will when the couple divorced also applied to the revocable trust. The lower court found that it did not. Clymer (P) appealed.

ISSUE: Does a state statute that terminates a spouse's interest in the other spouse's will when the couple divorces apply to a revocable pour-over trust that is funded entirely by the will of the deceased spouse?

HOLDING AND DECISION: (Hennessey, C.J.) Yes. A state statute that terminates a spouse's interest in the other spouse's will when the couple divorces also applies to a revocable pour-over trust that is funded entirely by the will of the deceased spouse. Like many other states, Massachusetts has a statute that terminates a spouse's interest in the other spouse's will upon divorce. Here, Clara's trust was unfunded during her lifetime and it would only be funded from the residuary of her will at the time of her death. Accordingly, it was clear that the will and the trust were part of a single testamentary scheme. It would be incongruous to revoke Mayo's (D) interest in the will but not the revocable trust that was only funded via the will's residuary provision. Accordingly, the statute terminating the interest in the will also terminates the spouse's interest in the revocable trust that is entirely funded through the will at the testator's death. Reversed.

ANALYSIS

The court noted that its holding was confined only to those revocable trusts that received their funding entirely from the will at the time of the testator's death. The court found that this holding was consistent with the legislative purposes behind enactment of the state statute terminating one spouse's interest in the other spouse's will upon divorce. The statute was enacted to conform the law to the expectations of people that upon divorce, the couple's financial interests will be completely separated.

Quicknotes

POUR-OVER PROVISION A provision pursuant to a testamentary instrument, providing that the residuary estate be distributed to a different testamentary instrument; i.e., will to trust or trust to will.

REVOCABLE TRUST A trust where the settlor reserves the right to revoke the trust.

Cook v. Equitable Life Assurance Society

Administrator of estate (D) v. Decedent's life insurance company (P)

Ind. Ct. App., 428 N.E.2d 110 (1981)

NATURE OF CASE: Appeal from lower court decision finding that decedent's use of a will to modify the beneficiary of his life insurance policy was ineffective.

FACT SUMMARY: Decedent Douglas Cook's life insurance policy named his first wife as beneficiary. After his divorce and remarriage, Cook drafted a holographic will that attempted to change the beneficiary of the insurance policy to his new wife and child.

RULE OF LAW

An attempt to change the beneficiary of a life insurance policy by will or other testamentary instrument will be ineffectual because that type of modification fails to follow the prescribed method as stated in the insurance policy.

FACTS: Douglas Cook's life insurance policy named his former wife Doris as beneficiary. After Douglas and Doris divorced, Douglas married Margaret Cook (D). The two of them had a son, Daniel (D). After his remarriage, Douglas created a handwritten will that attempted to change the beneficiary of his life insurance policy to Margaret (D) and Daniel (D). After his death, the life insurance company, Equitable Life Assurance Society (P), brought this interpleader action alleging that Douglas's attempt to change his life insurance policy via a will was ineffectual. The trial court agreed and granted summary judgment to Equitable Life (P). Margaret (D) and Daniel (D) appealed.

ISSUE: Is an attempt to change the beneficiary of a life insurance policy by will or other testamentary instrument ineffectual because that type of modification fails to follow the prescribed method as stated in the insurance policy?

HOLDING AND DECISION: (Ratliff, J.) Yes. An attempt to change the beneficiary of a life insurance policy by will or other testamentary instrument will be ineffectual because that type of modification fails to follow the prescribed method as stated in the insurance policy. There are some exceptions to the strict rule requiring compliance with the policy's provisions for beneficiary changes. The insurance company may waive compliance. The insured may be unable to comply with the policy requirement due to infirmity or disability. Lastly, compliance may be excused if the deceased took the necessary steps to change the beneficiary but passed away before the change went into effect. Here, none of those exceptions apply. Douglas was not prevented in any way from modifying the beneficiary in accordance with the requirements of the policy. He also did not take any steps at all to attempt to comply with the policy. Insurance companies have a substantial interest in requiring their insureds to comply with specified procedures regarding the change of beneficiaries. This will prevent insurance companies from being subjected to claims of others of whom the insurance company has no notice or knowledge. It is also in the interest of the beneficiaries of policies to be entitled to prompt payment without the insurance company having to investigate competing claims from others. Here, Douglas's attempted modification to change his beneficiary did not include some type of notice to Equitable Life (P). While Douglas may have intended that the insurance proceeds of $3,154.00 dollars go to his new wife, the valid interests of insurance companies and the judiciary in support of settled expectations is primary and trumps his stated intentions. Affirmed.

ANALYSIS

This decision summarizes the prevailing view regarding modification of life insurance beneficiaries via a will. The concept of settled expectations for insurance companies and named beneficiaries is paramount. Any opposite decision would allow hosts of competing claims based upon alleged testamentary documents created by the testator. The law of contracts is present here as well. A life insurance policy is a contract and it can only be modified in accordance with the terms of the contract.

Quicknotes

TESTAMENTARY INSTRUMENT An instrument that takes effect upon the death of the maker.

Nunnenman v. Estate of Grubbs

Named beneficiary of IRA (P) v. Decedent's mother (D)

Ark. Ct. App., 374 S.W.3d 75 (2010)

NATURE OF CASE: Appeal from lower court decision finding that decedent's use of a will to modify the beneficiary of his individual retirement account was effective.

FACT SUMMARY: Decedent Donald Grubbs' individual retirement account (IRA) named a friend, Jeannie Nunnenman (P), as beneficiary. Just prior to his death, Grubbs drafted a brief will with assistance of counsel that left his entire estate to his mother, Shervena Grubbs (D). While the will did not mention the IRA account, Grubbs allegedly drafted a separate handwritten note that stated his mother should be the named beneficiary of his IRA.

RULE OF LAW

A change in the beneficiary of a life insurance policy or individual retirement account may be accomplished via a will so long as the language of the will specifically identifies the insurance policy or individual retirement account involved and evidences the testator's clear intent to change the beneficiary.

FACTS: Decedent Donald Grubbs named a friend, Jeannie Nunnenman (P), as the beneficiary of his individual retirement account (IRA). Six days prior to his death in 2009, Grubbs had an attorney draft a formal will for him. The will stated that his entire estate should go to his mother, Shervana Grubbs (D). Grubbs also allegedly drafted a separate handwritten note stating that his mother should be the beneficiary of his IRA. Allegedly, Shervana Grubbs (D) found this note in a Bible after Grubbs' death. The trial court found the note evidenced intent on Grubbs' part to change the beneficiary of his IRA to his mother. Nunnenman (P) appealed.

ISSUE: May a change in the beneficiary of a life insurance policy or individual retirement account be accomplished via a will so long as the language of the will specifically identifies the insurance policy or individual retirement account involved and evidences the testator's clear intent to change the beneficiary?

HOLDING AND DECISION: (Pittman, J.) Yes. A change in the beneficiary of a life insurance policy or individual retirement account may be accomplished via a will so long as the language of the will specifically identifies the insurance policy or individual retirement account (IRA) involved and evidences the testator's clear intent to change the beneficiary. The significant determination is whether the testamentary instrument clearly identifies the policy or IRA to be modified. Here, Grubbs' will, drafted with assistance of counsel, did not mention the IRA. Instead, it only stated that Grubbs' entire estate should be left to his mother. The will therefore was not effective in changing the beneficiary of the IRA. As to the handwritten note, the note is of dubious authenticity. Even if it was authentic, the existence of the formal last will and testament drafted just days before Grubbs' death revoked the holographic will. If the handwritten note is viewed simply as an attempt to modify the beneficiary of the IRA, it did not comply with the procedures as specified in the IRA. Grubbs was able to summon an attorney just days before his death to draft a will. If he wanted to modify the IRA's beneficiary, he had the opportunity to do so with the assistance of counsel. Reversed and remanded.

ANALYSIS

This decision summarizes the minority view regarding modifications of life insurance or individual retirement account (IRA) beneficiaries via a will. In these jurisdictions, the will or trust document must specifically identify the policy or IRA in order for the modification to be valid. Most jurisdictions do not allow modifications of such beneficiaries via a will.

Quicknotes

HOLOGRAPHIC WILL A will that is handwritten by the testator.

TESTAMENTARY INSTRUMENT An instrument that takes effect upon the death of the maker.

Egelhoff v. Egelhoff

Decedent's child (P) v. Decedent's ex-wife (D)

532 U.S. 141 (2001)

NATURE OF CASE: Appeal from decision distributing proceeds of insurance policy and pension plan.

FACT SUMMARY: Donna Rae Egelhoff (D) received the proceeds from an insurance plan and a pension plan provided by her ex-husband's employer after he died intestate from injuries incurred in a traffic accident. The decedent had not removed her name as beneficiary. The decedent's two children from a previous marriage, David and Samantha Egelhoff (P), his statutory heirs, sued Donna Egelhoff (D) for the proceeds from the plans.

RULE OF LAW

The Employee Retirement Income Security Act of 1974 preempts a state statute that provides for the automatic revocation of a spouse as the designated beneficiary of a nonprobate asset upon the couple's divorce.

FACTS: David A. Egelhoff had named his wife, Donna Rae Egelhoff (D), beneficiary of an insurance policy and a pension plan provided through his employer, Boeing Company. Both plans were governed by the Employee Retirement Income Security Act of 1974 (ERISA). Two months after the couple's divorce, David died intestate after a traffic accident. He had not removed Donna's (D) name as beneficiary under either plan. Donna (D) received $46,000 from the life insurance policy. David and Samantha Egelhoff (P), the decedent's children from a previous marriage and his statutory heirs, sued Donna (D) for the life insurance proceeds, relying on a Washington statute that provided that the designation of a spouse as beneficiary of a nonprobate asset would be revoked automatically upon the couple's divorce. David and Samantha (P) also filed a separate action to recover the pension plan proceeds. [The trial courts granted summary judgment for Donna (D), holding that both the insurance policy and the pension should follow ERISA's procedures. The appellate court consolidated the cases and concluded that ERISA did not preempt the state statute and that David and Samantha (P) were not entitled to the proceeds. The state supreme court affirmed. The United States Supreme Court granted review.]

ISSUE: Does the Employee Retirement Income Security Act of 1974 preempt a state statute that provides for the automatic revocation of a spouse as the designated beneficiary of a nonprobate asset upon the couple's divorce?

HOLDING AND DECISION: (Thomas, J.) Yes. The Employee Retirement Income Security Act of 1974 (ERISA) preempts a state statute that provides for the automatic revocation of a spouse as the designated beneficiary of a nonprobate asset upon the couple's divorce. Under ERISA's preemption section, 29 U.S.C. Section 1144(a), ERISA supersedes all state laws that relate to employee benefit plans that are covered by ERISA. The provision must be given broad effect. A state law "relates to" an ERISA plan, if there is a "connection with" the plan. Here, the Washington statute impermissibly restricts ERISA plan administrators' choice of rules in determining whom to designate as beneficiary. Hence, it has a connection with ERISA plans. Further, the statute interferes with ERISA's ability to administer a plan uniformly throughout the country. An ERISA administrator should not be burdened with the task of trying to find out if a purported beneficiary has in fact had her beneficiary's status revoked. Reversed and remanded.

DISSENT: (Breyer, J.) Merely because a state's law imposes some burden on the administration of an ERISA plan does not by itself mandate preemption. The statute at issue here is no different from many such state laws. It imposes at most an administrative burden, but in substance it promotes ERISA objectives—it transfers an employee's pension assets at death to those individuals whom the worker would likely have wanted to receive them. The assumption under the state statute here—that a divorced worker would prefer that a child rather than a divorced spouse receive those assets—is embodied in the uniform probate code and is consistent with human experience. The effect of the majority's holding that statute preempted is that the ex-wife will receive a windfall at the expense of the deceased's children. Applying the majority's rationale would also preempt other transfer statutes, such as those involving simultaneous deaths or spousal murder.

ANALYSIS

Although it is not federal common law, divorce sets aside a revocable beneficiary designation of a former spouse under both the Restatement (Third) of Property and the Uniform Probate Code.

Quicknotes

POWER OF REVOCATION The power to revoke an existing interest.

Varela v. Bernachea

Joint account holder (D) v. Joint account holder (P)

Fla. Dist. Ct. App., 917 So. 2d 295 (2005)

NATURE OF CASE: Appeal from judgment declaring a sole owner of a joint account.

FACT SUMMARY: Bernachea (P) added his girlfriend Varela (D) as a joint tenant with right of survivorship to his CMA account. When they broke up and Varela (D) subsequently withdrew $280,000 from the account, Bernachea (P) sued to settle ownership of the account.

RULE OF LAW

A gift is presumed when a joint bank account is established with the funds from one person, and the presumption can be overcome only through clear and convincing evidence to the contrary.

FACTS: Varela (D) and Bernachea (P), both Argentine citizens, began an affair in 2000. In 2001 Varela (D) moved in with Bernachea (P), and in early 2002 Bernachea (P) added Varela (D) to his Merrill Lynch CMA account as a joint tenant with a right of survivorship. Bernachea (P) never restricted access to the account, and Varela (D) could access the account with a check card or a written check. Bernachea (P) had a heart attack in late 2002, and while he was in the hospital his daughters threw Varela (D) out of Bernachea's (P) house. Varela (D) moved out, but wrote herself a check withdrawing $280,000 from the CMA account. When Bernachea (P) learned of the withdrawal, he had Merrill Lynch return the funds and he sued both Merrill Lynch and Varela (D) to settle ownership of the account. The trial court found that Bernachea (P) lacked donative intent and awarded him full ownership of the entire account. Varela (D) appealed.

ISSUE: Is a gift presumed when a joint bank account is established with the funds from one person, and can the presumption only be overcome through clear and convincing evidence to the contrary?

HOLDING AND DECISION: (Per curiam) Yes. A gift is presumed when a joint bank account is established with the funds from one person, and the presumption can be overcome only through clear and convincing evidence to the contrary. The only evidence in support of Bernachea's (P) claim that he lacked donative intent was his own dubious testimony. Bernachea's (P) account representative testified that he specifically explained the details of joint tenancy with right of survivorship in Spanish without any questions from Bernachea (P), a former attorney, and Bernachea (P) admitted that Varela (D) had the ability to make check card purchases and write checks on the CMA account. Clearly, Bernachea (P) did not rebut Varela's (D) gift presumption when he openly admitted that he gave Varela (D) access to their joint account via check card. The record does not support the trial court's finding, as a matter of law, that Bernachea (P) demonstrated an absence of donative intent. Reversed and remanded with instructions.

ANALYSIS

This case illustrates the dangers of making someone a joint tenant on an account. The Uniform Probate Code attempts to solve this problem by creating a presumption that funds in a joint account belong to the person who placed the funds into the account unless there is clear and convincing evidence to the contrary. However, some states go in the opposite direction and have a conclusive presumption that naming someone as a joint owner is a gift of the entire account.

Quicknotes

DONATIVE INTENT Donor's intent to make a gift.

JOINT BANK ACCOUNT A bank account in which two or more persons have equal interests, usually with right of survivorship.

JOINT TENANCY An interest in property whereby a single interest is owned by two or more persons and created by a single instrument; joint tenants possess equal interests in the use of the entire property and the last survivor is entitled to absolute ownership.

RIGHT OF SURVIVORSHIP Between two or more persons, such as in a joint tenancy relationship, the right to the property of a deceased passes to the survivor.

In re Estate of Kurrelmeyer

[Parties not identified.]

Vt. Sup. Ct., 895 A.2d 207 (2006)

NATURE OF CASE: Appeal of grant of summary judgment setting aside a trust.

FACT SUMMARY: Kurrelmeyer's wife Martina created a trust in Kurrelmeyer's name under a durable power of attorney and transferred Kurrelmeyer's home into the trust. When Kurrelmeyer died, his son asked the court to set aside the trust.

RULE OF LAW

A durable power of attorney that authorizes the attorney-in-fact to "execute and deliver any assignments, stock powers, deeds or trust instruments" allows the attorney-in-fact to create and fund a revocable living trust, the creation of which is not an invalid usurpation of the principal's will.

FACTS: Kurrelmeyer executed a durable power of attorney naming his wife Martina as his attorney-in-fact. In his durable power of attorney, Kurrelmeyer gave his attorney-in-fact the ability "to add all of my assets deemed appropriate by my said attorney to any trust of which I am the donor" and also granted the power to "execute and deliver any assignments, stock powers, deeds or trust instruments." When Kurrelmeyer became incompetent, Martina, pursuant to what she presumed to be her powers under the durable power of attorney, created a revocable living trust for Kurrelmeyer's lifetime benefit and she transferred a piece of his property into the trust. Under the terms of the trust, Martina was allowed to live on the property for the remainder of her life, the trust could pay expenses for the property's upkeep, upon Martina's request the property could be sold with the proceeds used as trust principal or to purchase a new home, and the entire trust principal was available for Martina's support at the trustee's discretion. These terms differed from Kurrelmeyer's will, which only provided Martina with a life estate in the property. Both the trust and the will distributed the remainder of Kurrelmeyer's estate to his children. When Kurrelmeyer's estate entered probate, his son objected to the exclusion of the trust's property from the inventory, and he asked the court to rescind the trust and distribute the property according to the terms of the will. The probate court rejected the request, but on appeal the superior court granted summary judgment in favor of Kurrelmeyer's children and set aside the trust. Martina appealed.

ISSUE: Does a durable power of attorney that authorizes the attorney-in-fact to "execute and deliver any assignments, stock powers, deeds, or trust instruments" allow the attorney-in-fact to create and fund a revocable living trust, the creation of which is not an invalid usurpation of the principal's will?

HOLDING AND DECISION: (Burgess, J.) Yes. A durable power of attorney that authorizes the attorney-in-fact to "execute and deliver any assignments, stock powers, deeds or trust instruments" allows the attorney-in-fact to create and fund a revocable living trust, the creation of which is not an invalid usurpation of the principal's will. As its title suggests, this power of attorney is indeed "general" and quite broad. The first subsection, empowering the attorney to add any and all assets to a trust of which they are the donor, does refer to a trust already in existence, but does not suggest a lack of authority to create a new trust when considered together with the second subsection granting the power "to execute and deliver . . . trust instruments." Furthermore, we do not agree that delegation of authority to create a trust through a durable power of attorney to serve the interests of the principal violates public policy as a matter of law, even when a trust's dispositive terms may serve a function similar to a will. When the principal expressly granted their attorney-in-fact the power to convey realty from their estate, the principal must have anticipated that the terms of their will might be so altered. It is not clear, then, why conveyance of the property to a trust would be a per se impermissible alteration of the will, when the power of attorney expressly authorized Martina to convey any real estate outright to others. Reversed and remanded for further proceedings to determine if Martina breached her fiduciary duty as an agent when she transferred the property into trust.

ANALYSIS

On remand the trial court upheld the trust and found that Martina did not breach her fiduciary duty. That decision was also appealed.

Quicknotes

DURABLE POWER OF ATTORNEY (DPOA) A written document pursuant to which one party confers the authority to act as an agent on their behalf to another party, who is known as the "attorney-in-fact"; that becomes effective immediately or upon the grantor becoming incapacitated; and that terminates immediately upon the grantor's death.

LIFE ESTATE An interest in land measured by the life of the tenant or a third party.

REVOCABLE TRUST A trust where trustor reserves the right to revoke the trust.

TRUST The holding of property by one party for the benefit of another.

CHAPTER 8

Limits on Freedom of Disposition: Protection of the Spouse and Children

Quick Reference Rules of Law

PAGE

1. *Sullivan v. Burkin.* The surviving spouse may not claim against the assets of a valid inter vivos trust created by the deceased spouse even when the deceased spouse retained substantial rights and powers under the trust instrument. *90*

2. *In re Estate of Myers.* Assets that are payable on death to a specific beneficiary, such as checking accounts, certificates of deposit and annuities, are not included in the elective share of the surviving spouse. *91*

3. *Reece v. Elliott.* The failure to disclose the value of an asset is not fatal to an antenuptial agreement where the parties thereto have entered the agreement freely, with full disclosure available, and with the assistance of separate, independent counsel. *92*

4. *Lambeff v. Farmers Co-operative Executors & Trustees Ltd.* Under Australia's Inheritance (Family Provision) Act, an independent adult child of a decedent, who was abandoned by the decedent as a child, has a claim of support (provision) against the decedent's estate where the child has done nothing disentitling and would have done better with proper support for the child's proper advancement in life. *93*

5. *In re Estate of Prestie.* An amendment to an inter vivos trust cannot rebut the presumption that a pour-over will is revoked as to an unintentionally omitted spouse. *94*

6. *Gray v. Gray.* Where a pretermitted child statute provides that an omitted child is not entitled to share in a testator parent's estate where at the time the will was executed the testator had one or more children and devised substantially all of the decedent's estate to the other parent of the omitted child, the omitted child is not nonetheless entitled to share in the estate where the other children are from a prior marriage. *96*

7. *In re Estate of Jackson.* The pretermitted heir statute, providing for children unintentionally left out of a decedent's will, does not apply to a decedent's revocable inter vivos trust. *98*

Sullivan v. Burkin

Widow (P) v. Successor trustree (D)

Mass. Sup. Jud. Ct., 460 N.E.2d 572 (1984)

NATURE OF CASE: Appeal from a dismissal of a complaint for determination of estate assets.

FACT SUMMARY: Sullivan (P) contended that the value of real estate placed in trust by her late husband should be considered part of his estate for purposes of providing her a portion of the estate.

RULE OF LAW

The surviving spouse may not claim against the assets of a valid inter vivos trust created by the deceased spouse even when the deceased spouse retained substantial rights and powers under the trust instrument.

FACTS: Sullivan's (P) husband, the decedent, executed during his life a deed of trust by which he transferred real estate to a trust with himself as sole trustee. The net income of the trust was payable to him during his life, and the trustee was instructed to pay to him all or such part of the principal that he might request. Upon his death, the trust indicated that the trustee was to pay the principal amount and any undistributed income to third parties. Sullivan executed a will wherein he stated that he intentionally neglected to make any provision for his wife, Sullivan (P). Following her husband's death, Sullivan (P) made a claim against the estate, contending that the property in the trust should be considered part of the estate. Burkin (D) was the successor in interest to the third parties to whom the decedent left the residue of the trust. The probate court held that a valid inter vivos trust was created and that the property of the trust was not to be considered part of the estate. Sullivan (P) appealed.

ISSUE: May a surviving spouse claim against the assets of a valid inter vivos trust created by the deceased spouse even when the deceased spouse retained substantial rights and powers under the trust instrument?

HOLDING AND DECISION: (Wilkins, J.) No. The surviving spouse may not claim against the assets of a valid inter vivos trust created by the deceased spouse even when the deceased spouse retained substantial rights and powers under the trust instrument. Merely because the inter vivos trust was testamentary does not indicate that it was invalid. Merely because the settlor retained a broad power to modify or revoke the trust, the law of the state is quite clear in upholding inter vivos trusts which become testamentary in nature. Further, Sullivan (P) has no special interest that should be recognized in breaking the trust. As a result, because this trust was created under the then-established law, the assets of the trust cannot be applied to the estate. Affirmed.

ANALYSIS

The court indicated quite clearly that although it felt obligated to apply the general rule in this case, it announced that in the future any inter vivos trust created or amended after the date of this opinion shall no longer follow the previously announced rule. In the future, if the settlor retains the same type of substantial rights the decedent did in the principal case, then the assets of the trust will be considered part of the estate for purposes of distribution to the heirs of the estate.

Quicknotes

INTER VIVOS TRUST Property that is held by one person for the benefit of another and that is created by an instrument that takes effect during the life of the grantor.

REMAINDER INTEREST An interest in land that remains after the termination of the immediately preceding estate.

SUCCESSOR TRUSTEE A trustee who succeeds a previous trustee.

In re Estate of Myers

Named beneficiaries of checking account (P) v. Decedent's husband (D)

Iowa Sup. Ct., 825 N.W.2d 1 (2012)

NATURE OF CASE: Appeal from lower court decision finding that decedent's checking account, a certificate of deposit and an annuity should be included in the elective share of the decedent's surviving spouse.

FACT SUMMARY: Decedent Karen Myer's assets included a checking account, a certificate of deposit and an annuity that all named her children as beneficiaries in case of her death. The lower court determined that those accounts should be included in Karen Myer's husband's elective share.

RULE OF LAW

Assets that are payable on death to a specific beneficiary, such as checking accounts, certificates of deposit and annuities, are not included in the elective share of the surviving spouse.

FACTS: Decedent Karen Myer's assets included a checking account, a certificate of deposit and an annuity that all named her children (P) as beneficiaries in case of her death. Her husband, Howard (D), became the sole owner of their real estate because he and Karen were joint tenants with rights of survivorship. The checking account and certificate of deposit were worth $91,000 and the annuity was worth $18,000. After Karen's death, Howard (D) chose to receive his statutory elective share of Karen's estate in lieu of what he would have received via her will. The trial court found that the decedent's checking account, a certificate of deposit and an annuity should be included in the elective share of the decedent's surviving spouse. Karen's children (P) appealed.

ISSUE: Are assets that are payable on death to a specific beneficiary, such as checking accounts, certificates of deposit and annuities, included in the elective share of the surviving spouse?

HOLDING AND DECISION: (Waterman, J.) No. Assets that are payable on death to a specific beneficiary, such as checking accounts, certificates of deposit and annuities, are not included in the elective share of the surviving spouse. Prior case law held that a revocable trust with named beneficiaries other than the spouse should be included in the surviving spouse's elective share. The decedent had discretion to revoke or modify the trust during their lifetime and the property would properly be considered part of the decedent's estate. However, in 2009, the state legislature modified the elective share statute. The statute does not include any assets that are payable on death (POD) such as checking accounts. POD accounts are nonprobate assets. The legislative history of the 2009 amendment reveals the legislature intended to prevent POD accounts from being included in the surviving spouse's elective share. Accordingly, Karen Myer's three POD accounts will not be considered part of Howard's (D) elective share. Reversed and remanded.

ANALYSIS

The purpose of elective share statutes is to prevent spouses from disinheriting their surviving spouse. The statute allows the surviving spouse to elect a one-third or one-half share of the decedent's estate in lieu of what they would receive under the will. Each state's elective share statute is different. Some states include POD accounts as part of the elective share on the grounds that excluding them would frustrate the purpose of the statute.

Quicknotes

ELECTIVE SHARE Election by the surviving spouse to take either what the deceased spouse gave under the will or a share of the deceased spouse's estate as set forth by statute.

Reece v. Elliott

Widow (P) v. Executrix (D)

Tenn. Ct. App., 208 S.W.3d 419 (2006)

NATURE OF CASE: Appeal from dismissal of declaratory judgment action to have antenuptial agreement invalidated.

FACT SUMMARY: Ms. Reece (P) claimed that the antenuptial agreement she entered with Mr. Reece, who died intestate, was invalid because the value of stock held by Mr. Reece had not been disclosed.

RULE OF LAW

The failure to disclose the value of an asset is not fatal to an antenuptial agreement where the parties thereto have entered the agreement freely, with full disclosure available, and with the assistance of separate, independent counsel.

FACTS: Mr. Reece and Ms. Reece (P) entered an antenuptial agreement. They had each previously been married, had children from their prior marriages, and had their own property. The agreement indicated that they each waived their right to the separate property of the other, and that they had each consulted with independent counsel and that a full disclosure of assets had been made. The value of some of the assets disclosed by each party was not stated, including certain stock owned by Mr. Reece. Although Ms. Reece (P) and her counsel had the opportunity to inquire about the value of this stock, Ms. Reece did not do so because she fully understood this asset would not belong to her in the event of Mr. Reece's death, and that she would have no interest in it. Mr. Reece died intestate, and Ms. Reece (P) brought a declaratory judgment action against the executrixes (D) of his estate to invalidate the antenuptial agreement on the grounds that it did not state the value of the stock, which, it turned out, was substantial. The trial court ruled that the agreement was enforceable, since it was obvious from looking at Mr. Reece's list of property that he was a wealthy man, without taking into account the value of the stock, since all assets were revealed on the list and Ms. Reece (P) could have investigated any items that she wanted to. The court reasoned that it was not important that the value of some of the assets had not been identified because they both agreed the assets would go to their respective children. The state's intermediate appellate court granted review.

ISSUE: Is the failure to disclose the value of an asset fatal to an antenuptial agreement where the parties thereto have entered the agreement freely, with full disclosure available, and with the assistance of separate, independent counsel?

HOLDING AND DECISION: (Franks, J.) No. The failure to disclose the value of an asset is not fatal to an antenuptial agreement where the parties thereto have entered the agreement freely, with full disclosure available, and with the assistance of separate, independent counsel. State law favors the enforcement of antenuptial agreements where they have been entered into "voluntarily and knowledgeably." The term "knowledgeably" means that there was full and fair disclosure of the nature, extent and value of the proponent spouse's holdings, or that such disclosure was unnecessary because the other spouse had independent knowledge of the same. Also, "full and fair" disclosure depends on the facts of each particular case. While specific appraisals are not a necessity, the spouse must have a general knowledge of the proponent spouse's overall net worth and must not have been misled when entering the agreement. Representation by independent counsel also is a strong indication that the agreement has been entered into freely and knowingly. Here, Ms. Reece (P) had full knowledge that her husband was a man of wealth, as shown by the list of assets that was provided; she consulted with independent counsel and clearly understood that the agreement meant she would have no claim to any of Mr. Reece's assets; she admitted that Mr. Reece was never dishonest with her, and was very straightforward and open with her about his financial dealings and never misled her. For these reasons, Ms. Reece (P) was not misled, and the agreement is enforceable and binding. Affirmed.

ANALYSIS

A fairly straightforward and effective way of avoiding the disclosure issue presented by this case would have been for the parties to have attached a net worth schedule of assets, liabilities, and income to the agreement itself. The value of the assets, where not apparent from the face of the assets (e.g., cash), should be determined through a good-faith, independent valuation.

Quicknotes

ANTENUPTIAL AGREEMENT An agreement entered into by two individuals, in contemplation of their impending marriage, to determine their rights and interests in property upon dissolution or death.

Lambeff v. Farmers Co-operative Executors & Trustees Ltd.

Decedent's daughter (P) v. Estate's executors (D)

So. Australia Sup. Ct., 56 S.A.S.R. 323, 1991 WL 1121294 (1991)

NATURE OF CASE: Claim for maintenance against decedent's estate under Australia's Inheritance (Family Provision) Act.

FACT SUMMARY: Lambeff (P), decedent's daughter, who was abandoned by decedent when she was ten, claimed that she was entitled to support (provision) in the form of a legacy out of decedent's estate under Australia's Inheritance (Family Provision) Act because decedent had failed to support her "advancement in life."

RULE OF LAW

Under Australia's Inheritance (Family Provision) Act, an independent adult child of a decedent, who was abandoned by the decedent as a child, has a claim of support (provision) against the decedent's estate where the child has done nothing disentitling and would have done better with proper support for the child's proper advancement in life.

FACTS: Lambeff (P) was abandoned by decedent when she was ten. Decedent left Lambeff (P) and her mother and started another family, in which he had two sons. Lambeff (P) was not married, had a steady job, and had considerable equity in a flat. Decedent's will left his entire estate to his two sons, after payment of all debts and funeral expenses. Both sons had families to support and few assets. Lambeff (P) claimed that she was entitled to support (provision) under Australia's Inheritance (Family Provision) Act, which provides in pertinent part that a decedent's family member who is left without adequate provision for proper advancement in life may make a claim for support against the decedent's estate, which may be granted at the court's discretion.

ISSUE: Under Australia's Inheritance (Family Provision) Act, does an independent adult child of a decedent, who was abandoned by the decedent as a child, have a claim of support (provision) against the decedent's estate where the child has done nothing disentitling and would have done better with proper support for the child's proper advancement in life?

HOLDING AND DECISION: (Matheson, J.) Yes. Under Australia's Inheritance (Family Provision) Act, an independent adult child of a decedent, who was abandoned by the decedent as a child, has a claim of support (provision) against the decedent's estate where the child has done nothing disentitling and would have done better with proper support for the child's proper advancement in life. The statute's words "advancement in life" have a wide meaning and are not restricted to early childhood. In every case, the court must place itself in the testator's position and consider what they should have done as a "wise and just" testator. Here, although it is true that Lambeff (P) has done reasonably well in life without her father's support, she would have done better with proper support for her advancement in life. Given all the circumstances of the case—that she is independent and that the sons need to support families and do not have many assets—the legacy to Lambeff (P) should be modest. It is ordered that she be paid a legacy of $20,000 out of the estate.

ANALYSIS

The model under which this case was decided is known as the Family Maintenance Model, which gives courts the power to determine the morality of both the decedent's dispositive scheme and survivors' claims. Proponents argue that this performs a vital social welfare function. Critics assert that such judicial discretion is a "terrible price" to pay for improved support of dependents in that it would introduce complexity and unpredictability, undermine estate planning, and hamper the orderly transfer of property rights.

Quicknotes

LEGACY A disposition of real or personal property in the form of a gift, as stipulated in a donor's will.

In re Estate of Prestie

Decedent's wife (P) v. Decedent's son (D)

Nev. Sup. Ct., 138 P.3d 520 (2006)

NATURE OF CASE: Appeal from order adopting a probate commissioner's report and recommendation that decedent's will be revoked.

FACT SUMMARY: Maria (P), wife of W.R., who was deceased, contended that W.R.'s pour-over will, which he had made before remarrying her, should statutorily be revoked as to her because she married W.R. without entering into a marriage contract and because the will did not contain a provision providing for her or a provision expressing an intention to not provide for her. However, W.R., before remarrying Maria, had amended the accompanying inter vivos trust, which had named his son Scott (D) as beneficiary and trustee, to provide for Maria.

RULE OF LAW

An amendment to an inter vivos trust cannot rebut the presumption that a pour-over will is revoked as to an unintentionally omitted spouse.

FACTS: Maria (P) and W.R. were married, then divorced two years later, but remained friendly. Eventually, W.R. purchased a condominium. Then he simultaneously executed a pour-over will and an inter vivos trust. The pour-over will devised W.R.'s entire estate to the trust. W.R.'s son, Scott (D), was named both the trustee and a beneficiary of the inter vivos trust. Neither the will nor the inter vivos trust provided for Maria (P). A few years later, Maria (P) moved in with W.R., who amended the inter vivos trust to grant Maria (P) a life estate in his condominium upon his death. A few weeks later, Maria (P) and W.R. were married for a second time. W.R. passed away approximately nine months later. Maria (P) eventually petitioned for a one-half intestate succession share of W.R.'s estate on the ground that W.R.'s will was revoked as to her by a statutory provision relating to the revocation of a will by marriage. A probate commissioner recommended that because W.R.'s will was executed before he remarried Maria (P) and because the amendment granting Maria (P) a life estate in the condominium was to the inter vivos trust, not to W.R.'s will, so that the will did not provide for her, the will be revoked as to her. The trial court subsequently adopted the commissioner's recommendation, and Scott (D) appealed. The state's highest court granted review.

ISSUE: Can an amendment to an inter vivos trust rebut the presumption that a pour-over will is revoked as to an unintentionally omitted spouse?

HOLDING AND DECISION: (Hardesty, J.) No. An amendment to an inter vivos trust cannot rebut the presumption that a pour-over will is revoked as to an unintentionally omitted spouse. The statute relating to revocation of a will by marriage provides that "If a person marries after making a will and the spouse survives the maker, the will is revoked as to the spouse, unless provision has been made for the spouse by marriage contract, or unless the spouse is provided for in the will, or in such a way mentioned therein as to show an intention not to make such provision. . . ." This statutory provision is unambiguous and the facts on their face satisfy its elements, so that a presumption of revocation is created. The trust amendment did not create a marriage contract and no other marriage contract provided for Maria (P). Moreover, W.R.'s will did not contain a provision providing for Maria (P) or a provision expressing an intent not to provide for her. The argument by Scott (D) that the inter vivos trust amendment bars Maria's (P) claim is rejected, since a fundamental rule of statutory construction is that the mention of one thing implies the exclusion of another. Applying this rule, it is clear that the revocation of a will under one chapter of the probate statute is unrelated to a trust proceeding governed by another chapter. Additionally, the trust section makes reference to other chapters, but makes no mention of the will chapter. Because the legislature made reference to other chapters, it can be inferred that it intentionally excluded mention of the will chapter. Affirmed.

ANALYSIS

The sole purpose of the revocation presumption statute is to guard against the unintentional disinheritance of the surviving spouse. Not all states take the approach used by the state (Nevada) here. Those states that reject the revocation presumption typically leave the elective share provisions as the principal protection for the surviving spouse. However, in many jurisdictions the elective share might limit the surviving spouse to one-third of the estate. The Uniform Probate Code in § 2-301 provides that a premarital will reflects the testator's intent to the extent that it provides for the testator's issue from previous relationships, but also provides a rebuttable presumption that this intent is negated upon remarriage.

Continued on next page.

Quicknotes

INTER VIVOS TRUST Property that is held by one person for the benefit of another and that is created by an instrument that takes effect during the life of the grantor.

LIFE ESTATE An interest in land measured by the life of the tenant or a third party.

POUR-OVER PROVISION A provision pursuant to a testamentary instrument, providing that the residuary estate be distributed to a different testamentary instrument, i.e., will to trust or trust to will.

STATUTORY CONSTRUCTION The examination and interpretation of statutes.

Gray v. Gray

Executor (P) v. Omitted descendant (D)

Ala. Sup. Ct., 947 So. 2d 1045 (2006)

NATURE OF CASE: Appeal from judgment that an omitted descendant is entitled to a share of decedent's estate.

FACT SUMMARY: The executor (P) of John Gray's (John's) estate contended that Jack Gray (Jack) (D), John's son born after John's will was executed who was omitted from the will, was not entitled to a share of John's estate under the state's pretermitted child statute, even though John had divorced Jack's (D) mother before he died.

RULE OF LAW

Where a pretermitted child statute provides that an omitted child is not entitled to share in a testator parent's estate where at the time the will was executed the testator had one or more children and devised substantially all of the decedent's estate to the other parent of the omitted child, the omitted child is not nonetheless entitled to share in the estate where the other children are from a prior marriage.

FACTS: John Gray (John) was married to Mary Gray (Mary) at the time he executed his last will. He had two children from a prior marriage; however, the will devised all of his estate to Mary and did not include his two children. Three years later, John and Mary had Jack Gray (Jack) (D). Five years thereafter, John and Mary divorced, and, as part of the divorce proceedings, certain of John's inheritances, assets and disbursements would be placed in trust for Jack (D). Under state law, even though John's will devised all of his estate to Mary, Mary would not inherit under John's will upon his death because of the divorce. John died five years later without having changed his will. The executor (P) of John's estate probated the will, and Jack (D) claimed that he was entitled to a share of John's estate under the state's pretermitted child statute, which provides that "[i]f a testator fails to provide in his will for any of his children born or adopted after the execution of his will, the omitted child receives a share in the estate equal in value to that which he would have received if the testator had died intestate." The statute, however, has three exceptions. The executor (P) argued that two of these applied, namely that the pretermitted child is not entitled to a share of the estate because: "(2) When the will was executed the testator had one or more children and devised substantially all his estate to the other parent of the omitted child; or (3) The testator provided for the child by transfer outside the will and the intent that the transfer be in lieu of a testamentary provision be reasonably proven." Jack (D) argued that the first of these two exceptions was inapplicable because it did not appear to contemplate a situation wherein the testator has children, divorces their mother, remarries, executes a will that makes no provision for any children whatsoever, and then has a child with that second wife. The probate court held for Jack (D), and the executor (P) appealed. The state's highest court granted review.

ISSUE: Where a pretermitted child statute provides that an omitted child is not entitled to share in a testator parent's estate where at the time the will was executed the testator had one or more children and devised substantially all of the decedent's estate to the other parent of the omitted child, is the omitted child nonetheless entitled to share in the estate where the other children are from a prior marriage?

HOLDING AND DECISION: (See, J.) No. Where a pretermitted child statute provides that an omitted child is not entitled to share in a testator parent's estate where at the time the will was executed the testator had one or more children and devised substantially all of the decedent's estate to the other parent of the omitted child, the omitted child is not nonetheless entitled to share in the estate where the other children are from a prior marriage. The statutory exception involved is neither ambiguous nor absurd, and therefore must be given effect as written. It does not, like the other exceptions, require a determination of intent. It states only two conditions for excluding an omitted child from an intestate share of the testator's estate: (1) the testator had one or more children at the time they executed the will, and (2) the testator's will devised substantially all of the testator's estate to the other parent of the omitted child. Because the statute is one of substance and is in derogation of the common law, it must be construed strictly. Jack's (D) argument, therefore, fails. The fact that John's other children were from a prior marriage is immaterial; the exception's two requirements are met: when John executed his will, he had two children by a prior marriage, and his will devised all of his estate to Jack's (D) mother Mary. If the legislature wishes to change the statute to apply to children in being at the time the will is executed, it may do so, but currently the statute unambiguously applies only to children born after the will's execution. Therefore, Jack (D) is not entitled to share in John's estate. Reversed and remanded.

Continued on next page.

ANALYSIS

The majority asserts that the result reached under the exception at issue would not reach a level of absurdity requiring the court to conclude that the legislature meant something other than what its words convey. For example, the legislature might well have assumed that in a case like this one it could anticipate that the child would be protected in the divorce proceeding, either directly or by a distribution of a share of the marital assets to the custodial parent. In this case, in fact, Jack (D) was provided for in the divorce proceeding by the creation of a trust. In addition, to adopt the dissent's construction, that the exception was intended to apply only to a child "then in being," would be to give to the statute a meaning opposite of what it said. While statutes in some jurisdictions are expressly made applicable to children alive when the will was executed as well as afterborn (or after-adopted) children, the statute at issue here by its terms was applicable only to afterborn/adopted children. Similarly, the Uniform Probate Code applies only to afterborn/adopted children.

Quicknotes

PRETERMITTED Omitted; usually refers to an heir who is unintentionally omitted from a testator's will.

In re Estate of Jackson

Decedent's son (P) v. Trustees of decedent's trust (D)

Okla. Sup. Ct., 194 P.3d 1269 (2008)

NATURE OF CASE: Plaintiff's appeal from lower court decision finding that assets of decedent's revocable inter vivos trust are not subject to the state's pretermitted heir statute.

FACT SUMMARY: Decedent Walter Jackson created a trust that named the Butlers (D) as trustees. Jackson did not leave a will. Upon Jackson's death, his son, Johnny Benjamin (P), argued that the state's pretermitted heir statute entitled him to the proceeds of the revocable trust.

RULE OF LAW

The pretermitted heir statute, providing for children unintentionally left out of a decedent's will, does not apply to a decedent's revocable inter vivos trust.

FACTS: Jackson died without leaving a will. During his life, he created a revocable inter vivos trust that named Robena Butler (D) and Harris Butler (D) as trustees. Upon his death, Johnny Benjamin (Benjamin) (P), Jackson's son and sole surviving heir, petitioned the court for disgorgement of the trust assets. The state's pretermitted heir statute allows children unintentionally left out of a will to receive the same proceeds as those children named in the will. Benjamin (P) argued the state's pretermitted heir statute applied to the proceeds of a revocable trust just as it did to a will. The lower court found the statute did not encompass living trusts and denied Benjamin's (P) petition. After an intermediate appellate court affirmed, the Oklahoma Supreme Court granted Benjamin's petition for further appellate review.

ISSUE: Does the pretermitted heir statute, providing for children unintentionally left out of a decedent's will, apply to a decedent's revocable inter vivos trust?

HOLDING AND DECISION: (Taylor, J.) No. The pretermitted heir statute, providing for children unintentionally left out of a decedent's will, does not apply to a decedent's revocable inter vivos trust. The statute specifically refers only to circumstances where a decedent fails to name a child in their will. The statute makes no reference to a similar scenario involving a revocable living trust. Benjamin (P) argued the pretermitted heir statute is similar to statutes providing for disinherited spouses, known also as forced heir statutes or elective share statutes. Those statutes provide disinherited spouses with a right of election to a statutorily created minimum amount of the decedent's estate. Differences abound between the statutes. The pretermitted heir statute does not guarantee a child with a minimum amount of the decedent's estate. Also, unlike the forced heir statutes, a testator can disinherit a child if the will clearly expresses that intent. A testator can also leave one child a small amount, while that would not be allowed in the case of a spouse. Accordingly, Benjamin's (P) arguments that the pretermitted heir statute is similar to the forced heir statute are incorrect. The pretermitted heir statute does not reference revocable trusts. The statute also does not provide children with the same protection as the forced heir statute does for disinherited spouses. Affirmed.

ANALYSIS

Most jurisdictions limit the coverage of pretermitted heir statutes to wills only. Some states have allowed them to cover revocable trusts as well where it is evident the testator left a child out of the trust unintentionally. Other states are removing references to wills and trusts and using the term "testamentary instrument." This will allow forced heir statutes and pretermitted heir statutes to reach a broader spectrum of testamentary documents.

Quicknotes

INTER VIVOS TRUST Property that is held by one person for the benefit of another and that is created by an instrument that takes effect during the life of the grantor.

PRETERMITTED Omitted; usually refers to an heir who is unintentionally omitted from a testator's will.

TESTAMENTARY INSTRUMENT An instrument that takes effect upon the death of the maker.

CHAPTER 9

Trusts: Fiduciary Administration

Quick Reference Rules of Law

	PAGE
1. *Hartman v. Hartle.* A trustee breaches the duty of loyalty to the beneficiaries when the trustee engages in self-dealing.	*100*
2. *In re Gleeson's Will.* A trustee cannot deal with the trust property in the trustee's individual capacity.	*101*
3. *In re Rothko.* A trustee must refrain from placing the trustee in a position where the trustee's personal interest or that of a third person does or may conflict with the interest of the beneficiaries.	*102*
4. *Marsman v. Nasca.* Where a trust gives the trustee a discretionary power to pay amounts of the principal for the comfortable support and maintenance of a beneficiary, the trustee has a duty to inquire into the financial resources of that beneficiary so as to recognize the beneficiary's needs.	*103*
5. *In re Estate of Janes.* A fiduciary, in executing their duties as a trustee, is required to invest the assets of a trust as a prudent person would in the management of their own affairs.	*104*
6. *Matter of Will of Kline.* The Massachusetts Principal and Income Act (MPIA) permits a trustee to adjust between principal and income to ensure fair and reasonable distribution of the trust to all of the beneficiaries.	*105*
7. *Wilson v. Wilson.* A trust instrument may not override a beneficiary's right to information that is reasonably necessary for the beneficiary to enforce the beneficiary's rights under the trust or to prevent or redress a breach of trust.	*107*
8. *Allard v. Pacific National Bank.* A trustee, when disposing of important trust property, should inform the beneficiaries and attempt to obtain the highest possible price.	*109*
9. *National Academy of Sciences v. Cambridge Trust Co.* If a person makes a representation of fact as of the person's own knowledge and such representation is not true as to a subject matter susceptible of ascertainable knowledge, if the party to whom it is made relies and acts upon it as true and sustains damage by it, it is fraud, for which the party making it is responsible.	*110*

Hartman v. Hartle

Daughter of testatrix (P) v. Executor (D)

N.J. Ch., 122 A. 615 (1923)

NATURE OF CASE: Bill in equity to set aside the sale of property by executors for fraud and illegality.

FACT SUMMARY: After an executor (D) indirectly sold property to his wife, who resold the property at a substantial profit, Hartman (P), testatrix's daughter, filed a complaint to set aside the original sale.

RULE OF LAW

A trustee breaches the duty of loyalty to the beneficiaries when the trustee engages in self-dealing.

FACTS: Testatrix died leaving five children. She named her two sons-in-law (D) as executors. In her will, testatrix expressly directed the executors (D) to sell her real estate. The proceeds were to be divided equally among her children. However, part of the real estate was sold for $3,900 to Geick, a son of the testatrix. He bought it for his sister, Dieker, the wife of one of the executors (D). Dieker then resold the property for $5,500. Hartman (P), another of the testatrix's daughters, filed a complaint to set aside the first sale for fraud and illegality. She contended that the sale of the property by the executors (D) to Dieker, the wife of one of them, without previous authority from the court, was illegal and void.

ISSUE: Does a trustee breach the duty of loyalty to the beneficiaries when the trustee engages in self-dealing?

HOLDING AND DECISION: (Foster, V.C.) Yes. A trustee breaches the duty of loyalty to the beneficiaries when the trustee engages in self-dealing. It is the settled law of this state that a trustee cannot purchase from themself at their own sale and that the spouse is under the same disability, unless leave to do so has been previously obtained under an order of the court. In view of the fact that the property is now owned by innocent purchasers, a resale cannot be ordered, but, as an alternative, Dieker and the executors (D) will be held to pay one-fifth of their profit on the resale to Hartman (P). Decree so ordered.

ANALYSIS

Once it is shown that a trustee has engaged in self-dealing, the no-further-inquiry rule is triggered; the trustee will be liable for any profit realized, without inquiry by the court as to the trustee's good faith or the transaction's reasonableness. The trustee may assert two defenses – that either the self-dealing was approved by the settlor, or was fully disclosed to the beneficiaries, who then gave their consent. The strict no-further-inquiry rule is justified by the fiduciary relationship between the trustee and the beneficiaries, which is held to a higher standard than arm's-length transactions.

Quicknotes

DUTY OF LOYALTY A fiduciary's duty to refrain from self-dealing or taking a position that is adverse to the best interests of the party that the fiduciary is serving.

In re Gleeson's Will

Trustee of decedent's trust (P) v. Beneficiaries of the trust (D)

Ill. App. Ct., 124 N.E.2d 624 (1955)

NATURE OF CASE: Beneficiaries' appeal from lower court decision finding that the trustee did not deal with the trust in his individual capacity.

FACT SUMMARY: Mary Gleeson's will placed a 160-acre farm into a trust for the benefit of her three children. Con Colbrook (P) was the trustee. Prior to her death, Gleeson leased the farm to Colbrook (P). Upon her death, Colbrook (P) and his partner continued to lease the farm even though Colbrook (P) was the trustee of the trust property containing the 160-acre farm.

RULE OF LAW

A trustee cannot deal with the trust property in the trustee's individual capacity.

FACTS: Mary Gleeson's will placed a 160-acre farm into a trust for the benefit of her three children, Helen Black (D), Bernadine Gleeson (D), and Thomas Gleeson (D). Con Colbrook (P) was named trustee of the trust. Prior to her death, Gleeson leased the farm to Colbrook (P) and his business partner. Gleeson died fifteen days prior to the end of the lease. After the lease expired, Colbrook (P) held over as tenants under the lease for another year. It is undisputed Colbrook (P) and his partner made a profit during their time as tenants of the farm. After Gleeson's death, Colbrook (P) petitioned the court to be appointed as trustee of the trust. Gleeson's beneficiaries (D) objected on the ground that Colbrook (P) improperly dealt with himself while he was trustee of the trust property. The lower courts rejected the beneficiaries' (D) objections. The beneficiaries (D) appealed.

ISSUE: Can a trustee deal with the trust property in the trustee's individual capacity?

HOLDING AND DECISION: (Carroll, J.) No. A trustee cannot deal with the trust property in the trustee's individual capacity. Colbrook (P) argues that the particular circumstances of this case should allow for an exception. In particular, he argues that because Gleeson passed away fifteen days prior to the end of the lease, he did not have time to find a suitable tenant for the farm and such tenants are difficult to find. However, there is no evidence Colbrook (P) attempted to find a new tenant in the fifteen-day interval. In addition, Colbrook's (P) arguments that he transacted the lease in good faith and that he conferred openly with the trust beneficiaries (D) do not aid him. According to the settled principle, Colbrook (P) needed to decide whether to retain his tenancy or act as a trustee. It was improper for him to do both. Reversed and remanded.

ANALYSIS

Typically, a trustee's simple good faith and openness about their dealings with trust property will not shield the trustee from liability. A trustee can only deal with trust property in their individual capacity if the settlor or the beneficiaries of the trust expressly authorize it or the trustee obtains judicial approval.

Quicknotes

SETTLOR The grantor or donor of property that is to be held in trust for the benefit of another.

TRUSTEE A person or entity entrusted as a fiduciary to execute a trust and keep or administer the assets of the trust for the benefit of trust beneficiaries.

In re Rothko

Daughter of decedent (P) v. Executors of decedent's estate (D)

N.Y. Ct. App., 372 N.E.2d 291 (1977)

NATURE OF CASE: Appeal from award of damages for breach of trust.

FACT SUMMARY: Kate Rothko (P), the decedent's daughter, contended that the three executors of the estate had violated their fiduciary duties by entering into contracts with businesses in which they had an interest and selling the decedent's paintings for less than their full value.

RULE OF LAW

A trustee must refrain from placing the trustee in a position where the trustee's personal interest or that of a third person does or may conflict with the interest of the beneficiaries.

FACTS: Mark Rothko, an abstract expressionist painter whose works through the years gained him an international reputation of greatness, died testate on February 25, 1970, leaving an estate consisting of 798 paintings of tremendous value. During a period of three weeks after the will was admitted to probate, the three executors, Reis (D), Stamos (D), and Levine (D), dealt with all 798 paintings. The executors agreed to sell to Marlborough A.G. (MAG), a Liechtenstein corporation, 100 of the paintings. The executors also consigned to Marlborough Gallery, Inc. (MNY) approximately 700 paintings. After Kate Rothko (P), the decedent's daughter, brought an action to remove the executors, it was established that Reis (D), in addition to being one of the executors of the estate, was a director, secretary, and treasurer of MNY; that it was to the advantage of Stamos (D), as an aspiring artist, to curry favor with MNY; and that Levine (D), while not acting in self-interest or bad faith, nonetheless failed to exercise ordinary prudence in the performance of his fiduciary obligations since he was aware of the actual and potential conflicts of interests which existed. The trial court also held that the present value of the paintings was the proper measure of damages. All three executors and the two corporations then brought this appeal, contending, inter alia, that there was no breach of fiduciary duty since they had acted in good faith and the plan was fair and that the measure of damages should be based upon the value of the paintings at the time of sale.

ISSUE: Must a trustee refrain from placing the trustee in a position where the trustee's personal interest or that of a third person may or does conflict with the interest of the beneficiaries?

HOLDING AND DECISION: (Cooke, J.) Yes. A trustee must refrain from placing the trustee in a position where the trustee's personal interest or that of a third person does or may conflict with the interest of the beneficiaries. The duty of loyalty imposed on the fiduciary prevents them from accepting employment from a third party that is entering into a business transaction with the trust or estate. An executor who knows that a co-executor is committing breaches of trust and not only fails to exert efforts directed toward prevention but accedes to them is legally accountable even though the executor was acting on the advice of counsel. If the trustee is authorized to sell trust property but in breach of trust sells it for less than they should receive, the trustee is liable for the value of the property at the time of the sale less the amount that they received. The trustee may be held liable for appreciation damages if it was their duty to retain the property upon the theory that the beneficiaries are entitled to be placed in the same position they would have been in had the breach not consisted of a sale of property that should have been retained. Here, there is no doubt that Reis (D) and Stamos (D) had a conflict of interest regarding MNY or that Levine (D) knew of such conflict and ignored it. Further, Rothko (P) is entitled to appreciation damages due to the wrongful acts of the executors. Affirmed.

ANALYSIS

In addressing the issue of appreciation damages, Professor Scott states: "If the trustee is guilty of a breach of trust in selling trust property for an inadequate price, he is liable for the difference between the amount he should have received and the amount which he did receive. He is not liable, however, for any subsequent rise in value of the property sold." See 3 Scott, *Trust* (3d ed.) § 208.6, pp. 1689–1690.

Quicknotes

CONFLICT OF INTEREST Ethical problems that arise, or may be anticipated to arise, between an attorney and their client if the interests of the attorney, another client, or a third-party conflict with those of the present client.

DUTY OF LOYALTY A fiduciary's duty to refrain from self-dealing or taking a position that is adverse to the best interests of the party that the fiduciary is serving.

TRUSTEE A person or entity entrusted as a fiduciary to execute a trust and keep or administer the assets of the trust for the benefit of trust beneficiaries.

Marsman v. Nasca

Wife of beneficiary (P) v. Trustee (D)

Mass. App. Ct., 573 N.E.2d 1025 (1991)

NATURE OF CASE: Appeal from judgment imposing constructive trust for breach of trust.

FACT SUMMARY: Because Farr (D), as trustee of Cappy Marsman's trust, did not inquire into Cappy's financial circumstances, Cappy was forced to give up the house he lived in as a means of solving his financial difficulties.

RULE OF LAW

Where a trust gives the trustee a discretionary power to pay amounts of the principal for the comfortable support and maintenance of a beneficiary, the trustee has a duty to inquire into the financial resources of that beneficiary so as to recognize the beneficiary's needs.

FACTS: Sara Marsman set up a trust that provided for her husband, Cappy, after her death. Farr (D), as trustee, had discretionary power to pay out amounts of the principal as he deemed advisable, but failed to adequately explain that power to Cappy. Because Cappy was denied access to the principal, financial difficulties caused him to transfer his house to Sara's daughter, Sally, and her husband, Marlette (D), reserving a life estate for himself. After Cappy's death, Marlette (D), now sole owner due to Sally's death, told Margaret (P), Cappy's second wife, to vacate the premises. Margaret (P) brought an action in the probate court, which held that Farr (D) had breached his duty to inquire into Cappy's finances. Marlette (D) was ordered to convey the house to Margaret (P), and Farr (D) was ordered to reimburse Marlette (D) for upkeep expenses. Marlette (D) and Farr (D) appealed.

ISSUE: Where a trust gives the trustee a discretionary power to pay amounts of the principal for the comfortable support and maintenance of a beneficiary, does the trustee have a duty to inquire into the financial resources of that beneficiary so as to recognize the beneficiary's needs?

HOLDING AND DECISION: (Dreben, J.) Yes. Where a trust gives the trustee a discretionary power to pay amounts of the principal for the comfortable support and maintenance of a beneficiary, the trustee has a duty to inquire into the financial resources of that beneficiary so as to recognize the beneficiary's needs. A life beneficiary is to be maintained in accordance with their normal standard of living. Had Farr (D) met his duties either of inquiry or of distribution under the trust, Cappy would not have lost his home. Sally and Marlette (D) cannot be charged as constructive trustees of the property, but the payments of principal that would have made it possible for Cappy to keep the house can be deemed to be a constructive trust in favor of his estate. Vacated and remanded for a determination of the amount to be paid Cappy's estate from the trust.

ANALYSIS

Here, Farr (D) was directed by the trust agreement to pay Cappy enough for his "comfortable support," yet Farr (D) failed to do so. Prudence and reasonableness are the standard of conduct for trustees of a discretionary trust. However, a desire to save for a beneficiary's future medical needs does not warrant a persistent policy of miserliness toward those beneficiaries.

Quicknotes

CONSTRUCTIVE TRUST A trust that arises by operation of law whereby the court imposes a trust upon property lawfully held by one party for the benefit of another, as a result of some wrongdoing by the party in possession so as to avoid unjust enrichment.

DISCRETIONARY TRUST A trust pursuant to which the trustee is authorized to make decisions regarding the investment of the trust funds and the distribution of such funds to beneficiaries.

EXCULPATORY CLAUSE A clause in a contract relieving one party from liability for certain unlawful conduct.

TENANCY BY THE ENTIRETY The ownership of property by a husband and wife whereby they hold undivided interests in the property with right of survivorship.

TRUSTEE A person or entity entrusted as a fiduciary to execute a trust and keep or administer the assets of the trust for the benefit of trust beneficiaries.

In re Estate of Janes

Testator's spouse (P) v. Trustee (D)

N.Y. Ct. App., 681 N.E.2d 332 (1997)

NATURE OF CASE: Appeal from award of damages for negligent retention of trust assets.

FACT SUMMARY: Mrs. Janes (P) argued that the trustee (D) appointed to oversee her husband's testamentary trusts violated its fiduciary duty to maintain a diversified portfolio of the trust's investments by retaining a majority of the assets in Kodak stock.

RULE OF LAW

A fiduciary, in executing their duties as a trustee, is required to invest the assets of a trust as a prudent person would in the management of their own affairs.

FACTS: Rodney Janes, the testator, died in 1973, leaving an estate valued at $3.5 million. The estate held $2.5 million in stocks, 71 percent of which were shares in Eastman Kodak Company. Janes's will devised his estate to three trusts. The first trust was composed of 50 percent of the estate, granting Mrs. Janes (P) the income for life and a general power of appointment as to the principal. Second, Janes created a charitable trust consisting of 25 percent of the assets of the estate. The rest of his assets were placed in a trust designating income to Mrs. Janes (P) for life and the remainder to the charitable trust. At the time of Janes's death, the Kodak stock was valued at $135 per share. By the end of 1973, however, the value of the shares had fallen to $109 per share. By 1978, the value of the stock had declined even further, to $40 per share. The surrogate court held that the estate's trustee (D) had violated its fiduciary duty by retaining the Kodak stock and employed a "lost profits" measure of damages. The appellate division affirmed, but modified the measure of damages used, concluding that the proper damages should be calculated as the difference between the stock's value at the time it should have been sold and its value when it was actually sold. Both parties appealed.

ISSUE: Is a fiduciary, in executing their duties as a trustee, required to invest the assets of a trust as a prudent person would in the management of their own affairs?

HOLDING AND DECISION: (Levine, J.) Yes. A fiduciary, in executing their duties as a trustee, is required to invest the assets of a trust as a prudent person would in the management of their own affairs. The trustee's predominate objectives must be the maintenance of the trust assets and the acquisition of a sufficient income. In determining whether the trustee has satisfied their duty to invest the trust assets prudently, the court must consider the attendant facts and circumstances. This requires the court to examine the trustee's thoughts and actions in respect to each investment of the trust property, at the moment the act or omission occurred. While the court may not evaluate the trustee's decision based on the result of the investment, the court must necessarily consider the trustee's overall performance in managing the trust assets. The holding of a large percentage of the trust assets in one investment is prima facie evidence of imprudence. However, the individual investment must be examined in relation to several factors. These include the total value of the estate, relevant cost of living expenses, economic conditions, the beneficiaries' need, the asset's marketability, and potential tax liabilities. This requires the court to examine the individual investment in relation to the performance and circumstances of the trust as a whole. Here the trustee (D) failed to discharge its duties as would a prudent investor in the management of their own affairs. The appellate division was correct in setting damages as the amount of value lost to the trust by virtue of the improvident investment. This requires the court to determine the difference, between what the value of the stock was on the date that it should have been sold, and the value of the stock when it was in fact sold or at the date of the accounting. Applying this formula to the present case, the proper measure of damages is $4,065,029. Affirmed.

ANALYSIS

The determination of the date and value at which the investment should have been sold presents a difficult issue for resolution by the court. The court states that such action should be taken within a "reasonable" time period. The discernment of what constitutes a "reasonable" time necessarily depends upon the facts and circumstances of the individual case, and is determined consistent with the prudent investor standard.

Quicknotes

CHARITABLE TRUST A trust that is established for the benefit of a class of persons or for the public in general.

DUTY TO DIVERSIFY Duty of a trustee, in the administration of the trust, to diversify the investments made with the trust's funds or property.

POWER OF APPOINTMENT Power, created by another person in connection with a gratuitous transfer (often in trust) residing in a person (as trustee or otherwise), to affect the disposition or distribution of the property.

TRUSTEE A person or entity entrusted as a fiduciary to execute a trust and keep or administer the assets of the trust for the benefit of trust beneficiaries.

Matter of Will of Kline

Son of decedent's daughter (P) v. Trustee (D)

Mass. Sup. Ct., 244 N.E.3d 1011 (2024)

NATURE OF CASE: Appeal of order granting summary judgment in favor of trustee in action challenging trust distributions.

FACT SUMMARY: Robert Friedman (D), a trustee, adjusted between principal and income to adequately balance trust distributions among the trust beneficiaries to offset the disproportionate impact of a long-term investing strategy. Peter Judson (P), a remainder beneficiary, argued that this adjustment was against the terms of the decedent's will, which authorized distributions of principal to a beneficiary only under emergency circumstances.

RULE OF LAW

The Massachusetts Principal and Income Act (MPIA) permits a trustee to adjust between principal and income to ensure fair and reasonable distribution of the trust to all of the beneficiaries.

FACTS: Helyn Kline died with a will that created separate trusts for the benefit of her daughters. One of those daughters, Denise Jo Levy, is the income beneficiary of the trusts, meaning that she receives distributions of the trusts' net income. Additionally, Kline's will stated that Levy was entitled to a portion of the principal that the trustees "in their absolute discretion, may deem necessary for any emergency affecting" Levy, but noted that principal distributions should only be made to Levy under "the most extraordinary circumstances," and further stated that these distributions would likely not be required. Levy's three sons, Stephen, William, and Peter Judson (P) were remainder beneficiaries.

Peter (P) filed a petition with the Probate and Family Court alleging that Levy had received improper distributions in excess of the trusts' net income. The trustee, Robert Friedman (D), objected, arguing that while the trusts' principal had grown significantly, their income had "not kept pace," meeting only approximately two percent of the principal's value in 2021. The trustee argued that if he had shifted to an investment strategy that resulted in higher annual rates of income to benefit Levy, it would have also resulted in lower long-term returns that would have harmed Peter (P) and his brothers as remaindermen. Additionally, the trustee (D) stated that this alternative strategy would have carried negative tax implications for the remaindermen. The court granted summary judgment in favor of the trustee (D) and Levy, agreeing that the trustee was authorized under the MPIA to adjust between principal and income "for the benefit of all beneficiaries" and denied Peter's (P) cross-motion in which he argued that Levy was not facing an emergency situation that would allow the reallocation of the principal. Peter (P) appealed. The state's highest court took the case for review.

ISSUE: Does the Massachusetts Principal and Income Act permit a trustee to adjust between principal and income to ensure fair and reasonable distribution of the trust to all of the beneficiaries?

HOLDING AND DECISION: (Wendlandt, J.) Yes. The Massachusetts Principal and Income Act (MPIA) permits a trustee to adjust between principal and income to ensure fair and reasonable distribution of the trust to all of the beneficiaries. A central purpose of the MPIA, which is based on the Uniform Principal and Income Act, is to guide trustees in carrying out their sometimes-conflicting duties of investing assets prudently and administering the trust in a manner that treats current and future beneficiaries fairly. To address this, the MPIA allows a trustee to adjust trust assets between principal and income to offset the implications of an ultimately prudent but presently lopsided investment strategy. There are three prerequisites for this adjustment: (1) the trustee must invest and manage the trust assets prudently; (2) "the terms of the trust must describe the amount that may or must be distributed to a beneficiary by referring to the trust's income"; and (3) the trust does not contain a "different provision" that bars exercise of the power to adjust and the trustee determines that they cannot administer the trust impartially without adjusting between principal and income. Notably, a trustee who is a beneficiary of a trust cannot adjust between principal and income, though there is an exception stating that an uninvolved co-trustee can make the adjustment unless the terms of the trust prohibit it.

Here, analysis centers on whether the provisions of the will stating that Levy is entitled to a distribution of principal only in an emergency constitute a "different provision" under the MPIA. Because these provisions address only distributions of principal but not adjustments of principal and income, they do not qualify as a "different provision" that would bar the trustee from adjusting.

Regarding whether Levy is barred from making the adjustment because she is a trustee who is a beneficiary, Friedman (D) could make these distributions as co-trustee under the MPIA's exception. Affirmed.

Continued on next page.

ANALYSIS

The Uniform Principal and Income Act was updated by the Uniform Law Commission in 2018 and became the Uniform Fiduciary Income and Principal Act. The updated act addresses the modernization of trusts, which no longer differentiate so clearly between income and principal interests and instead focus on investing for the greatest total return with equitable adjustment between principal and income for fair results.

Quicknotes

REMAINDER BENEFICIARY A person who is to receive property that is held in trust after the termination of a preceding income interest.

TRUSTEE A person or entity entrusted as a fiduciary to execute a trust and keep or administer the assets of the trust for the benefit of trust beneficiaries.

Wilson v. Wilson

Trust beneficiary (P) v. Trustee (D)

N.C. Ct. App., 690 S.E.2d 710 (2010)

NATURE OF CASE: Appeal from grants of protective order, partial declaratory judgment, summary judgment, and award of costs for defendants in action for breach of trustee's fiduciary duties.

FACT SUMMARY: The beneficiaries (the sons) (P) of irrevocable trusts created by Wilson, Jr. (D) (their father) contended that the trusts' trustee, Wilson, Sr. (D) (their grandfather) breached his fiduciary duty by allowing Wilson, Jr. (D) to take control of trust assets, which resulted in substantial depreciation of trust assets; failing to distribute income as required; and failing to provide them with a complete accounting, notwithstanding that the trust instruments attempted to override such a duty by stating that the trustee "shall not be required by any law, rule or regulation to prepare or file for approval any inventory, appraisal or regular or periodic accounts or reports with any court or beneficiary."

RULE OF LAW

A trust instrument may not override a beneficiary's right to information that is reasonably necessary for the beneficiary to enforce the beneficiary's rights under the trust or to prevent or redress a breach of trust.

FACTS: Wilson, Jr. (D) created two irrevocable trusts, one each for his two sons (P). The trust instruments for each trust provided that the trustee "shall not be required by any law, rule or regulation to prepare or file for approval any inventory, appraisal or regular or periodic accounts or reports with any court or beneficiary." Wilson, Jr. (D) named his father, Wilson, Sr. (D) as trustee of each trust. Fifteen years after the trusts were established, the beneficiary-sons (P) brought suit, alleging a breach of fiduciary duty. They requested, among other things, that the trustee be required to provide a full, complete, and accurate accounting of the trusts from the date of their creation, claiming that Wilson, Sr. (D) had allowed Wilson, Jr. (D) to take control of the trusts' assets, and that Wilson, Jr. (D) subsequently invested the assets in his personal business ventures, which were highly speculative and resulted in a substantial depreciation of assets. The sons (P) further alleged that Wilson, Sr. (D) breached his statutory duty by failing to distribute income to the sons (P) as required by the terms of the trust instruments. Wilson, Sr. (D) and Wilson, Jr. (D), in their answer, invoked the trust provision excusing the trustee from providing an accounting. The trial court, agreeing that this provision overrode any statutory duty to provide an accounting, granted a protective order to Wilson, Sr. (D) and Wilson, Jr. (D), and also granted to them partial declaratory judgment and summary judgment. The sons (P) appealed, and the state's intermediate appellate court granted review.

ISSUE: May a trust instrument override a beneficiary's right to information that is reasonably necessary for the beneficiary to enforce the beneficiary's rights under the trust or to prevent or redress a breach of trust?

HOLDING AND DECISION: (Wynn, J.) No. A trust instrument may not override a beneficiary's right to information that is reasonably necessary for the beneficiary to enforce the beneficiary's rights under the trust or to prevent or redress a breach of trust. The state's trust code requires a trustee to act in good faith, and provides that the terms of the trust cannot prevail over the power of the court to act in the interests of justice. The code also recognizes that a trustee generally has a duty to account for the trust property to the beneficiaries. Commentary to the code concluded that a settlor is free to override the provisions regarding certain information to be furnished to the beneficiaries by directing the trustee not to provide a beneficiary with any of the information otherwise required. More specifically, and in keeping with state case law precedent (*Taylor v. Nationsbank,* 521, 481 S.E.2d 358 (1997)), the commentary concluded that trust beneficiaries are entitled to view the trust instrument from which their interest is derived so long as that right is not waived by the settlor through an explicit provision in the trust to the contrary. In granting the defendants' motions, the trial court relied on this commentary to conclude that Wilson, Sr. (D) was not required to disclose the information requested by the trust beneficiaries (P). The trial court's reliance on the commentary, however, was misplaced, because that commentary, and *Taylor,* was limited to the beneficiaries' entitlement to view the trust instrument. The *Taylor* court noted that the beneficiary is always entitled to such information as is reasonably necessary to enable them to enforce their rights under the trust or to prevent or redress a breach of trust, and it held that the information plaintiffs sought, namely documents relating to the trust instrument including prior revoked drafts of the trust, was not reasonably necessary to enforce the plaintiffs rights. That is not the case here, since the information sought by the sons (P) is reasonably necessary to enable them to enforce their rights under the trusts. Code provisions that permit a trustee to override the disclosure of certain information cannot override the duty of the trustee to act in good faith, nor

Continued on next page.

can they obstruct the power of the court to take such action as may be necessary in the interests of justice. Such action would clearly encompass the power of the court to compel discovery where necessary to enforce the beneficiary's rights under the trust or to prevent or redress a breach of trust, any contrary provision in the trust instrument notwithstanding. Therefore, the trial court erred by relying on the commentary to the state's statutes, which is not binding. Because the information sought by the sons (P) was reasonably necessary to enforce their rights under the trusts, it could not legally be withheld, notwithstanding the terms of the trust instruments. Any other conclusion would render the trusts unenforceable by those it was meant to benefit.

ANALYSIS

The pertinent trust code provision at issue departed from the Uniform Trust Code approach, and instead incorporated the rule from section 173 of the Restatement (Second) of Trusts (1959) requiring trustees to give beneficiaries certain information upon request and to permit the beneficiaries to inspect trust documents. This rule, however, is not listed as a mandatory rule that prevails over the terms of the trust instrument. Nevertheless, as this decision illustrates, this rule cannot override a trustee's duty to act in good faith, or a court's power to take such action as may be necessary in the interests of justice. This result is consistent with how other jurisdictions have approached this question, viewing any notion of a trust without accountability as a contradiction in terms. Thus, under the Restatement approach, a trust instrument may lawfully relieve a trustee from the necessity of keeping formal accounts, and, when such a provision is found in a trust instrument, a beneficiary cannot expect to receive reports concerning the trust estate. However, even when such a provision is made a part of the trust instrument, the trustee will, nevertheless, be required in a suit for an accounting to show that they faithfully performed their duty and will be liable to whatever remedies may be appropriate if they were unfaithful to their trust.

Quicknotes

GOOD FAITH An honest intention to abstain from taking advantage of another.

IRREVOCABLE TRUST A trust that is not capable of being revoked after it is established.

PROTECTIVE ORDER Court order protecting a party against potential abusive treatment through use of the legal process.

TRUSTEE A person or entity entrusted as a fiduciary to execute a trust and keep or administer the assets of the trust for the benefit of trust beneficiaries.

Allard v. Pacific National Bank

Beneficiaries (P) v. Trustee bank (D)

Wash. Sup. Ct., 663 P.2d 104 (1983)

NATURE OF CASE: Appeal of denial of challenge to trustee's disposition of trust property.

FACT SUMMARY: Pacific National Bank (D), trustee, sold certain trust property without informing the beneficiaries or trying to sell on the open market.

RULE OF LAW

A trustee, when disposing of important trust property, should inform the beneficiaries and attempt to obtain the highest possible price.

FACTS: Pacific National Bank (the Bank) (D) was a trustee of a trust. The only significant trust asset was a parcel of developed real estate. The lessee of the property, which had a purchase right of first refusal, offered to purchase the property. After some negotiations, a sale was consummated. The beneficiaries were not informed of this until after the sale. The beneficiaries brought an action for breach of fiduciary duty, contending that the property should have been offered in the open market. The trial court held in favor of the Bank (D), and the beneficiaries appealed.

ISSUE: When disposing of important trust property, should a trustee inform the beneficiaries and attempt to obtain the highest possible price?

HOLDING AND DECISION: (Dolliver, J.) Yes. A trustee, when disposing of important trust property, should inform the beneficiaries and attempt to obtain the highest possible price. A trustee owes the beneficiaries the highest degree of loyalty and good faith. Inherent in this is that beneficiaries be apprised of important trust asset transactions. Even where, as here, consent of the beneficiaries is unnecessary for a trustee to dispose of trust assets, the beneficiaries have a right to know of pending property dispositions. For instance, they may wish to purchase the property themselves. Also, attempting to obtain the highest possible price is incumbent upon the trustee. Here, since the Bank (D) never tried to sell on the open market, it cannot be known if the highest price was obtained. Reversed and remanded.

ANALYSIS

A subissue in this case involved the expected standard of care of the Bank (D). The court noted that some commentators have contended that a professional trustee should be held to a higher standard than a nonprofessional one. The court did not rule on this, however, because the trust instrument itself delineated the proper standard of care.

Quicknotes

BREACH OF FIDUCIARY DUTY The failure of a fiduciary to observe the standard of care exercised by professionals of similar education and experience.

National Academy of Sciences v. Cambridge Trust Co.

Remainderman (P) v. Bank (D)

Mass. Sup. Jud. Ct., 346 N.E.2d 879 (1976)

NATURE OF CASE: Appeal from a petition seeking revocation of seven decrees allowing the trustee's accounting.

FACT SUMMARY: The National Academy of Sciences (P), a remainderman under a trust, brought an action seeking revocation of seven court decrees allowing accounts of the Cambridge Trust Company (D), the trustee.

RULE OF LAW

If a person makes a representation of fact as of the person's own knowledge and such representation is not true as to a subject matter susceptible of ascertainable knowledge, if the party to whom it is made relies and acts upon it as true and sustains damage by it, it is fraud, for which the party making it is responsible.

FACTS: The will of Troland left all of his real and personal property to be held in trust by the Cambridge Trust Company (the Bank) (D), with the net income to be paid to his wife, provided she did not remarry. On his wife's remarriage or death, the Bank (D) was to transfer the trust and trusteeship to the National Academy of Sciences (the Academy) (P). The Bank (D) paid income from the trust to the widow until her death in 1967. However, it turned out that in 1945, the widow had remarried without the Bank's (D) knowledge. Thereafter, the Academy (P) brought an action seeking revocation of the Bank's (D) accounting. The judge revoked the accounting and ordered restoration to the trusts of those amounts erroneously delivered to the decedent's widow. The appellate court affirmed, and the Bank (D) appealed.

ISSUE: If a person makes a representation of fact as of the person's own knowledge and such representation is not true as to a subject matter susceptible of ascertainable knowledge, if the party to whom it is made relies and acts upon it as true and sustains damage by it, is it fraud, for which the party making it is responsible?

HOLDING AND DECISION: (Reardon, J.) Yes. If a person makes a representation of fact as of the person's own knowledge and such representation is not true as to a subject matter susceptible of ascertainable knowledge, if the party to whom it is made relies and acts upon it as true and sustains damage by it, it is fraud, for which the party making it is responsible. This principle is well settled. In this case, the marital status of Mrs. Troland/Flynn was a fact susceptible of precise knowledge. The Bank (D) made representations concerning this fact of its own knowledge when it had no such knowledge, and the Academy (P), to whom the representations were made, relied on them to its detriment. The Bank (D) exerted no effort at all to ascertain if Mrs. Troland had remarried even to the extent of annually requesting a statement or certificate from her to that effect. Affirmed.

ANALYSIS

To avoid expensive accountings, provisions are often inserted in a trust instrument providing that judicial accountings should be dispensed with and accounts rendered periodically to the adult income beneficiaries of the trust. In the case of testamentary trusts, a few courts have indicated that a testator will not be permitted to dispense with statutorily required accountings. (Bogert & Bogert, *Trusts & Trustees*, § 973, 2d ed. 1962.) In the case of inter vivos trusts, which are not placed under judicial supervision by statutes, it would appear that a "no judicial accounting" provision does not contravene public policy.

Quicknotes

CONSTRUCTIVE FRAUD Breach of a duty at law or in equity that tends to deceive another to whom the duty is owed, resulting in damages.

FIDUCIARY DUTY A legal obligation to act for the benefit of another, including subordinating one's personal interests to that of the other person.

CHAPTER 10

Trusts: Alienation and Modification

Quick Reference Rules of Law

PAGE

1. *Scheffel v. Krueger.* Spendthrift trust assets are not reachable by tort creditors even when the beneficiary's conduct constitutes a criminal act, unless the beneficiary is also the settlor or the assets were fraudulently transferred to the trust. *112*

2. *Huber v. Huber.* (1) In a federal bankruptcy action, where the bankruptcy debtor has chosen one state's law to govern a self-settled trust for the purpose of protecting the debtor's assets because the debtor's home state does not recognize the validity of such asset protection trusts, the transfer of assets to the trust will be invalidated where the debtor as trust settlor, the great majority of trust assets, and the trust beneficiaries are all located in the home state. (2) In a federal bankruptcy action, a bankruptcy debtor's transfers to a self-settled trust may be avoided under state law as fraudulent where, pursuant to state law, it is shown by clear and satisfactory proof that the debtor acted with actual intent to hinder, delay, or defraud a creditor without receiving a reasonably equivalent value in exchange for the transfer. *113*

3. *In re Estate of Brown.* An active trust may not be terminated, even with the consent of all the beneficiaries, if a material purpose of the settlor remains to be accomplished. *116*

4. *In re Riddell.* Equitable deviation may be used to modify a trust's administrative or distributive provisions or to permit the trustee to deviate from such a provision, where circumstances not anticipated by the settlor have changed and the modification or deviation will further the primary purposes of the trust and is consistent with law or policy. *117*

5. *Hodges v. Johnson.* A trustee, who makes unequal distributions among beneficiaries and/or eliminates a beneficiary's non-vested interest in an irrevocable trust through decanting, violates the statutory duty of impartiality when the trustee fails to consider the beneficiaries' beneficial interests and fails to treat the beneficiaries equitably in light of the purposes and terms of the trust. *119*

6. *Davis v. U.S. Bank National Association.* (1) Under UTC § 706(b)(4), all remainder beneficiaries of a trust do not have to be joined in a petition to remove a trustee for the court to have subject matter jurisdiction. (2) Under UTC § 303(6), a parent may represent a minor child in seeking to remove a trustee where there is no inherent conflict of interest between the parent and child as to such removal, and their interests are substantially identical. (3) Under UTC § 706(b)(4), a trustee may be removed where the qualified beneficiaries seeking such removal have presented factually supported evidence that such removal will inure to the beneficiaries' benefit, and where the trust does not prohibit such removal. *121*

Scheffel v. Krueger

Creditor (P) v. Trust beneficiary (D)

N.H. Sup. Ct., 782 A.2d 410 (2001)

NATURE OF CASE: Appeal of dismissal of trustee process action.

FACT SUMMARY: Scheffel (P) was awarded a judgment against Krueger (D) and attempted to reach trust assets of which Krueger (D) was the beneficiary.

RULE OF LAW

Spendthrift trust assets are not reachable by tort creditors even when the beneficiary's conduct constitutes a criminal act, unless the beneficiary is also the settlor or the assets were fraudulently transferred to the trust.

FACTS: Scheffel (P) was awarded damages in a tort action against Krueger (D) for his sexual assault of her minor child and subsequent broadcast of the act over the Internet. Scheffel (P) sought an attachment of Krueger's (D) beneficial interest in the Kyle Krueger Irrevocable Trust (Trust). The Trust was established by Krueger's (D) grandmother, and its terms direct the trustee to pay all of the net income from the trust to Krueger (D) at least quarterly, or more frequently if he requests. The trustee is also authorized to pay any of the principal to Krueger (D) if in the trustee's sole discretion the funds are necessary for the maintenance, support, and education of Krueger (D). Krueger (D) cannot touch the principal until 2016 and is prohibited from making any voluntary or involuntary transfers of his interest in the Trust. The Trust specifically provides that the Trust proceeds cannot be assigned or given to creditors or reached by any legal or equitable process in satisfaction of any debt or liability prior to its receipt by Krueger (D). Scheffel (P) filed a trustee process action against Citizens Bank NH (D), the trustee defendant. Citizens (D) argued that the spendthrift provision barred the claim and moved to release the attachment and dismiss the claim. The Superior Court ruled that under RSA 564:23 (1997) the spendthrift provision is enforceable and dismissed Scheffel's (P) trustee process action. Scheffel (P) appealed.

ISSUE: Are spendthrift trust assets reachable by tort creditors even when the beneficiary's conduct constitutes a criminal act, unless the beneficiary is also the settlor or the assets were fraudulently transferred to the trust?

HOLDING AND DECISION: (Duggan, J.) No. Spendthrift trust assets are not reachable by tort creditors even when the beneficiary's conduct constitutes a criminal act, unless the beneficiary is also the settlor or the assets were fraudulently transferred to the trust. The legislature did intend RSA 564:23 to shield trust assets from tort creditors, even when the beneficiary's conduct constitutes a criminal act, unless the exceptions apply. According to RSA 564:23, a spendthrift trust, is enforceable unless the beneficiary is also the settlor or the assets were fraudulently transferred to the trust. In the present case, neither of these exceptions applies. Moreover, the Trust instrument is a valid spendthrift trust because it contains a provision that does not allow the beneficiary to transfer their right to future payments, and a creditor shall not be able to subject the beneficiary's interest to the payment of its claim. Furthermore, the statute plainly states that a creditor of a beneficiary shall not be able to subject the beneficiary's interest to the payment of its claim. Therefore, the legislature did not intend that a tort creditor should be exempted from a spendthrift provision. Since the legislature did make two other exemptions, we must presume that no others were intended. In addition, no rule of public policy is available to overcome the statutory rule. The legislature has enacted a statute repudiating the public policy exception sought by Scheffel (P) and the court cannot question the wisdom of the statute. Lastly, the Trust's purpose, to provide for Krueger's support, maintenance, and education, may still be fulfilled while Krueger (D) is incarcerated and after he is released; therefore the Trust should not be terminated. Affirmed.

ANALYSIS

This case is a prime example of how a spendthrift trust can be used not only as an estate-planning tool, but can also protect beneficiaries from creditors. In *Wilcox v. Gentry*, 867 P.2d 281 (Kan. 1994), the judgment creditors were able to garnish the payments from the trust because the trust was a discretionary trust with no spendthrift clause. Unlike in New Hampshire, where the present case occurred, in certain jurisdictions spendthrift trusts cannot protect beneficiaries from creditors in some situations. For example, in *Bacardi v. White*, 463 So. 2d 218 (Fla. 1985), disbursements from a spendthrift trust could be garnished to enforce judgments for alimony.

Quicknotes

SPENDTHRIFT TRUST A trust formed for the beneficiary's support, but with restrictions imposed so as to safeguard against the beneficiary's abuse.

Huber v. Huber

Bankruptcy trustee (P) v. Bankruptcy debtor (D)

493 B.R. 798 (Bankr. W.D. Wash. 2013)

NATURE OF CASE: Cross motions for summary judgment in chapter 11 bankruptcy action.

FACT SUMMARY: To shield his assets, Donald Huber (Debtor) (D) set up an asset protection asset trust (APT) in Alaska, because Washington, the state in which he lived and in which his assets were located, did not permit APTs. When Debtor (D) subsequently filed for bankruptcy protection, the Bankruptcy Trustee (P) sought to have the transfer of assets to Debtor's (D) APT voided, and to avoid the transfers as fraudulent. Debtor (D) contended that Alaska law should govern the validity of his transfers to the APT, and also argued that his intent was not fraudulent, insofar as he had set up the APT as an estate planning vehicle, so that the transfers to the APT should not be avoided as fraudulent transfers.

RULE OF LAW

(1) In a federal bankruptcy action, where the bankruptcy debtor has chosen one state's law to govern a self-settled trust for the purpose of protecting the debtor's assets because the debtor's home state does not recognize the validity of such asset protection trusts, the transfer of assets to the trust will be invalidated where the debtor as trust settlor, the great majority of trust assets, and the trust beneficiaries are all located in the home state.

(2) In a federal bankruptcy action, a bankruptcy debtor's transfers to a self-settled trust may be avoided under state law as fraudulent where, pursuant to state law, it is shown by clear and satisfactory proof that the debtor acted with actual intent to hinder, delay, or defraud a creditor without receiving a reasonably equivalent value in exchange for the transfer.

FACTS: Donald Huber (Debtor) (D) had been involved in real estate development and management in the Puget Sound area of the state of Washington for decades. In 1968, he founded United Western Development (UWD), through which he carried out most of his business activities. In 2007 and 2008, the real estate business nationwide suffered a downturn as a result of the subprime mortgage crisis. In 2009, Debtor (D), with the help of his son, Kevin Huber (Kevin) and an attorney (Snow), set up an asset protection trust (APT) (the Donald Huber Family Trust) (the Trust) that was created in Alaska. He did so because Washington has a strong public policy against APTs and does not permit them. The Trust instrument expressly acknowledged that one of its goals was to "protect a portion of [Debtor's (D)] assets from [his] creditors." Debtor (D) transferred the great majority of his assets to an Alaskan company that was owned 99 percent by the APT. All but one asset (a $10,000 certificate of deposit) were assets based in Washington. Also, none of the beneficiaries of the Trust were located in Alaska. In 2011, Debtor (D) filed for Chapter 11 bankruptcy protection. Although the APT was created in Alaska and designated the law of Alaska as the controlling law, the Bankruptcy Trustee (P) argued that the APT should be invalidated under Washington law, which does not recognize APTs. Under the applicable federal choice-of-law doctrine, the law of the state designated by the settlor to govern the validity of the trust controls, provided the state has a substantial relation to the trust and the application of its laws does not violate a strong public policy. The Bankruptcy Trustee (P) also sought to have the transfers Debtor (D) made to the Trust avoided as fraudulent under Washington law. The parties cross-moved for summary judgment as to each issue.

ISSUE:

(1) In a federal bankruptcy action, where the bankruptcy debtor has chosen one state's law to govern a self-settled trust for the purpose of protecting the debtor's assets because the debtor's home state does not recognize the validity of such asset protection trusts, will the transfer of assets to the trust be invalidated where the debtor as trust settlor, the great majority of trust assets, and the trust beneficiaries are all located in the home state?

(2) In a federal bankruptcy action, may a bankruptcy debtor's transfers to a self-settled trust be avoided under state law as fraudulent where, pursuant to state law, it is shown by clear and satisfactory proof that the debtor acted with actual intent to hinder, delay, or defraud a creditor without receiving a reasonably equivalent value in exchange for the transfer?

HOLDING AND DECISION: (Snyder, J.)

(1) Yes. In a federal bankruptcy action, where the bankruptcy debtor has chosen one state's law to govern a self-settled trust for the purpose of protecting the debtor's assets because the debtor's home state does not recognize the validity of such asset protection trusts, the transfer of assets to the trust will be invalidated where the debtor as trust settlor, the great majority of trust assets, and the trust beneficiaries are all located in the home state. Federal choice-of-law

Continued on next page.

rules apply in federal bankruptcy actions. This circuit follows the approach of the Restatement (Second) of Conflict of Laws (1971) (Restatement). Under that approach, the Debtor's (D) choice of Alaska law designated in the Trust should be upheld if Alaska has a substantial relation to the Trust, and if application of Alaska law will not violate a strong public policy of the state with which the trust has its most significant relationship. A state has a substantial relation to a trust if at the time the trust is created: (1) the trustee or settlor is domiciled in the state; (2) the assets are located in the state; and (3) the beneficiaries are domiciled in the state. Here, Alaska had a very minimal relation to the settlor, trust assets, and beneficiaries. To the contrary, Washington is where Debtor (D) resided, where the vast majority of trust assets were located, where the beneficiaries resided, where the Debtor's (D) creditors were located, and where the attorney who prepared the Trust documents and transferred the assets into the Trust was located. Therefore, Washington is the state with the most significant relationship to the Trust. Washington has a strong public policy against self-settled asset protection trusts, and, under Washington law, transfers made to such self-settled trusts are void as against existing or future creditors. Accordingly, Washington law must be applied here. Under Washington law, Debtor's (D) transfers of assets into the Trust were void, and the Bankruptcy Trustee (P) is entitled to summary judgment as a matter of law to the extent the Bankruptcy Trustee (P) seeks to have the transfers invalidated.

(2) Yes. In a federal bankruptcy action, a bankruptcy debtor's transfers to a self-settled trust may be avoided under state law as fraudulent where, pursuant to state law, it is shown by clear and satisfactory proof that the debtor acted with actual intent to hinder, delay, or defraud a creditor without receiving a reasonably equivalent value in exchange for the transfer. Under Washington law, which follows the Uniform Fraudulent Transfer Act (UFTA), circumstantial evidence of intent may be considered, and, in determining whether actual intent exists, a court may consider 11 factors, or badges of fraud, set forth by statute, and may consider other evidence impacting on intent. Here, several of the statutory badges of fraud are present. These are that Debtor (D) was threatened with litigation when the transfers occurred; the transfers were of substantially all the Debtor's (D) assets; and Debtor (D) retained control of the transferred property. The evidence also established that as a self-settled trust, the transfer from Debtor (D) to the Trust was to an insider. For the same reason, Debtor (D) conceded that he did not receive consideration for transferring his assets to the Trust. Additionally, the evidence established that by transferring the property into the Trust, Debtor (D) was attempting to remove the assets from creditors' reach. Additionally, the Bankruptcy Trustee's (P) evidence showed that in the face of the declining real estate market, Debtor's (D) inability to secure funding, and mounting debt, Debtor (D) was concerned that he would lose all of his assets to his creditors. Thus, the evidence is overwhelming that Debtor (D) was desperate to protect and shield his assets. Debtor (D) counters that his denial that he had fraudulent intent is sufficient to raise an issue of material fact. However, Debtor (D) failed to present evidence of his intent, and, although his deposition testimony stated he established the Trust for estate planning purposes, this testimony does not directly address or deny the evidence submitted by the Trustee (P) establishing that Debtor (P) wanted to protect his assets in light of his increasingly bleak financial situation. Debtor's (D) desire to provide for his children and grandchildren through estate planning by protecting his assets, which they would otherwise stand to inherit, is not mutually exclusive of the desire to shield his assets from creditors. Accordingly, estate planning alone does not create an issue of fact as to intent. For these reasons, there is no genuine dispute as to any material fact. Summary judgment as a matter of law is granted to the Bankruptcy Trustee (P) on the UFTA/state-law claim based on actual fraudulent intent.

ANALYSIS

Under the Uniform Fraudulent Transfer Act (UFTA), which has been widely adopted by the states, it is actual fraud to make a transfer with the intent to hinder, delay, or defraud creditors, whereas it is constructive fraud to make a transfer without receiving equivalent value if the transfer leaves the debtor with insufficient assets to pay anticipated debts. In assessing evidence of the requisite intent of actual fraud, courts consider "badges of fraud," which are circumstances so commonly associated with fraudulent transfers that their presence gives rise to an inference of intent. As this case shows, some of these badges are (1) actual or threatened litigation against the debtor; (2) a purported transfer of all or substantially all of the debtor's property; (3) insolvency or other unmanageable indebtedness on the part of the debtor; (4) a special relationship between the debtor and the transferee; and, after the transfer, (5) retention by the debtor of the property involved in the putative transfer. Whereas the presence of a single badge of fraud may spur mere suspicion, the confluence of several

Continued on next page.

can constitute conclusive evidence of actual intent to defraud, absent significantly clear evidence of a legitimate supervening purpose.

Quicknotes

ASSET An item of real or personal property that is owned and has tangible value.

BANKRUPTCY TRUSTEE Individual charged with the administration of the bankruptcy estate.

CONSTRUCTIVE FRAUD Breach of a duty at law or in equity that tends to deceive another to whom the duty is owed, resulting in damages.

FRAUDULENT TRANSFER The conveyance of title to property with the intent to defraud creditors or with the intent to deceive others.

INSOLVENT One's liabilities exceed one's assets; inability to pay one's debts.

MATERIAL FACT A fact without the existence of which a transaction or contract would not have been entered, or an action not taken.

SELF-SETTLED TRUST A trust set up by the same person who is to receive the benefits from the trust; it is usually set up to avoid creditors.

In re Estate of Brown

Beneficiary (P) v. Court (D)

Vt. Sup. Ct., 528 A.2d 752 (1987)

NATURE OF CASE: Appeal from judgment terminating trust.

FACT SUMMARY: The lifetime beneficiaries (P) of Brown's trust petitioned the court (D) to terminate the trust.

RULE OF LAW

An active trust may not be terminated, even with the consent of all the beneficiaries, if a material purpose of the settlor remains to be accomplished.

FACTS: Andrew Brown died, passing his entire estate into a trust. The trust income and principal were to be used to provide an education for the children of his nephew, Woolson Brown. After that purpose was accomplished, the trust income and principal were to be used for the care and maintenance of Woolson and his wife so that they could live in the style to which they were accustomed. At their death, the remainder was to pass to Woolson's children. The trustee complied with the terms of the trust by using the proceeds for the education of Woolson's children and applying the proceeds to benefit Woolson and his wife after the education purpose was completed. Woolson and his wife petitioned the probate court for termination of the trust, arguing that the sole remaining purpose of the trust was to maintain their lifestyle and that the distribution of the assets was necessary to accomplish this purpose. The remaindermen, Woolson's children, filed consents to the proposed termination. The probate court denied Woolson's petition to terminate, and Woolson appealed. The superior court reversed, concluding that the only material trust purpose, the education of the children, had been accomplished. The trustee appealed.

ISSUE: May an active trust be terminated, even with the consent of all the beneficiaries, if a material purpose of the settlor remains to be accomplished?

HOLDING AND DECISION: (Gibson, J.) No. An active trust may not be terminated, even with the consent of all the beneficiaries, if a material purpose of the settlor remains to be accomplished. Here, the termination cannot be compelled because a material purpose remains to be accomplished. The trust instrument had two purposes. First, it provided for the education of Woolson's children. It is clear that the educational purpose of the trust was achieved. The second purpose was the assurance of lifelong income for the beneficiaries through the discretion of the trustee. The trustee has to use all the income and such part of the principal as is necessary for this purpose. This purpose would be defeated if termination of the trust were allowed. Reversed.

ANALYSIS

Some courts will allow the termination of a testamentary trust by a compromise agreement between the beneficiaries and heirs entered into soon after the testator's death. In one case, the court allowed such a compromise regardless of whether a material purpose of the trust was defeated by the trust's termination (*Budin v. Levy*, 343 Mass. 644, 180 N.E. 2d 74 (1982)).

Quicknotes

LIFE-INCOME BENEFICIARY A person who is the recipient of income generated by certain property for the duration of the person's life, the remainder of which is to pass on to another individual upon the income beneficiary's death.

REMAINDERMAN A person who has an interest in property to commence upon the termination of a present possessory interest.

RESIDUARY BENEFICIARIES Person specified pursuant to a will to receive the portion of the estate remaining following distribution of the assets and the payment of costs.

SPENDTHRIFT TRUST A trust formed for the beneficiary's support, but with restrictions imposed so as to safeguard against the beneficiary's abuse.

SUPPORT TRUST A trust pursuant to which the trustee is authorized only to distribute such funds as are required for the support of the beneficiary.

In re Riddell

[Parties not identified.]

Wash. Ct. App., 157 P.3d 888 (2007)

NATURE OF CASE: Appeal from denial of motion by trustee to create a special needs trust.

FACT SUMMARY: Ralph Riddell (Ralph), the trustee of a consolidated trust, contended that the trust should be modified to a special needs trust for his daughter, Nancy, who suffered from schizophrenia affective disorder and bipolar disorder, since that would preserve the settlor's (his parents') intent that Nancy attain a level of responsibility, stability, and maturity to handle the trust funds before receiving the distribution, and that due to Nancy's mental illness, allowing a distribution to her would defeat the settlors' intent and the trust's purpose.

RULE OF LAW

Equitable deviation may be used to modify a trust's administrative or distributive provision or to permit the trustee to deviate from such a provision, where circumstances not anticipated by the settlor have changed and the modification or deviation will further the primary purposes of the trust and is consistent with law or policy.

FACTS: Ralph Riddell's (Ralph's) parents established trusts for the benefit of Ralph, his wife, and Ralph's children, i.e., the settlors' grandchildren. The trusts provided that upon the death of Ralph and his wife, the grandchildren would receive the trust benefits until age 35, when the trusts would terminate and the trustee would distribute the principal to the grandchildren. Ralph's daughter, Nancy, who was over 35 and suffered from schizophrenia affective disorder and bipolar disorder, was not expected to live independently for the remainder of her life. Therefore, Ralph sought to create a "special needs" trust on her behalf, instead of distributing to her the trust principal, which was around $667,500. He filed a petition asking the trial court to consolidate the trusts and to modify the consolidated trust to create a "special needs" trust on Nancy's behalf, instead of distributing the trust principal to her. He argued that a special needs trust was necessary because, upon distribution, Nancy's trust funds would either be seized by the State to pay her extraordinary medical bills or Nancy would manage the funds poorly due to her mental illness and lack of judgment. He argued that the modification would preserve and properly manage Nancy's funds for her benefit. The trial court granted the motion to consolidate the trusts, but denied the motion to modify. It stated that it did not have the power to modify the trust unless unanticipated events existed that were unknown to the settlor that would result in defeating the trust's purpose. The trial court found that the trust's purpose was "to provide for the education, support, maintenance, and medical care of the beneficiaries" and that a modification would only "permit[] the family to immunize itself financially from reimbursing the State for costs of [Nancy's medical] care." It stated that it would not allow a modification "merely because a change would be more advantageous to the beneficiaries." The trial court denied a motion by Ralph for reconsideration, and the state's intermediate appellate court granted review.

ISSUE: May equitable deviation be used to modify a trust's administrative or distributive provision, or to permit the trustee to deviate from such a provision, where circumstances not anticipated by the settlor have changed and the modification or deviation will further the primary purposes of the trust and is consistent with law or policy?

HOLDING AND DECISION: (Penoyar, J.) Yes. Equitable deviation may be used to modify a trust's administrative or distributive provision or to permit the trustee to deviate from such a provision, where circumstances not anticipated by the settlor have changed and the modification or deviation will further the primary purposes of the trust and is consistent with law or policy. Under state law, equitable deviation may be used to modify a trust's administrative or distributive provision, or to permit the trustee to deviate from such a provision, provided two prongs are satisfied: (1) changed circumstances not anticipated by the settlor and (2) the modification or deviation will further the purposes of the trust. This test adopts the Restatement (Third) of Trusts, which requires a lower threshold finding than the older Restatement and gives courts broader discretion in permitting deviation of a trust. A determination relating to the second prong is subjective and attempts to determine the settlor's primary purpose in establishing the trust. The reason to modify is to give effect to the settlor's intent, had the circumstances in question been anticipated. Here, there is no dispute that the circumstances had changed. The trial court found that the "stated" purpose of the trust was to provide for the beneficiaries' education, support, maintenance, and medical care. Thus, it found that the primary purpose was to provide for Nancy during her lifetime. Because the trust was to terminate at age 35, it was also the settlors' intent that Nancy has the money to dispose of as she saw fit, which would include any estate planning that she might choose to do. Thus, the changed circumstances have intervened to frustrate the settlors' intent,

Continued on next page.

since Nancy is unable to manage the funds or to pass them to her children, and since there is a great likelihood that the funds will be lost to the State for her medical care. It is clear that the settlors would have wanted a different result. In 1993, Congress provided for special needs trusts intended to care for the needs of persons with disabilities and preserve government benefits eligibility, while allowing families to provide for the supplemental needs of a disabled person that government assistance does not provide. The trial court in its ruling determined that the trust should not be modified to permit the family to shield itself from "reimbursing the State" for the costs of Nancy's medical care due to her disability. However, given that Congress permitted the creation of special needs trusts in order to allow disabled persons to continue to receive governmental assistance for their medical care, the trial court should not have considered any loss to the State in determining whether an equitable deviation was allowed since the law invites, rather than discourages, the creation of special needs trusts in just this sort of situation. Under 42 U.S.C. § 1396p(d)(4)(A), although the State receives all remaining trust amounts upon trust termination for medical assistance paid on behalf of the disabled beneficiary, the State is not entitled to receive payback upon termination of a third party special needs trust for medical assistance provided for the disabled beneficiary. Here, the trust was established and funded by the grandparents for the beneficiary Nancy; it is a third party special needs trust. The trust is not subject to State assistance payback and is not required to have a payback provision. On remand, the trial court should order such equitable deviation as is consistent with the settlors' intent in light of the changed circumstances. Reversed and remanded.

ANALYSIS

The Restatement (Third) of Trusts not only provides for equitable deviation, as in this case, but also provides for nonjudicial combination and division of trusts, and, similarly, for the termination of a trust if it is no longer economically viable.

Quicknotes

EQUITABLE DEVIATION DOCTRINE Allows for deviation from trust terms if the purposes of the trust would be defeated under the attendant circumstances.

Hodges v. Johnson

Trust beneficiary (P) v. Co-trustee (D)

N.H. Sup. Ct., 177 A.3d 86 (2017)

NATURE OF CASE: Appeal from ruling voiding trust decantings ab initio.

FACT SUMMARY: Beneficiaries (P) of two irrevocable trusts contended that the trusts' trustees violated their duty of impartiality when the trustees decanted the trusts to eliminate the beneficiaries' (P) interests, notwithstanding that, under the terms of the trusts, distributions to beneficiaries were discretionary and did not have to be equalized among the beneficiaries.

RULE OF LAW

A trustee, who makes unequal distributions among beneficiaries and/or eliminates a beneficiary's non-vested interest in an irrevocable trust through decanting, violates the statutory duty of impartiality when the trustee fails to consider the beneficiaries' beneficial interests and fails to treat the beneficiaries equitably in light of the purposes and terms of the trust.

FACTS: David Hodges, Sr. ("David Sr." or "settlor") created two irrevocable trusts. The trusts were funded with all the non-voting stock in Hodges Development Company (HDC), a relatively large and successful real estate holding and development company. The non-voting stock represented more than 98 percent of the company's stock. The purposes of the trusts were to provide for the continuation of HDC following his death by eliminating the need to liquidate HDC assets to pay estate taxes. The beneficiaries were his then-wife Joanne, his five children and stepchildren, and their descendants. After the trusts were established, family discord ensued. The settlor fired his stepson, Barry (P), and got into such a ferocious confrontation with his son, David Jr. (P), that the settlor moved out of the family home, and Barry (P) had a heart attack. The settlor hired armed guards to protect him at work from Barry (P), fired David Jr. (P), and divorced Joanne. Thereafter, the settlor approached the trustees about decanting the trusts to eliminate the interests of David Jr. (P) and his stepchildren Barry (P) and Patricia (P). During the settlor's lifetime, any distributions of income or principal were completely discretionary, and did not have to be equalized among beneficiaries. Following the death of the settlor and Joanne, the trusts were to be divided into five trusts, one for each child and stepchild. The settlor was advised that because the trusts were discretionary, the trustees could use the power to decant to create new distributee trusts that eliminated the three beneficiaries. The trustees effected this plan by instituting two decantings, the result of which was to specifically exclude David Jr. (P), Barry (P), and Patricia (P) from the definition of "descendants" contained in the trust documents. Subsequently, the trusts were again decanted to eliminate Joanne's beneficial interests. David Jr. (P), Barry (P), and Patricia (P) brought suit for a declaration that the decantings were void ab initio, and for removal of the trustees. The trial court ruled in their favor, invalidating the decantings on the ground that the trustees had accomplished them without considering the beneficiaries' interests under the trusts. The state's highest court granted review.

ISSUE: Does a trustee, who makes unequal distributions among beneficiaries and/or eliminates a beneficiary's non-vested interest in an irrevocable trust through decanting, violate the statutory duty of impartiality when the trustee fails to consider the beneficiaries' beneficial interests and fails to treat the beneficiaries equitably in light of the purposes and terms of the trust?

HOLDING AND DECISION: (Dalianis, C.J.) Yes. A trustee, who makes unequal distributions among beneficiaries and/or eliminates a beneficiary's non-vested interest in an irrevocable trust through decanting, violates the statutory duty of impartiality when the trustee fails to consider the beneficiaries' beneficial interests and fails to treat the beneficiaries equitably in light of the purposes and terms of the trust. The duty of impartiality does not mean that the trustee must treat the beneficiaries equally, but instead requires a trustee to treat the beneficiaries equitably in light of the purposes and terms of the trust. Thus, a trustee, who makes unequal distributions among beneficiaries and/or eliminates a beneficiary's non-vested interest in an irrevocable trust through decanting, violates the statutory duty of impartiality only when the trustee fails to treat the beneficiaries "equitably in light of the purposes and terms of the trust." Here, a key purpose of the trusts was to support the beneficiaries (P), but the trustees (D) failed to consider this trust purpose when they eliminated the beneficiaries' (P) future beneficial interests through decanting. Notwithstanding that the beneficiaries' (P) interests were discretionary, the trustees violated their duty of impartiality by not considering the three beneficiaries' beneficial interests when the trustees eliminated the beneficiaries' interests. Although it is true that the beneficiaries' (P) interests were contingent, non-vested, and mere expectancies, that alone is not dispositive of whether the trustees (P) fulfilled their duty of impartiality. That duty is owed to all beneficiaries, regardless

Continued on next page.

of whether their interests are present or future, vested or contingent. Additionally, the trustees' (D) argument that eliminating the beneficiaries' (P) future beneficial interests would promote the trusts' main purpose, to ensure that HDC continued after the settlor died, is unavailing because evidence adduced at trial showed that the settlor had put in place other safeguards for HDC's continuity that would not have been affected by retaining the beneficiaries' (P) interests in the trusts. Because the record supports the trial court's determination that the trustees (D) failed to give any consideration to the beneficiaries' (P) future beneficial interest when the trustees decanted the trust, thereby violating their duty of impartiality, the trial court's decision is not erroneous. Affirmed.

ANALYSIS

The trial court in this case determined that the trusts' primary purpose was to "hold family business assets and provide for continuation of the family business after the death of its founder." The New Hampshire Supreme Court, however, read into the trust documents another, broader purpose, namely "to support the beneficiaries," and then concluded that the trustees (D) violated the duty of impartiality by not considering that specific purpose. Arguably, such an expansive interpretation of the settlor's purpose was not one that was evident from the trust documents, or from the settlor's dealings with the trustees, and certainly was not a purpose placed on the record by the trial court. Therefore, in the absence of this "support" purpose, it is arguable that the trustees (D) did not violate their duty of impartiality, because eliminating the plaintiff beneficiaries' (P) future beneficial interests through decanting, while retaining two of the original beneficiaries, was entirely consistent with the primary purpose of the trusts as found by the trial court.

Quicknotes

CONTINGENT EQUITABLE INTEREST A beneficiary's interest in a trust that is based on the uncertain happening of another event.

DECANT A TRUST Pour the assets from one irrevocable trust that has undesirable terms into another irrevocable trust that has more desirable terms.

DISCRETIONARY TRUST A trust pursuant to which the trustee is authorized to make decisions regarding the investment of the trust funds and the distribution of such funds to beneficiaries.

FUTURE INTEREST An interest in property the right to possession or enjoyment of which is to take place at some time in the future.

IRREVOCABLE TRUST A trust that is not capable of being revoked after it is established.

PRESENT INTEREST A trust interest in which the beneficiary has the immediate benefit of proceeds of the trust.

TRUST The holding of property by one party for the benefit of another.

TRUSTEE A person or entity entrusted as a fiduciary to execute a trust and keep or administer the assets of the trust for the benefit of trust beneficiaries.

VESTED INTEREST A present right to property, although the right to the possession of such property may not be enjoyed until a future date.

Davis v. U.S. Bank National Association

Trust beneficiary (P) v. Trustee (D)

Mo. Ct. App., 243 S.W.3d 425 (2007)

NATURE OF CASE: Appeal from summary judgment for plaintiff in action seeking the replacement of a trustee and removal of trust assets.

FACT SUMMARY: Davis (P), the income beneficiary of his grandfather's Trust, petitioned under the state's Uniform Trust Code (UTC), in his name and those of his children ("Son" and "Daughter"), the residual beneficiaries, to have the current trustee (Trustee) (D) removed and replaced by U.S. Trust Company of Delaware (UST), and to have the Trust assets moved to UST. The Trustee (D) contended that Davis's (P) failure to join all of the remainder beneficiaries of the trust as parties to his lawsuit deprived the court of subject matter jurisdiction; that Davis (P) could not virtually represent Son and Daughter because their interests inherently conflicted; and that Davis (P) failed to show that removal of the Trustee (D) would best serve all the beneficiaries' interests.

RULE OF LAW

(1) Under UTC § 706(b)(4), all remainder beneficiaries of a trust do not have to be joined in a petition to remove a trustee for the court to have subject matter jurisdiction.

(2) Under UTC § 303(6), a parent may represent a minor child in seeking to remove a trustee where there is no inherent conflict of interest between the parent and child as to such removal, and their interests are substantially identical.

(3) Under UTC § 706(b)(4), a trustee may be removed where the qualified beneficiaries seeking such removal have presented factually supported evidence that such removal will inure to the beneficiaries' benefit, and where the trust does not prohibit such removal.

FACTS: Davis's (P) grandfather established a Trust under which Davis (P), as the income beneficiary of the Trust, was entitled to receive the entire net income of the Trust for life. Upon his death, the principal of the Trust was to be divided among his then living children in equal shares and distributed to each child. Davis (P) had two children ("Son" and "Daughter"). The Trust also provided that if Davis (P) had no surviving children upon his death, Davis's (P) share would pass to various remainder beneficiaries. For many years, the Trustee (D) was located in Missouri, whereas Davis (P) was a resident of Pennsylvania. Eventually, Davis (P) petitioned under the state's Uniform Trust Code (UTC), in his name and those of Son and Daughter, to have the current Trustee (D) removed and replaced by U.S. Trust Company of Delaware (UST), and to have the Trust assets moved to UST. As part of his petition, Davis (P) presented evidence that UST's fees would be over $10,000 less per year and UST would permit an independent investment adviser; there would be no state income tax on trust income; he was a 30-minute car drive away from UST; and the proposed investment advisor had a complete understanding of Davis (P) and his family's unique personal financial situation and how the Trust coordinated with his family's financial objectives. The trial court granted summary judgment to Davis (P), and the Trustee (D) appealed, claiming that summary judgment should not have been granted because a conflict of interest existed between Davis (P) and Son and Daughter, so that Davis (P) could not represent the interests of Son and Daughter; Davis (P) had failed to name necessary and indispensable parties to the lawsuit; Davis (P) had failed to show removal of the Trustee (D) would best serve the interests of the beneficiaries; removal of the Trustee (D) would be inconsistent with a material purpose of the Trust; and discovery was needed. The state's intermediate appellate court granted review.

ISSUE:

(1) Under UTC § 706(b)(4), must all remainder beneficiaries of a trust be joined in a petition to remove a trustee for the court to have subject matter jurisdiction?

(2) Under UTC § 303(6), may a parent represent a minor child in seeking to remove a trustee where there is no inherent conflict of interest between the parent and child as to such removal, and their interests are substantially identical?

(3) Under UTC § 706(b)(4), may a trustee be removed where the qualified beneficiaries seeking such removal have presented factually supported evidence that such removal will inure to the beneficiaries' benefit, and where the trust does not prohibit such removal?

HOLDING AND DECISION: (Sullivan, J.)

(1) No. Under UTC § 706(b)(4), all remainder beneficiaries of a trust do not have to be joined in a petition to remove a trustee for the court to have subject matter jurisdiction. Instead, UTC § 706(b)(4) provides that only "qualified" beneficiaries must be joined. A qualified beneficiary means a beneficiary who, on the date the beneficiary's qualification is determined is a permissible distributee. Here, Son and Daughter were the permissible distributees at the time of the

Continued on next page.

filing of the suit, and, as such, Davis (P) and Son and Daughter are all of the qualified beneficiaries of the Trust. The remote remainder beneficiaries of the Trust are not qualified beneficiaries. Accordingly, all of the qualified beneficiaries were before the court, which, therefore, had subject matter jurisdiction. Affirmed as to this issue.

(2) Yes. Under UTC § 303(6), a parent may represent a minor child in seeking to remove a trustee where there is no inherent conflict of interest between the parent and child as to such removal, and their interests are substantially identical. Here, Davis (P) and Son and Daughter have substantially identical interests which are not in conflict with regard to removing the Trustee (D) and implementing UST as Trustee. Even if there is a conflict of interest between Davis (P) and his children as to some issues unrelated to trustee removal (the Trustee (D) asserts there is an inherent conflict of interest between income beneficiaries and residual beneficiaries) the conflict must be "with respect to a particular question or dispute." As such, whether there is a conflict of interest must be determined on a case-by-case basis. There is no such conflict here as relates to the removal of Trustee (D). Therefore, Davis (P) could virtually represent his children in seeking such removal. Affirmed as to this issue.

(3) Yes. Under UTC § 706(b)(4), a trustee may be removed where the qualified beneficiaries seeking such removal have presented factually supported evidence that such removal will inure to the beneficiaries' benefit, and where the trust does not prohibit such removal. Here, Davis (P) presented evidence that UST's annual fees would be close to 24 percent lower than those being charged by Trustee (D), and Trustee (D) did not dispute this figure, but merely called it speculative and hearsay. Under the UTC, the petitioner only has to show that the change in trustee will somehow inure to their and the other beneficiaries' benefit—and Davis (P) has done that. Trustee (D) also claims that the change in trustee is inconsistent with the material purpose of the Trust as the Trust clearly did not contemplate the change, but does contemplate keeping the same Trustee in the same state. This argument is speculative and without any evidentiary support. It is also irrelevant, because the UTC provides for the change of trustee as long as the terms of the Trust do not prohibit it. Here, the terms of the Trust do not include such a prohibition. Accordingly, there are no further factual disputes, so that discovery is not needed. Affirmed as to this issue.

ANALYSIS

UTC § 706 changes traditional trust law by permitting a "no-fault" change of trustee where the beneficiaries request such a change and can, as in this case, show that some benefit will inure to the beneficiaries as a result. Under traditional law, the beneficiaries did not have the right to request such a change. Nonetheless, the UTC § 706 may be overridden by contradictory terms in the trust instrument.

Quicknotes

JURISDICTION The authority of a court to hear and declare judgment in respect to a particular matter.

REMAINDER BENEFICIARY A person who is to receive property that is held in trust after the termination of a preceding income interest.

CHAPTER 11

Trusts: Charitable Purposes, Cy Pres, and Supervision

Quick Reference Rules of Law

PAGE

1. *Shenandoah Valley National Bank v. Taylor.* For a charitable trust to be valid, it must provide relief for the poor or needy or otherwise benefit or advance the social interest of the community. *124*

2. *In re Neher's Will.* Where a will gives real property for a general charitable purpose, the gift may be reformed cy pres when compliance with a particular purpose grafted onto the general purpose is impracticable. *125*

3. *Smithers v. St. Luke's-Roosevelt Hospital Center.* The estate of a donor of a charitable gift has standing to sue the donee to enforce the terms of the gift. *126*

Shenandoah Valley National Bank v. Taylor

Trustee (D) v. Heir-at-law (P)

Va. Sup. Ct. App., 63 S.E.2d 786 (1951)

NATURE OF CASE: Appeal from judgment holding that a testamentary trust was not charitable, and, therefore, was void.

FACT SUMMARY: A testator created a perpetual trust, the income of which was to be paid in equal shares to each student in a particular grade school just before Christmas and Easter. Although the payments were purportedly for educational purposes, an heir challenged the validity of the trust as not being a valid charitable trust, and contended that as a private trust, it was subject to, and violative of, the Rule Against Perpetuities, so that it was void.

RULE OF LAW

For a charitable trust to be valid, it must provide relief for the poor or needy or otherwise benefit or advance the social interest of the community.

FACTS: The terms of the testator's will left the bulk of his $86,000 estate to the Shenandoah Valley National Bank (D), as trustee, to administer as a perpetual trust. The trust funds were to be invested and the income was to be paid to all first-, second-, and third-grade students in a particular local grade school. The payments were to be made in equal shares to each student directly and were to be distributed just before the Christmas and Easter vacations. The trust directed that the money so distributed was to be used by each student for the furtherance of the student's education. Although the testator had no children or other close relatives, Taylor (P), a distant relative and heir, brought suit challenging the validity of the trust as not being charitable, and asserting that as a private trust, it was subject to, and violative of, the Rule Against Perpetuities, so that it was void. The trial court agreed with Taylor (P), and the state's highest court granted review.

ISSUE: For a charitable trust to be valid, must it provide relief for the poor or needy or otherwise benefit or advance the social interest of the community?

HOLDING AND DECISION: (Miller, J.) Yes. For a charitable trust to be valid, it must provide relief for the poor or needy or otherwise benefit or advance the social interest of the community. There is a fundamental difference between a trust that is charitable and one that is benevolent. A benevolent trust, while it may be praiseworthy, is a private enterprise and is subject to the Rule Against Perpetuities. A charitable trust is public and is not subject to the rule. For a perpetual charitable trust to be valid, it must provide relief to the poor or needy or otherwise benefit or advance the social interest of the community. The most common examples of such interests include the relief of poverty, the advancement of education, the advancement of religion, the promotion of health, and governmental or municipal purposes. The keystone is the accomplishment of a purpose that is beneficial to the community. While the testator's scheme would surely delight the recipients, there is no way that the stated purpose of educational advancement can be assured. The timing of the payments and the ages of the children practically assure the opposite. This trust cannot be classified as charitable, and, as it violates the Rule Against Perpetuities, it must fail. Affirmed.

ANALYSIS

A perpetual charitable trust may validly be directed toward a small ascertainable group so long as the recipients are qualified as to actual need. Such provisions as providing for the support of needy widows and children of the deceased ministers of a particular church have been upheld, for example. Where no need test is applied, the group benefited must be needy by definition, such as young seamstresses (upheld at a time before minimum wage laws). Generally, the larger the class is, the less strict the application of the needs test.

Quicknotes

CHARITABLE TRUST A trust that is established for the benefit of a class of persons or for the public in general.

PERPETUAL TRUST A trust that is to continue for as long as its purpose is necessary.

RULE AGAINST PERPETUITIES The doctrine that a future interest that is incapable of vesting within 21 years of lives in being at the time it is created is immediately void.

TESTAMENTARY TRUST A trust, created by will and effective only after the grantor's death, since the assets that comprise the corpus of the trust are assumed to vest at that time.

In re Neher's Will

[Parties not identified.]

N.Y. Ct. App., 18 N.E.2d 625 (1939)

NATURE OF CASE: Appeal from the denial of a petition for a decree to construe and reform a charitable gift.

FACT SUMMARY: When Red Hook Village (P) found it did not have the resources to establish and maintain a hospital on property willed to the village (P) by Ella Neher, the village (P) petitioned the court for permission to establish an administration building designated as the "Herbert Neher Memorial Hall."

RULE OF LAW

Where a will gives real property for a general charitable purpose, the gift may be reformed cy pres when compliance with a particular purpose grafted onto the general purpose is impracticable.

FACTS: Ella Neher's will gave her home in Red Hook Village (P) to the village (P) to be used as a memorial to the memory of her husband. She further directed that the property be used as a hospital to be known as the "Herbert Neher Memorial Hospital." The village (P) accepted the gift, but later discovered that it was without the resources necessary to establish and maintain a hospital on the property. Furthermore, a modern hospital in a neighboring village adequately served the needs of both communities. Instead, the village (P) petitioned the court for leave to erect and maintain a building for the administration purposes of the village (P), to be designated as the "Herbert Neher Memorial Hall." The court denied the petition. The appellate division affirmed. The village (P) appealed.

ISSUE: Where a will gives real property for a general charitable purpose, may the gift be reformed cy pres when compliance with a particular purpose grafted onto the general purpose is impracticable?

HOLDING AND DECISION: (Loughran, J.) Yes. Where a will gives real property for a general charitable purpose, the gift may be reformed cy pres when compliance with a particular purpose grafted onto the general purpose is impracticable. When taken as a whole the true construction of the paragraph outlining the gift in Neher's will is that the paramount intention was to give the property for a general charitable purpose rather than a particular charitable purpose. Neher's gift to the village (P) did not specify what sort of medical or surgical care should be provided. The direction grafted on to the general gift, that the property be used for a hospital, may be ignored where, as here, the village (P) finds compliance with that direction impracticable due to a lack of resources. Reversed and remanded.

ANALYSIS

Application of the doctrine of cy pres allows a charitable trust to continue rather than fail. The doctrine's application occurs where the court can discern a primary general charitable intent and where the altered charitable purpose falls within the general charitable intent of the settlor. Such reformation allows the donor's general intent to be carried out even where changes unforeseen by the settlor eliminate the need for the gift's original intended use.

Quicknotes

CHARITABLE TRUST A trust that is established for the benefit of a class of persons or for the public in general.

DOCTRINE OF CY PRES Equitable doctrine applied in order to give effect to an instrument, which would be unlawful if enforced strictly, as close to the drafter's intent as possible without violating the law.

Smithers v. St. Luke's-Roosevelt Hospital Center

Estate's administratrix (P) v. Charitable donee (D)

N.Y. App. Div., 723 N.Y.S.2d 426 (2001)

NATURE OF CASE: Appeal from dismissal for lack of standing to enforce terms of a charitable gift.

FACT SUMMARY: Smithers (P), administratrix for her husband's estate, brought suit to enforce the terms of a charitable gift made by her deceased husband to St. Luke's Roosevelt Hospital Center (the "Hospital") (D). The gift was restricted for the purpose of establishing an alcoholism center and maintaining it in its own building.

RULE OF LAW

The estate of a donor of a charitable gift has standing to sue the donee to enforce the terms of the gift.

FACTS: Mr. Smithers made a $10 million gift to St. Luke's Roosevelt Hospital Center (the Hospital) (D), which was dedicated for the purpose of establishing an alcoholism rehabilitation center. One of the conditions of the gift was that the center be housed in its own building, separate from the Hospital (D). Years of investigation by the state Attorney General (D) revealed that the Hospital (D) had misappropriated funds from the charitable fund to fund other hospital projects. The Attorney General (D) entered into an agreement with the Hospital (D), whereby the Hospital (D) agreed not to use gift funds for any purpose other than to benefit the center and to return to the gift fund proceeds from any sale of the building in which the center was housed. Smithers (P), administratrix for Mr. Smithers' estate, filed a claim against both the Hospital (D) and the Attorney General (D) to enforce the terms of her deceased husband's gift. She sought an accounting of the funds of the gift, and also sought an injunction preventing the Hospital (D) from selling the building in which the rehabilitation center was housed, or, alternatively, preventing disbursement of the funds from the sale. The Hospital (D) and the Attorney General (D) moved to dismiss, and the trial court granted the defendants' motions. The appellate division granted review.

ISSUE: Does the estate of a donor of a charitable gift have standing to sue the donee to enforce the terms of the gift?

HOLDING AND DECISION: (Ellerin, J.) Yes. The estate of a donor of a charitable gift has standing to sue the donee to enforce the terms of the gift. Standing to enforce the terms of charitable gifts is not exclusive to the Attorney General (D). Here, Smithers (P) is bringing her suit as administratrix of her husband's estate, not on her own behalf or on behalf of the Center's beneficiaries. Therefore, the general rule barring beneficiaries from suing charitable corporations has no application here. The donor of a charitable gift is in a better position than the Attorney General (D) to be vigilant and, if they are so inclined, to enforce their own intent. Mr. Smithers was the founding donor of the Smithers Center, which he established to carry out his vision of "first class alcoholism treatment and training." In his agreement with the Hospital (D) Mr. Smithers reserved to himself the right to veto the Hospital's (D) project plans and staff appointments for the Smithers Center. Mr. and Mrs. Smithers (P) remained actively involved in the affairs of the Smithers Center until his death, and she thereafter. During his lifetime, when Mr. Smithers found that his intent was not carried out by the Hospital (D), he decided not to donate the balance of the gift. It was only when the Hospital (D) expressly agreed to the various restrictions imposed by Mr. Smithers that he completed the gift. The Hospital's (D) subsequent unauthorized deviation from the terms of the completed gift commenced during Mr. Smithers's lifetime and was discovered shortly after he died. To hold that, in her capacity as her late husband's representative, Smithers (P) has no standing to institute an action to enforce the terms of the gift is to contravene the well-settled principle that a donor's expressed intent is entitled to protection and the longstanding recognition under state law of standing for a donor such as Mr. Smithers. There is thus a need for co-existent standing for the Attorney General (D) and the donor; the Attorney General's (D) interest in enforcing gift terms is not necessarily congruent with that of the donor. Therefore, the distinct but related interests of the donor and the Attorney General (D) are best served by continuing to accord standing to donors to enforce the terms of their own gifts concurrent with the Attorney General's (D) standing to enforce such gifts on behalf of the beneficiaries thereof. Reversed on the standing issue.

DISSENT: (Friedman, J.) When a charitable gift is made, without any provision for a reversion of the gift to the donor or their heirs, the interest of the donor and the donor's heirs is permanently excluded. Accordingly, in the absence of a right of reverter, the right to seek enforcement of the terms of a charitable gift is restricted to the Attorney General (D). This general rule is consistent with the common-law rule, and with the approach found in the Restatement (Second) of Trusts. Such a rule is necessary to avoid "vexatious litigation" by parties who do not have a tangible stake in the outcome of the litigation. It is

Continued on next page.

uncontroverted that the estate was not the donor of the gift. Thus even if pure donor standing were recognized, (as the majority concludes) this could not be a basis for granting standing to Mr. Smithers's estate. To the extent that Mr. Smithers may have had standing based upon his right to exercise discretionary control over the gift, i.e., via the right to appoint key staffing positions, that right was personal to him, abated upon his death, and did not devolve to his estate.

ANALYSIS

The approach taken by the court in this case finds support in the Uniform Trust Code, which provides that "[t]he settlor of a charitable trust, among others, may maintain a proceeding to enforce the trust." Of course, this can be interpreted as granting only a personal right in the donor, not one that survives the donor's death.

Quicknotes

CHARITABLE TRUST A trust that is established for charitable purposes.

DONEE A person to whom a gift is made.

DONOR A person who voluntarily gives a gift of real or personal property or value.

GIFT A transfer of property to another person that is voluntary and that lacks consideration.

CHAPTER 12

Trusts: Powers of Appointment

Quick Reference Rules of Law

PAGE

1. *Irwin Union Bank & Trust Co. v. Long.* An unexercised power of appointment may not be reached by a creditor of the trustee. *130*

2. *Cessac v. Stevens.* To properly exercise a power of appointment provided for in a trust, which requires a specific reference to the power of appointment to validate it, a decedent must at least make a reference in the will to the power of appointment held by the decedent. *131*

3. *Timmons v. Ingrahm.* A technical legal term used in a testamentary instrument should be accorded its usual legal definition unless it is clear the testator employed the term in a different sense. *133*

4. *Brown v. Miller.* A trust provision granting a beneficiary the right to request payment from the trustee of additional amounts of trust principle from time to time grants the beneficiary unrestricted power to use some or all of the trust proceeds for the beneficiary's benefit. *134*

Irwin Union Bank & Trust Co. v. Long

Bank (D) v. Ex-wife of trustee (P)

Ind. Ct. App., 312 N.E.2d 908 (1974)

NATURE OF CASE: Appeal from order allowing execution on a portion of a trust corpus.

FACT SUMMARY: The trial court ordered that four percent of the trust corpus of a trust held as trustee by Irwin Union Bank and Trust (D) was subject to execution in favor of his ex-wife (P).

RULE OF LAW

An unexercised power of appointment may not be reached by a creditor of the trustee.

FACTS: Philip Long was made the beneficiary of a trust by his mother and was granted a right of appointment of four percent of the trust corpus. Long was subsequently sued by his wife, Victoria Long (P), for divorce, and a judgment in the amount of $15,000 was entered in favor of Victoria (P). Victoria (P) then filed an action to execute upon four percent of the trust corpus in which she contended that because Philip had a right of appointment with regard to this percentage of the trust, it could be reached by his creditors. The trial court, over the objections of the trustee Irwin Union Bank and Trust Co. (Union Bank) (D) that an unexercised right of appointment cannot be reached by creditors, issued the writ of execution. Union Bank (D) appealed.

ISSUE: May an unexercised power of appointment be reached by creditors of the trust's beneficiary?

HOLDING AND DECISION: (Lowdermilk, J.) No. An unexercised power of appointment may not be reached by creditors of the beneficiary. In the absence of a statute, the unexercised general right of appointment cannot be reached by creditors, as to hold to the contrary would allow creditors to force the exercise of said power upon the beneficiary. If the beneficiary chooses not to exercise the power, creditors cannot force the beneficiary to do so. Where the power is a special power, the appointee derives no benefit therefrom, and, therefore, it cannot be reached by the creditors. As a result, the trial court erred in granting the writ of execution. Reversed and remanded.

ANALYSIS

In *Irwin Union Bank & Trust Co. v. Long*, the court cites *Gilman v. Bell*, 99 Ill. 144 (1881), and the Restatement (Second) Property donative transfers. The basis upon which *Irving* is determined is that a right of appointment is not property. Because the beneficiary does not derive any benefit from it, it cannot be attached by his creditors. The power of appointment is personal to the beneficiary and therefore cannot be alienated. As a result, it lacks a fundamental element of the concept of property and therefore cannot be attached.

Quicknotes

POWER OF APPOINTMENT Power, created by another person in connection with a gratuitous transfer (often in trust) residing in a person (as trustee or otherwise), to affect the disposition or distribution of the property.

TRUST CORPUS The aggregate body of assets placed into a trust.

Cessac v. Stevens

Residuary beneficiary (D) v. Alternate trust beneficiary (P)

Fla. Ct. App., 127 So. 3d 675 (2013)

NATURE OF CASE: Appeal from judgment that will did not properly exercise trust powers of appointment.

FACT SUMMARY: Decedent's will named Joanne Cessac (D) as the residuary beneficiary of decedent's estate, and referenced three trusts as being part of decedent's estate, but failed to specifically reference powers of appointment in the trusts as required by the trusts' donor. Marcia Stevens (P), decedent's daughter, who was named as a beneficiary under the trusts in the event decedent failed to exercise the powers of appointment, contended that because decedent only mentioned the trusts, but not the powers, the trust assets were not part of decedent's estate.

RULE OF LAW

To properly exercise a power of appointment provided for in a trust, which requires a specific reference to the power of appointment to validate it, a decedent must at least make a reference in the will to the power of appointment held by the decedent.

FACTS: Decedant Sally Christiansen (Sally) was the beneficiary of three trusts created by her father. The trusts each included a provision authorizing Sally to direct who would receive the assets in the trusts upon her death. This power of appointment provided that it would be effective if Sally's will made "specific reference to the power herein granted." The trusts also provided that if Sally failed to exercise the powers, the assets would go to her children. Sally's will, however, only made reference to the trusts, but did not specifically reference the powers of appointment. The will named Joanne Cessac (Cessac) (D) as the residuary beneficiary of Sally's estate. Marcia Stevens (Stevens) (P), Sally's daughter, who as a child of Sally was an alternate beneficiary under the trusts, petitioned the probate court for a declaratory judgment that because Sally's will only mentioned the trusts, but not the powers of appointment, the trust assets were not part of Sally's estate. The probate court agreed with Stevens (P), concluding that Sally's will did not include a valid exercise of the powers of appointment provided in the trusts because it "failed to reference the power of appointment in the Trusts as required by the grantor." The state's intermediate appellate court granted review.

ISSUE: To properly exercise a power of appointment provided for in a trust, which requires a specific reference to the power of appointment to validate it, must a decedent at least make a reference in the will to the power of appointment held by the decedent?

HOLDING AND DECISION: (Wetherell, J.) Yes. To properly exercise a power of appointment provided for in a trust, which requires a specific reference to the power of appointment to validate it, a decedent must at least make a reference in the will to the power of appointment held by the decedent. The state's only precedent that is on point held that strict compliance with a trust donor's requirements for the proper exercise of a power of appointment is necessary to effectuate the power, and that intent to exercise the power is immaterial. Similarly, merely referencing a trust that contains a power, while not following the donor's requirements for validating the power, as in the case at bar, will invalidate the exercise of the power of appointment. Here, Sally's will cannot meet even an equitable construction standard that requires only reasonable substantive compliance with a donor's requirements for the exercise of a power, because Sally's will did not include even a general reference to the powers of appointment held by Sally. Without such a general reference, the will failed to even substantially comply with the "specific reference" requirements of the trusts. Accordingly, the trust assets did not become part of Sally's estate, and, in accordance with the trusts' directions, must pass to Sally's children rather than to Cessac (D). Affirmed.

ANALYSIS

The court in this case acknowledged the seemingly harsh result of its conclusion that Cessac (D) would not receive the assets Sally apparently intended for her to receive. However, as the court explained, this result is a function of the intent of the original donor (Sally's father), who had the right to place whatever restrictions he desired on the disposition of his property. Sally was obligated to comply with these restrictions, and compliance would not have been difficult here, as all that was necessary was some reference to powers of appointment in the will. As the Pennsylvania Supreme Court explained in *In re Estate of Schede*, 231 A.2d 135, 137 (Pa. 1967), the donor of a power, who is disposing of the donor's own property, may prescribe whatever ceremonies the donor pleases for its execution. Even though "these may be perfectly arbitrary, yet, being required by the creator of the power, they can be satisfied only by a strictly literal and precise performance of them."

Continued on next page.

Quicknotes

GRATUITOUS Something that is given without consideration received therefor.

POWER OF APPOINTMENT An authority granted by one person to another to affect the disposition or distribution of an estate or income in connection with a gratuitous transfer.

Timmons v. Ingrahm

Decedent's adopted children (P) v. Decedent's wife (D)

Fla. Dist. Ct. App., 36 So. 3d 861 (2010)

NATURE OF CASE: Appeal from lower court decision allowing decedent's wife to modify a family trust to effectively disinherit the decedent's adopted children.

FACT SUMMARY: Frank Timmons, Sr.'s, will created two trusts, a Marital Trust for the benefit of his wife, Myrtle Ingrahm (D), and a Family Trust created for Timmons Sr.'s two adopted children (P) and the four children of Ingrahm (D) from a prior marriage. Ingrahm (D) petitioned the court to remove the adopted children (P) from the Family Trust.

RULE OF LAW

A technical legal term used in a testamentary instrument should be accorded its usual legal definition unless it is clear the testator employed the term in a different sense.

FACTS: Frank Timmons, Sr.'s, will created two trusts, a Marital Trust for the benefit of his wife, Myrtle Ingrahm (D), and a Family Trust created for Timmons Sr.'s two adopted children (P) and the four children of Ingrahm (D) from a prior marriage. Timmons Sr.'s adopted children, Frank Timmons, Jr. (P) and Jacquelyn Forman (P), were his children from a prior marriage. Ingrahm (D) did not adopt them as her own children. Similarly, Ingrahm's (D) four children were from her prior marriage. Timmons Sr. did not adopt them when he married Ingrahm (D). Ingrahm (D) served as trustee of both trusts. The trusts provided that Ingrahm (D) was the sole income beneficiary of both trusts during her lifetime. Upon her death, the remaining proceeds of the Marital Trust would pour over into the Family Trust. The trust assets would be divided in equal shares among his children then living. The will specifically defined "children" as Timmons Sr.'s adopted children and the four children of Ingrahm (D). After Timmons Sr.'s death, Ingrahm (P) sought to use the limited power of appointment in the Family Trust to remove Frank Timmons, Jr. (P) and Jacquelyn Forman (P) as beneficiaries. The relevant provision in the Family Trust stated that Ingrahm (D) had a limited power to deliver any or all of the trust principle to any of "my then living lineal descendants." Ingrahm (D) executed a brief document entitled Exercise of Limited Power of Appointment that expressly removed Frank Timmons, Jr. (P) and Jacquelyn Forman (P) from the Family Trust. Frank Timmons, Jr. (D) and Jacquelyn Forman (D) brought suit against Ingrahm (D) for breach of a fiduciary duty and for an accounting. Specifically, their argument was that because the limited power of appointment referred to Timmons Sr.'s "lineal" descendants, the power could only be exercised in favor of them and not her four children. The lower court granted summary judgment to Ingrahm (D). Frank Timmons, Jr. (D) and Jacquelyn Forman (D) appealed, and the state's intermediate appellate court granted review

ISSUE: Should a technical legal term used in a testamentary instrument be accorded its usual legal definition unless it is clear the testator employed the term in a different sense?

HOLDING AND DECISION: (Evander, J.) Yes. A technical legal term used in a testamentary instrument should be accorded its usual legal definition unless it is clear the testator employed the term in a different sense. "Lineal descendant" is defined to mean any person in any generational level down an individual's descending line. Adopted children are included in the definition. Ingrahm (D) argues that because Timmons Sr.'s will defines children to include her four children, the term "lineal" descendant in the Family Trust encompasses her four children. The argument is flawed. Although Timmons Sr.'s will provided a different definition of the term "children" to specifically include his wife's four children, the Family Trust did not redefine the legal definition of lineal descendant. In addition, there is no language in the will providing Ingrahm (D) with the power to disinherit Timmons Sr.'s children. Accordingly, there is no evidence that Timmons Sr. intended to expand the definition of lineal descendant beyond its customary usage. Accordingly, Ingrahm (D) had no power to use her limited power of appointment for the benefit of her children. Reversed and remanded.

ANALYSIS

The guiding principle for the interpretation of testamentary instruments is to ascertain the intent of the testator. A second principle is that a court should not rewrite a will or a trust unless there is clear evidence there was a mistake. Here, to find in favor of Timmons Sr.'s adopted children, the court relied on the legal hook that Timmons Sr. did not redefine lineal descendants to include the children of his wife. Practically speaking, the court also relied on Timmons Sr.'s intent that his children should not be disinherited by his wife after his death.

Quicknotes

TESTAMENTARY INSTRUMENT An instrument that takes effect upon the death of the maker.

Brown v. Miller

Decedent's estate (D) v. Decedent's son (P)

Fla. Dist. Ct. App., 2 So. 3d 321 (2008)

NATURE OF CASE: Appeal from lower court decision invalidating decedent's transfer of seven million dollars from a trust created by his wife into a trust for his exclusive benefit.

FACT SUMMARY: Elinor Miller created several trusts during her lifetime, including a trust called Trust A-2. Her trust document allowed her husband, Bill Miller, as primary beneficiary, to remove amounts of principal from Trust A-2 "from time to time" during his lifetime for his benefit. Before his death in 2004, Bill Miller transferred the balance of over seven million dollars from Trust A-2 to the newly created Bill Miller Trust.

RULE OF LAW

A trust provision granting a beneficiary the right to request payment from the trustee of additional amounts of trust principle from time to time grants the beneficiary unrestricted power to use some or all of the trust proceeds for the beneficiary's benefit.

FACTS: Elinor Miller created several trusts during her lifetime, including a trust called Trust A-2. Her trust document allowed her husband, Bill Miller, as primary beneficiary, to remove amounts of principal from Trust A-2 "from time to time" during his lifetime for his benefit. Elinor's trust stated that upon Bill Miller's death, the remainder of the A-2 trust, not appointed or used by Bill Miller, would be held in trust for Thomas Miller III (P), Elinor and Bill's son. Before his death in 2004, Bill Miller transferred $420,000 from Trust A-2 to the newly created Bill Miller Trust. He then transferred the remaining balance of seven million dollars from Trust A-2 to the Bill Miller Trust. After Bill's death, Thomas Miller III (P) petitioned the court to invalidate Bill Miller's transfers from Trust A-2 on the grounds they were inconsistent with the trust language in Elinor's original trust document. The lower court agreed and granted him partial summary judgment. Bill Miller's estate (D) appealed. The state's intermediate appellate court granted review.

ISSUE: Does a trust provision granting a beneficiary the right to request payment from the trustee of additional amounts of trust principle from time to time grant the beneficiary unrestricted power to use some or all of the trust proceeds for the beneficiary's benefit?

HOLDING AND DECISION: (Evander, J.) Yes. A trust provision granting a beneficiary the right to request payment from the trustee of additional amounts of trust principle from time to time grants the beneficiary unrestricted power to use some or all of the trust proceeds for the beneficiary's benefit. Thomas Miller III (P) argues that the language permitting Bill Miller to request additional trust proceeds "from time to time" does not mean he could remove the trust proceeds "in one fell swoop." First, the parties agree the elder Miller made two different transfers, as opposed to one. Second, many other courts have found that the language, "from time to time," does not serve as a limitation on the beneficiary's right to receive any or all of the trust proceeds. Elinor's trust manifested her clear intent that Bill Miller be able to receive any or all of the Trust A-2 proceeds at any time. In addition, Thomas Miller III (P) argues Elinor's trust only allowed her husband to receive trust proceeds, and not a separate trust entity created by her husband. The argument is flawed. The Bill Miller Trust was revocable by Bill Miller during his lifetime. He therefore effectively controlled the trust assets. Accordingly, a donation from Trust A-2 to the Bill Miller Trust was a donation to Bill Miller himself. Because Elinor's trust document clearly gave Bill Miller the authority to remove trust proceeds, the lower court erred in granting partial summary judgment to Thomas Miller III (P). Reversed and remanded.

ANALYSIS

Most jurisdictions agree that the language "from time to time" provides beneficiaries with the authority to remove any and all trust proceeds in any manner. As with all trusts, the intent of the testator is paramount. Here, Elinor's trust also stated that Thomas Miller III (P) would only receive trust funds that were not expended or appointed by Bill Miller during his lifetime.

Quicknotes

PARTIAL SUMMARY JUDGMENT Judgment rendered by a court in response to a motion by one of the parties, claiming that the lack of a question of material fact in respect to one of the issues warrants disposition of that issue without going to the jury.

REVOCABLE TRUST A trust where trustor reserves the right to revoke the trust.

CHAPTER 13

Trusts: Construction and Future Interests

Quick Reference Rules of Law

PAGE

1. *Tait v. Community First Trust Co.* The interest of a beneficiary of an inter vivos trust vests at the time the settlor creates the trust, and that interest does not lapse when the beneficiary predeceases the settlor. *136*

2. *Clobberie's Case.* If a bequest is "to be paid" at the happening of a certain event, the money passes to the estate of the beneficiary even if the beneficiary dies before the contingency occurs. *137*

3. *Dewire v. Haveles.* A class gift creates a joint tenancy with rights of survivorship unless a contrary intent is manifested in the will. *138*

4. *Estate of Woodworth.* The identity of heirs entitled to trust assets must be determined at the date of death of the named ancestor who predeceased the life tenant, not at the date of death of the life tenant. *140*

Tait v. Community First Trust Co.

Children of deceased trust beneficiaries (P) v. Trustee (P)

Ark Sup. Ct., 425 S.W.3d 684 (2012)

NATURE OF CASE: Appeal from decision finding that the interests of deceased trust beneficiaries lapsed when they predeceased the settlor of the trust.

FACT SUMMARY: William Fowler and Annie Fowler created the Fowler Family Trust. The trust stated that after their deaths, the remaining trust property would pass to various children and stepchildren. Three of the named beneficiaries died before William Fowler, having survived his wife, passed away in 2011. The descendants of the deceased beneficiaries claimed they had a vested right to a portion of the trust proceeds.

RULE OF LAW

The interest of a beneficiary of an inter vivos trust vests at the time the settlor creates the trust, and that interest does not lapse when the beneficiary predeceases the settlor.

FACTS: William Fowler and Annie Fowler created the Fowler Family Trust. The trust stated that after their deaths, the remaining trust property would pass to various children and stepchildren. Annie Fowler died in 1999. Three of the named beneficiaries then died before William Fowler passed away in 2011. The descendants of the deceased beneficiaries, Debbie Tait (D), Kerry Jones (D), Leanna Lackey (D) and Lesia Winters (D), claimed the interest in the trust survived the death of their parents and should pass on to them as descendants. The trustee of the trust, Community First Trust Co. (P), petitioned the court to construe the trust. It argued the interests of the deceased beneficiaries lapsed because they predeceased William Fowler. The lower court agreed with Community First Trust (P). Tait (D) and the children of the other deceased beneficiaries appealed. The state's highest court granted review.

ISSUE: Does the interest of a beneficiary of an inter vivos trust vest at the time the settlor creates the trust, and does that interest not lapse when the beneficiary predeceases the settlor?

HOLDING AND DECISION: (Goodson, J.) Yes. The interest of a beneficiary of an inter vivos trust vests at the time the settlor creates the trust, and that interest does not lapse when the beneficiary predeceases the settlor. A contrary line of cases has held that the interest of a trust beneficiary does not vest until the death of the settlor of the trust; accordingly, if a beneficiary predeceases the settlor of the trust, the beneficiary's interest lapses. The modern rule is that the interest vests at the time the trust is created, even though it is subject to the settlor's power to revoke or modify the trust document during the settlor's lifetime. Stated otherwise, a delay in enjoyment of the trust proceeds does not imply that the beneficiary must survive the settlor. Accordingly, the lower court's order finding that the beneficiaries' interest in the trust lapsed when they predeceased William Fowler was in error. Because the court finds that the interest does not lapse, the court does not need to consider Tait's (D) alternative argument that the state's anti-lapse statute applies to revocable trusts as it does to wills. Reversed and remanded.

ANALYSIS

The rule followed in most states is that a beneficiary need not survive the settlor for their interest to pass on to their descendants, unless the trust document expressly states that the beneficiary must survive for the future interest to vest.

Quicknotes

INTER VIVOS TRUST Property that is held by one person for the benefit of another and that is created by an instrument that takes effect during the life of the grantor.

VESTED INTEREST A present right to property, although the right to the possession of such property may not be enjoyed until a future date.

Clobberie's Case

[Parties not identified.]

Ch., 86 Eng. Rep. 476, 2 Ventris 342 (1677)

NATURE OF CASE: Suit seeking an order construing a bequest.

FACT SUMMARY: Money was bequeathed to a woman at her age of twenty-one years or day of marriage, to be paid with interest. The woman died without marrying or attaining the age of twenty-one.

RULE OF LAW

If a bequest is "to be paid" at the happening of a certain event, the money passes to the estate of the beneficiary even if the beneficiary dies before the contingency occurs.

FACTS: Money was bequeathed to a certain woman at her age of twenty-one years or day of marriage, to be paid to her with interest. She died prior to marrying or attaining the age of twenty-one. It was argued that the bequest, instead of lapsing, should pass to the executor of her estate.

ISSUE: If a bequest is "to be paid" at the occurrence of a stated event, but the beneficiary dies before the contingency occurs, does the bequest pass to the beneficiary's estate?

HOLDING AND DECISION: (Lord Finch, Ch.) Yes. If a bequest is "to be paid" at the happening of a certain event, the money passes to the estate of the beneficiary even if the beneficiary dies before the contingency occurs. In this case, money was bequeathed to the woman at her age of twenty-one years or her wedding day and was to be paid with interest. Thus, upon her death, the money passed to the executor of her estate. If the money had merely been bequeathed at the occurrence of a stated event, the death of the beneficiary prior to its occurrence would have resulted in the loss of the money. But, where the money is "to be paid" at the occurrence of the designated event, it shall pass to the beneficiary's executors despite the beneficiary's failure to survive until the event takes place. Therefore, the bequest to the woman in this case passes to her executor.

ANALYSIS

The rule in *Clobberie's Case* has long perplexed the student of future interests in property. The rule causes significantly different consequences to ensue from the minutest differences in language. The rule in *Clobberie's Case* is still applied by some courts, although it has been repeatedly modified and updated. Perhaps no case of comparable succinctness has enjoyed notoriety equivalent to that earned by *Clobberie's Case.*

Quicknotes

BEQUEST A transfer of property that is accomplished by means of a testamentary instrument.

Dewire v. Haveles

[Parties not identified.]

Mass. Sup. Jud. Ct., 534 N.E.2d 782 (1989)

NATURE OF CASE: Action to declare rights in a residuary trust.

FACT SUMMARY: Haveles contended the testator failed to manifest a contrary intent in his will that a right of survivorship should apply to a gift to the testator's grandchildren, and that, therefore, Dewire was not entitled to share in her father's legacy.

RULE OF LAW

A class gift creates a joint tenancy with rights of survivorship unless a contrary intent is manifested in the will.

FACTS: Thomas Dewire died, leaving a widow, a son named Thomas Jr., and three grandchildren. He placed his estate in a residuary trust, the income payable to his widow for life and, on her death, to his son, his widow, and Thomas Jr.'s children. The will also provided that the trust should terminate 21 years after the death of the testator's last grandchild. After the testator's death, Thomas Jr. had three more children by a second wife and then died. Thomas Jr. was survived by six children, including Thomas III, who served as trustee until his death. Thomas III left one child, Jennifer (Thomas Dewire's (the testator's) great granddaughter). Upon Thomas III's death, an action was brought to determine the rights of the remaining five grandchildren in the estate. The key question presented was to whom the one-sixth share of the trust income, once payable to Thomas, III, was now payable. The will contained no explicit provision concerning the distribution of income on the death of a grandchild while the gift of income to grandchildren continued, nor was there any statement as to what the trustee should do with trust income between the death of the last grandchild and the date assigned for termination of the trust 21 years later. Haveles contended that Jennifer could not take a share of the grandchildren's gift, as a class gift had been created for the grandchildren as a joint tenancy with rights of survivorship. Jennifer contended that a contrary intent was manifested in the original will to supersede the joint tenancy, and, therefore, that she was entitled to her father's share by right of representation to Thomas III's income interest in the trust created by the class gift. The state's highest court heard the case.

ISSUE: Does a class gift create a joint tenancy with rights of survivorship unless a contrary intent is manifested in the will?

HOLDING AND DECISION: (Wilkins, J.) Yes. A class gift creates a joint tenancy with rights of survivorship unless a contrary intent is manifested in the will. Here, the will manifested such a contrary intent. The testator provided that the trust should terminate 21 years after the death of his last grandchild. It is unlikely that the testator intended that trust income should be accumulated for 21 years, and such a construction should be avoided. Thus, because the testator must have intended for the income of the trust to be paid out during the term of its existence, the only logical recipients of that income would be the issue, by right of representation, of deceased grandchildren—the same group of people who would take the trust assets upon termination of the trust (assuming no violation of the Rule Against Perpetuities). In other words, because every other provision in the will concerning the distribution of trust income and principal (after the death of the testator and his wife) pointed to equal treatment of the testator's issue per stirpes, there was a sufficient contrary intent shown to overcome the rule of construction that the class gift of income to grandchildren was given to them as joint tenants with the right of survivorship. As a result, Jennifer is entitled to her father's share of the estate.

ANALYSIS

The court, addressing a side issue as to whether the will violated the Rule Against Perpetuities, indicated that the prospect that interests under the will could vest beyond the permissible limit of the Rule Against Perpetuities was not only theoretically possible, but was actuarially likely. The interests of the grandchildren in the trust income vested at their father's (Thomas Jr.'s) death (if not sooner) and, because he was a life in being at the testator's death, those interests vested within the period of the Rule. The gift over at the end of the class gift of income to the grandchildren, however, might not vest seasonably because another grandchild could have been born after the testator's death and could be the surviving grandchild. In this case, in fact, the three youngest grandchildren were born after the death of the testator but they were measuring lives for the term of the class gift. The parties agreed that the purported gift of the remainder to the lineal descendants of the testator's grandchildren "twenty-one years after the death of the last surviving" grandchild violated the Rule in its traditional form and would be void.

Continued on next page.

Quicknotes

CLASS GIFT A gift to a group of unspecified persons whose number, identity, and share of the gift will be determined sometime in the future.

JOINT TENANCY An interest in property whereby a single interest is owned by two or more persons and created by a single instrument; joint tenants possess equal interests in the use of the entire property, and the last survivor is entitled to absolute ownership.

RIGHT OF SURVIVORSHIP Between two or more persons, such as in a joint tenancy relationship, the right to the property of a deceased passes to the survivor.

RULE AGAINST PERPETUITIES The doctrine that a future interest that is incapable of vesting within 21 years of lives in being at the time it is created is immediately void.

Estate of Woodworth

[Parties not identified.]

Cal. Ct. App., 22 Cal. Rptr. 2d 676 (1993)

NATURE OF CASE: Appeal from an order rejecting a claim to the remainder of a testamentary trust.

FACT SUMMARY: Because the trustee was uncertain as to whether the heirs at law of the ancestor named to take the remainder of the Woodworth trust should be determined at the date of the named ancestor's death or at the date of the life tenant's death, the trustee petitioned the court for that determination.

RULE OF LAW

The identity of heirs entitled to trust assets must be determined at the date of death of the named ancestor who predeceased the life tenant, not at the date of death of the life tenant.

FACTS: Woodworth's will distributed a portion of his estate outright to his wife, Mamie Barlow Woodworth, with the balance to be administered as a testamentary trust with Mamie as the life tenant. Upon her death, any remainder of the trust estate was to go to Woodworth's sister, Elizabeth Plass, or to her heirs-at-law, if she no longer survived. Elizabeth died before Mamie but was survived by her husband, Ray Plass, a niece, and a nephew. Ray also died before Mamie, leaving the residue of his estate to the Regents of the University of California. At Mamie's death, the trustee petitioned the probate court as to the date for determining who would receive the distribution of the trust estate. Concluding that the heirs must be determined as of the date of death of the life tenant, Mamie, the court ordered the assets distributed to Elizabeth's niece and nephew. The regents appealed.

ISSUE: Must the identity of heirs entitled to trust assets be determined at the date of death of the named ancestor who predeceased the life tenant, not at the date of death of the life tenant?

HOLDING AND DECISION: (DiBiaso, J.) Yes. The identity of heirs entitled to trust assets must be determined at the date of death of the named ancestor who predeceased the life tenant, not at the date of death of the life tenant. Nothing in the language of the other provisions of the decree of distribution revealed Woodworth's intent or desire. The general rule favoring early vesting was well established long before Woodworth died. Nothing in the decree forecloses the possibility that Woodworth took into account the fact that Raymond Plass might succeed to a portion of the trust remainder. Moreover, the fact that the university, an entity, is not a relative of Elizabeth Plass or one of her heirs at law is not material. In addition, the language of the decree does not contain any expression of futurity in the description of the ancestor's heirs. Therefore, the regents have a claim to the assets of the trust. Reversed.

ANALYSIS

In the absence of any firm indication of testamentary intent, the rules of construction must be implemented in order to ensure uniformity and predictability in the law. This is preferable to carrying out a court's ad hoc sense of what is, with perfect hindsight, acceptable in a particular set of circumstances. Here, at the time of Elizabeth Plass's death, her "heir-at-law" was her husband, Ray.

Quicknotes

DEFEASIBLE FEE SIMPLE ESTATE A fee-simple interest in land that is subject to being terminated upon the happening of a future event.

LIFE ESTATE An interest in land, measured by the life of the tenant or a third party.

LIFE TENANT An individual whose estate in real property is measured either by that invidual's own life or by that of another.

REMAINDER An interest in land that remains after the termination of the immediately preceding estate.

TESTAMENTARY TRUST A trust created by will and effective only after the grantor's death, since the assets that comprise the corpus of the trust are assumed to vest at that time.

Note: There are no principal cases in Chapter 14 of the casebook.

CHAPTER 15

Wealth Transfer Taxation

Quick Reference Rules of Law

PAGE

1. *Old Colony Trust Co. v. United States.* The estate of a settlor of an inter vivos trust, who was a trustee until the date of the settlor's death, is to be charged with and, therefore, taxed on, the value of the principal the settlor contributed by virtue of reserved powers in the trust. *142*

2. *Estate of Vissering v. Commissioner.* A power vested in a trustee to invade the principal of the trust for their benefit is sufficient to find the decedent trustee to have a general power of appointment, unless the power is limited by an ascertainable standard related to health, education, support, or maintenance. *143*

Old Colony Trust Co. v. United States

Estate administrator (D) v. Federal government (P)

423 F.2d 601 (1st Cir. 1970)

NATURE OF CASE: Appeal from finding of estate tax deficiency.

FACT SUMMARY: Old Colony (D), the administrator of the estate of the unnamed decedent, contended that the estate should not include for estate tax purposes the principal contributed to an inter vivos trust established by the decedent, and of which the decedent had been the trustee until his death, where the trust terms gave the decedent-settlor-trustee the power to increase or stop payments to their son at any time.

RULE OF LAW

The estate of a settlor of an inter vivos trust, who was a trustee until the date of the settlor's death, is to be charged with and, therefore, taxed on, the value of the principal the settlor contributed by virtue of reserved powers in the trust.

FACTS: The decedent, unnamed in the case, established an inter vivos trust prior to his death in which the initial life beneficiary of the trust was the settlor's adult son. Eighty percent of the income was normally to be payable to the son and the balance added to the principal. Article 4 of the trust agreement permitted the trustees to increase the percentage of income payable to the son beyond the 80 percent "in their absolute discretion . . . when in their opinion such increase is needed in case of sickness, or desirable in view of changed circumstances." In addition, under Article 4 the trustees were given the discretion to cease paying income to the son and add it all to principal "during such period as the Trustees may decide that the stoppage of such payments is for his best interests." Article 7 gave the trustees broad administrative and management powers over the trust corpus. After the death of the settlor, who also had acted as the sole trustee of the trust, the government (P) sought to include the corpus of the trust in the estate of the settlor, contending that the settlor had possessed the ownership of the corpus because he could designate the persons who could enjoy its income and that until the date of his death he had an absolute right to alter, amend, or terminate the trust. After the trial court ruled for the government (P), the executor of the estate (D) appealed.

ISSUE: Is the estate of a settlor of an inter vivos trust, who was a trustee until the date of the settlor's death, to be charged with and, therefore, taxed on, the value of the principal the settlor contributed by virtue of reserved powers in the trust??

HOLDING AND DECISION: (Aldrich, J.) Yes. The estate of a settlor of an inter vivos trust, who was a trustee until the date of the settlor's death, is to be charged with and, therefore, taxed on, the value of the principal the settlor contributed by virtue of reserved powers in the trust. A settlor will not find the corpus of the trust included in the settlor's estate merely because the settlor named themself a trustee. The settlor must have reserved a power to themself that is inconsistent with the full termination of ownership. Trustee powers given for the administration or management of the trust must be equitably exercised for the benefit of the trust as a whole. It is difficult to see how a power can be subject to control by the probate court and exercisable only in what the trustee fairly concludes is in the interests of the trust and its beneficiaries as a whole and at the same time is an ownership power. However, under Article 4 of the trust, the trustees could increase the life tenant's income "in case of sickness, or . . . in view of changed circumstances." Alternatively, they could reduce it "for his best interests." Additional payments to a beneficiary, whenever in the beneficiary's best interests is a broad standard, showing the plain indicia of ownership. With the present settlor-trustee free to determine the standard himself, a finding of ownership was warranted. To put it another way, the cost of holding onto the strings may prove to be a rope burn. Affirmed.

ANALYSIS

In this case, the court held that the mere grant of administrative control to the trustees did not equate to indicia of ownership. In its decision, the court held that no aggregation of purely administrative powers can meet the government's amorphous test of "sufficient dominion and control" so as to be equated with ownership. The court also noted that trustee powers were not to be construed more broadly for tax purposes than a probate court would construe them for administrative purposes.

Quicknotes

INTER VIVOS TRUST Property that is held by one person for the benefit of another and which is created by an instrument that takes effect during the life of the grantor.

TRUST CORPUS The aggregate body of assets placed into a trust.

Estate of Vissering v. Commissioner

Representatives of decedent's estate (P) v. Tax commissioner (D)

990 F.2d 578 (10th Cir. 1993)

NATURE OF CASE: Appeal from a judgment including the assets of a trust in the gross estate of a cotrustee for estate tax purposes.

FACT SUMMARY: Because the tax court determined that Vissering, at the time of his death, held a general power of appointment over the assets of a trust of which he was a cotrustee, the tax court included the assets of the trust in Vissering's gross estate (P) for federal estate tax purposes. The estate's representatives (P) contended that Vissering did not have such a general power of appointment, because the trust terms limited such power by including an ascertainable standard related to health, education, support, or maintenance, where those terms provided that trust assets could be paid to Vissering when "required for [his] continued comfort, support, maintenance, or education."

RULE OF LAW

A power vested in a trustee to invade the principal of the trust for their benefit is sufficient to find the decedent trustee to have a general power of appointment, unless the power is limited by an ascertainable standard related to health, education, support, or maintenance.

FACTS: Vissering and a bank were cotrustees of a trust created by his mother. The trust agreement authorized the trustees "to pay over, use, or expend, for the direct or indirect benefit of any of the beneficiaries, whatever amount or amounts of the principal of the Trust as may, in the discretion of the Trustees, be required for the continued comfort, support, maintenance, or education of said beneficiary." The tax court and the IRS, focusing on the word "comfort," found that Vissering held a general power of appointment at the time of his death that was not limited by an ascertainable standard. Therefore, the tax court agreed with the IRS that the assets of the trust were to be included in his gross estate for federal estate tax purposes. The estate (P) appealed, and the federal Tenth Circuit granted review.

ISSUE: Is a power vested in a trustee to invade the principal of the trust for their benefit sufficient to find the decedent trustee to have a general power of appointment, unless the power is limited by an ascertainable standard related to health, education, support, or maintenance?

HOLDING AND DECISION: (Logan, C.J.) Yes. A power vested in a trustee to invade the principal of the trust for their benefit is sufficient to find the decedent trustee to have a general power of appointment, unless the power is limited by an ascertainable standard related to health, education, support, or maintenance. A trust document permitting invasion of principal for comfort, without further qualifying language, creates a general power of appointment. Here, however, there is modifying language in the trust at issue. "Comfort," in context, does not permit an unlimited power of invasion because such power is permitted only to "continue" such comfort, i.e., to continue Vissering's current standard of living. Moreover, invasion of the corpus is permitted only to the extent "required," not to the extent "determined" or "desired," to "continue" such "comfort." Thus, the tax court erred in finding that Vissering had a general power of appointment includable in his estate (P). Reversed and remanded.

ANALYSIS

The court of appeals undertook a de novo review. Since the trust was created in Florida, specifying that Florida law controlled, the court of appeals looked to what it believed the Florida courts would hold. The estate (P) argued unsuccessfully that Vissering (P) was not a trustee at the time of death because he had been judged incapacitated by a New Mexico court.

Quicknotes

CONTINGENT BENEFICIARY A third party who is the recipient of the benefit of a transaction undertaken by another, the receipt of which is based on the uncertain happening of another event.

POWER OF APPOINTMENT Power, created by another person in connection with a gratuitous transfer (often in trust) residing in a person (as trustee or otherwise), to affect the disposition or distribution of the property.

REMAINDER BENEFICIARY A person who is to receive property that is held in trust after the termination of a preceding income interest.

Glossary

Common Latin Words and Phrases Encountered in the Law

A FORTIORI: Because one fact exists or has been proven, therefore a second fact that is related to the first fact must also exist.

A PRIORI: From the cause to the effect. A term of logic used to denote that when one generally accepted truth is shown to be a cause, another particular effect must necessarily follow.

AB INITIO: From the beginning; a condition that has existed throughout, as in a marriage that was void ab initio.

ACTUS REUS: The wrongful act; in criminal law, such action sufficient to trigger criminal liability.

AD VALOREM: According to value; an ad valorem tax is imposed upon an item located within the taxing jurisdiction calculated by the value of such item.

AMICUS CURIAE: Friend of the court. Its most common usage takes the form of an amicus curiae brief, filed by a person who is not a party to an action but is nonetheless allowed to offer an argument supporting their legal interests.

ARGUENDO: In arguing. A statement, possibly hypothetical, made for the purpose of argument is one made arguendo.

BILL QUIA TIMET: A bill to quiet title (establish ownership) to real property.

BONA FIDE: True, honest, or genuine. May refer to a person's legal position based on good faith or lacking notice of fraud (such as a bona fide purchaser for value) or to the authenticity of a particular document (such as a bona fide last will and testament).

CAUSA MORTIS: With approaching death in mind. A gift causa mortis is a gift given by a party who feels certain that death is imminent.

CAVEAT EMPTOR: Let the buyer beware. This maxim is reflected in the rule of law that a buyer purchases at their own risk because it is their responsibility to examine, judge, test, and otherwise inspect what they are buying.

CERTIORARI: A writ of review. Petitions for review of a case by the United States Supreme Court are most often done by means of a writ of certiorari.

CONTRA: On the other hand. Opposite. Contrary to.

CORAM NOBIS: Before us; writs of error directed to the court that originally rendered the judgment.

CORAM VOBIS: Before you; writs of error directed by an appellate court to a lower court to correct a factual error.

CORPUS DELICTI: The body of the crime; the requisite elements of a crime amounting to objective proof that a crime has been committed.

CUM TESTAMENTO ANNEXO, ADMINISTRATOR (ADMINISTRATOR C.T.A.): With will annexed; an administrator c.t.a. settles an estate pursuant to a will in which they are not appointed.

DE BONIS NON, ADMINISTRATOR (ADMINISTRATOR D.B.N.): Of goods not administered; an administrator d.b.n. settles a partially settled estate.

DE FACTO: In fact; in reality; actually. Existing in fact but-not officially approved or engendered.

DE JURE: By right; lawful. Describes a condition that is legitimate "as a matter of law," in contrast to the term "de facto," which connotes something existing in fact but not legally sanctioned or authorized. For example, de facto segregation refers to segregation brought about by housing patterns, etc., whereas de jure segregation refers to segregation created by law.

DE MINIMUS: Of minimal importance; insignificant; a trifle; not worth bothering about.

DE NOVO: Anew; a second time; afresh. A trial de novo is a new trial held at the appellate level as if the case originated there and the trial at a lower level had not taken place.

DICTA: Generally used as an abbreviated form of obiter dicta, a term describing those portions of a judicial opinion incidental or not necessary to resolution of the specific question before the court. Such nonessential statements and remarks are not considered to be binding precedent.

DUCES TECUM: Refers to a particular type of writ or subpoena requesting a party or organization to produce certain documents in their possession.

EN BANC: Full bench. Where a court sits with all justices present rather than the usual quorum.

EX PARTE: For one side or one party only. An ex parte proceeding is one undertaken for the benefit of only one party, without notice to, or an appearance by, an adverse party.

EX POST FACTO: After the fact. An ex post facto law is a law that retroactively changes the consequences of a prior act.

EX REL.: Abbreviated form of the term "ex relatione," meaning upon relation or information. When the state brings an action in which it has no interest against an individual at the instigation of one who has a private interest in the matter.

FORUM NON CONVENIENS: Inconvenient forum. Although a court may have jurisdiction over the case, the action should be tried in a more conveniently located court, one to which parties and witnesses may more easily travel, for example.

GUARDIAN AD LITEM: A guardian appointed by the court to represent a minor or incompetent person in a legal action.

HABEAS CORPUS: You have the body. The modern writ of habeas corpus is a writ directing that a person (body) being detained (such as a prisoner) be brought before the court so that the legality of the person's detention can be judicially ascertained.

IN CAMERA: In private, in chambers. When a hearing is held before a judge in the judge's chambers or when all spectators are excluded from the courtroom.

IN FORMA PAUPERIS: In the manner of a pauper. A party who proceeds in forma pauperis because of their poverty is one who is allowed to bring suit without liability for costs.

INFRA: Below, under. A word referring the reader to a later part of a book. (The opposite of supra.)

IN LOCO PARENTIS: In the place of a parent.

IN PARI DELICTO: Equally wrong; a court of equity will not grant requested relief to an applicant who is in pari delicto, or as much at fault in the transactions giving rise to the controversy as is the opponent of the applicant.

IN PARI MATERIA: On like subject matter or upon the same matter. Statutes relating to the same person or things are said to be in pari materia. It is a general rule of statutory construction that such statutes should be construed together, i.e., looked at as if they together constituted one law.

IN PERSONAM: Against the person. Jurisdiction over the person of an individual.

IN RE: In the matter of. Used to designate a proceeding involving an estate or other property.

IN REM: A term that signifies an action against the res, or thing. An action in rem is basically one that is taken directly against property, as distinguished from an action in personam, i.e., against the person.

INTER ALIA: Among other things. Used to show that the whole of a statement, pleading, list, statute, etc., has not been set forth in its entirety.

INTER PARTES: Between the parties. May refer to contracts, conveyances, or other transactions having legal significance.

INTER VIVOS: Between the living. An inter vivos gift is a gift made by a living grantor, as distinguished from bequests contained in a will, which pass upon the death of the testator.

IPSO FACTO: By the mere fact itself.

JUS: Law or the entire body of law.

LEX LOCI: The law of the place; the notion that the rights of parties to a legal proceeding are governed by the law of the place where those rights arose.

MALUM IN SE: Evil or wrong in and of itself; inherently wrong. This term describes an act that is wrong by its very nature, as opposed to one which would not be wrong but for the fact that there is a specific legal prohibition against it (malum prohibitum).

MALUM PROHIBITUM: Wrong because prohibited, but not inherently evil. Used to describe something that is wrong because it is expressly forbidden by law but that is not in and of itself evil, e.g., speeding.

MANDAMUS: We command. A writ directing an official to take a certain action.

MENS REA: A guilty mind; a criminal intent. A term used to signify the mental state that accompanies a crime or other prohibited act. Some crimes require only a general mens rea (general intent to do the prohibited act), but others, like assault with intent to murder, require the existence of a specific mens rea.

MODUS OPERANDI: Method of operating; generally refers to the manner or style of a criminal in committing crimes, admissible in appropriate cases as evidence of the identity of a defendant.

NEXUS: A connection to.

NISI PRIUS: A court of first impression. A nisi prius court is one where issues of fact are tried before a judge or jury.

N.O.V. (NON OBSTANTE VEREDICTO): Notwithstanding the verdict. A judgment n.o.v. is a judgment given in favor of one party despite the fact that a verdict was returned in favor of the other party, the justification being that the verdict either had no reasonable support in fact or was contrary to law.

NUNC PRO TUNC: Now for then. This phrase refers to actions that may be taken and will then have full retroactive effect.

PENDENTE LITE: Pending the suit; pending litigation underway.

PER CAPITA: By head; beneficiaries of an estate, if they take in equal shares, take per capita.

PER CURIAM: By the court; signifies an opinion ostensibly written "by the whole court" and with no identified author.

PER SE: By itself, in itself; inherently.

PER STIRPES: By representation. Used primarily in the law of wills to describe the method of distribution where a person, generally because of death, is unable to take that which is left to them by the will of another, and therefore the person's heirs divide such property between them rather than take under the will individually.

PRIMA FACIE: On its face, at first sight. A prima facie case is one that is sufficient on its face, meaning that the evidence supporting it is adequate to establish the case until contradicted or overcome by other evidence.

PRO TANTO: For so much; as far as it goes. Often used in eminent domain cases when a property owner receives partial payment for their land without prejudice to their right to bring suit for the full amount they claim their land to be worth.

QUANTUM MERUIT: As much as one deserves. Refers to recovery based on the doctrine of unjust enrichment in those cases in which a party has rendered valuable services or furnished materials that were accepted and enjoyed by another under circumstances that would reasonably notify the recipient that the rendering party expected to be paid. In essence, the law implies a contract to pay the reasonable value of the services or materials furnished.

QUASI: Almost like; as if; nearly. This term is essentially used to signify that one subject or thing is almost analogous to another but that material differences between them do exist. For example, a quasi-criminal proceeding is one that is not strictly criminal but shares enough of the same characteristics to require some of the same safeguards (e.g., procedural due process must be followed in a parole hearing).

QUID PRO QUO: Something for something. In contract law, the consideration, something of value, passed between the parties to render the contract binding.

RES GESTAE: Things done. In evidence law, this principle justifies the admission of a statement that would otherwise be hearsay when it is made so closely to the event in question as to be said to be a part of it, or with such spontaneity as not to have the possibility of falsehood.

RES IPSA LOQUITUR: The thing speaks for itself. This doctrine gives rise to a rebuttable presumption of negligence when the instrumentality causing the injury was within the exclusive control of the defendant, and the injury was one that does not normally occur unless a person has been negligent.

RES JUDICATA: A matter adjudged. Doctrine which provides that once a court of competent jurisdiction has rendered a final judgment or decree on the merits, that judgment or decree is conclusive upon the parties to the case and prevents them from engaging in any other litigation on the points and issues determined therein.

RESPONDEAT SUPERIOR: Let the master reply. This doctrine holds the master liable for the wrongful acts of their servant (or the principal for their agent) in those cases in which the servant (or agent) was acting within the scope of the master's authority at the time of the injury.

STARE DECISIS: To stand by or adhere to that which has been decided. The common law doctrine of stare decisis attempts to give security and certainty to the law by following the policy that once a principle of law as applicable to a certain set of facts has been set forth in a decision, it forms a precedent that will subsequently be followed, even though a different decision might be made were it the first time the question had arisen. Of course, stare decisis is not an inviolable principle and is departed from in instances where there is good cause (e.g., considerations of public policy led the Supreme Court to disregard prior decisions sanctioning segregation).

SUPRA: Above. A word referring a reader to an earlier part of a book. (The opposite of infra.)

ULTRA VIRES: Beyond the power. This phrase is most commonly used to refer to actions taken by a corporation that are beyond the power or legal authority of the corporation.

Addendum of French Derivatives

CHATTEL: Tangible personal property.

CY PRES: Doctrine permitting courts to apply trust funds to purposes not expressed in the trust but necessary to carry out the settlor's intent.

IN PAIS: Not pursuant to legal proceedings.

PER AUTRE VIE: For another's life; during another's life. In property law, an estate may be granted that will terminate upon the death of someone other than the grantee.

PROFIT A PRENDRE: A license to remove minerals or other produce from land.

VOIR DIRE: Process of questioning jurors as to their predispositions about the case or parties to a proceeding in order to identify those jurors displaying bias or prejudice.

www.ingramcontent.com/pod-product-compliance
Lightning Source LLC
LaVergne TN
LVHW082339200926
848481LV00012B/3395